TOWARDS AN
IMPERFECT UNION

TOWARDS AN IMPERFECT UNION

A Conservative Case for the EU

Dalibor Rohac

ROWMAN & LITTLEFIELD
Lanham • Boulder • New York • London

Published by Rowman & Littlefield
A wholly owned subsidiary of
The Rowman & Littlefield Publishing Group, Inc.
4501 Forbes Boulevard, Suite 200, Lanham, Maryland 20706
www.rowman.com

Unit A, Whitacre Mews, 26-34 Stannary Street, London SE11 4AB,
United Kingdom

British Library Cataloguing in Publication Information Available

Library of Congress Cataloging-in-Publication Data
Names: Rohac, Dalibor, 1983-
Title: Towards an imperfect union : a conservative case for the EU / Dalibor
    Rohac.
Description: Lanham : Rowman & Littlefield, [2016] | Series: Europe today |
    Includes bibliographical references and index.
Identifiers: LCCN 2016014742 (print) | LCCN 2016016850 (ebook) | ISBN
    9781442270633 (cloth : alk. paper) | ISBN 9781442270640 (pbk. : alk.
    paper) | ISBN 9781442270657 (electronic)
Subjects: LCSH: European Union. | European cooperation.
Classification: LCC JN30 .R64 2016 (print) | LCC JN30 (ebook) | DDC
    341.242/2—dc23
LC record available at https://lccn.loc.gov/2016014742

♾ ™ The paper used in this publication meets the minimum requirements of
American National Standard for Information Sciences Permanence of Paper
for Printed Library Materials, ANSI/NISO Z39.48-1992.

Printed in the United States of America

CONTENTS

INTRODUCTION

The European Union (EU) has seen better days. "Not only has [Europe] not recovered from its post-2008 cold," says Martin Schulz, the president of the European Parliament, "beset by multiplying crises, it is now on the verge of developing pneumonia."[1] The continent's troubles are not just economic, although a lack of economic growth and chronically high rates of unemployment play an important role in Europe's overall malaise. The refugee crisis that hit the EU in 2015 has fueled nationalism, deepened the divisions between member states, and risks tearing the bloc apart altogether. Depending on one's point of view, the EU is "on the verge of collapse"[2] (investor and philanthropist George Soros); "stuck in a political trap"[3] (philosopher Jürgen Habermas); or "not in a good state"[4] (president of European Commission Jean-Claude Juncker). Even the usually measured World Economic Forum is distinctly pessimistic: "Europe's leaders are in crisis-fighting mode: reactive, improvising, often uncoordinated."[5]

It is difficult for critics of European integration to avoid a certain schadenfreude about Europe's misfortunes, not least because these might herald the demise of what they see as an unnecessary bureaucratic monster. Nigel Farage, leader of the Eurosceptic United Kingdom Independence Party, believes that the upcoming referendum about the UK's membership in the European Union will be a "tipping point," marking the end of the EU.[6]

What is more, Europe's troubles appear to vindicate the Eurosceptics' arguments. From the critics' perspective, the EU's woes are almost completely self-inflicted and result from the hubris of European political elites. The common currency; the rush towards federalization imposed on Europeans against the popular will expressed in referenda in France, the Netherlands, and Ireland; and burdensome European regulation are all coming back with a vengeance, threatening to undo the 70 years of moves towards "ever-closer union."

While there is plenty of blame to go around for Europe's political elites, conservatives and advocates of free markets are committing a grave error when they wish ill to European integration. Notwithstanding its recent and ongoing crises, the existence of the EU and of its precursors has been associated with a number of good outcomes, which should be particularly dear to those who believe in democratic capitalism. Throughout the history of the EU and its precursors, its member countries have been democratic and at peace—an anomaly by historical standards. Its benign influence contributed to the successful transition of a number of Central and Eastern European countries, with a total population of nearly 100 million, to democracy and markets. European integration has also put an end to protectionist barriers that have long divided European nations. What is more, through a concerted effort to reduce regulatory obstacles to trade and the movement of capital, services, and people, it has created the largest integrated marketplace in the world.

The EU's critics are quick to point out that these achievements cannot be attributed fully, or perhaps at all, to the integration project. Peace and free trade in Europe do not require a quasi-federal government in Brussels. In this book, I provide a twofold response to that objection. First, I remind conservative critics of the EU of a foundational principle of conservative thought: *epistemic humility*. Establishing reliable causal links is notoriously difficult in history and in the social sciences, especially if they pertain to large, one-off events that lack obvious counterfactuals. That applies to the link between European integration and Europe's peace and prosperity. The uncertainty about what came first (the EU or prosperity) should make conservatives wary of large, irreversible changes to existing political institutions, including those governing the EU. This is because such changes are susceptible to ushering in unintended, unforeseen consequences that will be well beyond our control and could destroy peace, democracy, and prosperity on the European continent.

But there is also a second line of response to the EU's conservative critics, which I pursue in this book. As a matter of fact, we do have ample historical evidence of what the Europe of sovereign nation-states, unencumbered by the EU, looked like. That evidence lends little credence to the notion that there is no need for common European political institutions to keep the continent free and at peace. The pre-EU Europe was a continent ravaged by wars and authoritarianism, as well as by economic nationalism and protectionism. In fact, even Friedrich August von Hayek, one of the most prominent free-market thinkers of the 20th century, recognized that an international federal structure was a necessary component of the architecture of a free and peaceful world. In short, I attempt to show in this book that instead of feeding the fantasy of an EU-less Europe, defenders of a free society need to come to the forefront of efforts to reform the European institutions that already exist. With their appreciation for a limited, accountable government and free enterprise, conservatives are naturally positioned to be a source of fresh ideas on how to close the EU's democratic deficit and how to make European integration an engine of Europe's prosperity again.

Like similar projects, this book cannot be fully dissociated from its author. I became interested in classical liberal thought and free-market economics at an early age, largely in light of the experience of my home country, Slovakia, in its transition from communism to democracy and the market economy. Very early on, I internalized the canonical criticisms of the European project. Before graduating from high school around 2000, I wrote an op-ed for the now-defunct Slovak weekly *Domino fórum* lambasting the EU for introducing the euro. At that time, I was extremely fond of Hayek's idea of currency competition, squarely incompatible with the project of the common currency. With some effort, it might be possible to dig out the article, which did not take any prisoners in its critique of European elites, from the annals of the early days of the Slovak Internet. In 2009, I spent the summer interning in the office of President Václav Klaus of the Czech Republic, who was at the time refusing to sign the Lisbon Treaty. When I joined the think tank world a year later, criticizing the EU became my daily bread first at the Legatum Institute in London and later at the Cato Institute in Washington, DC. I have written extensively about its outdated competition policy,[7] the moral hazard created by bailouts in the Eurozone[8] and the costs of the common European currency,[9] the corrupting influence of the EU structural funds,[10] and the Common Agricultural Policy.[11]

I stand by most of these criticisms. However, in the past two years, I have come to the realization that, for all its flaws, the European project has been beneficial for the continent, especially when compared with plausible alternatives. The event that made me revisit my Eurosceptic beliefs was Kyiv's Maidan. It reminded me, in the first instance, of the importance of the prospect of political integration for the success of postcommunist transitions elsewhere in the region. In the second instance, it reminded me that free societies do not exist in a geopolitical vacuum. To an Anglo-Saxon reader, this observation might appear uninteresting or trivial, but it resonates strongly with the experience of many on the European continent. To a varying extent, the countries of Central and Eastern Europe share a painful history of war, occupation, ethnic cleansing, and totalitarianism—sometimes self-inflicted and sometimes perpetrated by Europe's great powers. These countries also share an understanding, albeit clouded by the current rise of populist nationalism in the region, that the only way to avoid a repetition of such events is to join the community of Western liberal democracies. Britons might easily imagine a peaceful, democratic, and prosperous future outside the EU. However, for many denizens of the European continent, a demise of Europe's political order represents an existential threat. For that reason, I have come to the firm belief that the right choice for Europeans is to keep the EU together.

While I am solely responsible for the errors in the book, I am indebted to countless individuals for their support and feedback, which helped to turn this project into reality. First and foremost, my thanks goes to Susan McEachern, my editor at Rowman & Littlefield, for taking her chances with a previously unpublished author and for overseeing the editing and publication process with an extraordinary degree of efficiency. I also thank Erik Jones and Ron Tiersky for including the manuscript in the *Europe Today* series.

I benefited from conversations with Jeff Gedmin, Fredrik Erixon, Tyler Cowen, Alex Teytelboym, Pavol Hardoš, Warren Coats, Anne Applebaum, Ken Weinstein, Tim Harford, Robert Hahn, Ivan Mikloš, Michael Žantovský, Charles Gati, Nigel Ashford, Andrei Illarionov, Lady Elizabeth Roberts, Diego Zuluaga Laguna, Dominique Lazanski, Lars Christensen, and many others. I am equally grateful for critical reactions to this and my earlier writings by those who do not share my perspective on European affairs, including my former colleague at the Cato Institute, Marian L. Tupy, the Heritage Foundation's Nile Gardiner and Ted Bromund, and Petr Mach.

The origins of this book can be traced back to a short article that I wrote for *Reason* magazine's website in September 2014.[12] I thank J. D. Tucille for shepherding it through the publication process. Ian Vásquez, at the time my colleague at the Cato Institute, provided me with extremely helpful comments on the first draft. Many ideas presented in this book originated in other pieces that I wrote for various other outlets. For their kind help with these, I thank Max Strasser, then at *Foreign Policy*,[13] Adrian Ho at the *Wall Street Journal*,[14] Iain Martin at *CapX*,[15] Joe Gregory at the *New York Times*,[16] Tunku Varadarajan at *Politico*,[17] Daniel Kennelly and Damir Marusic at *The American Interest*,[18] as well as Štefan Hríb, the founder and editor-in-chief of Slovakia's leading center-right weekly *Týždeň*, where I contribute a monthly column.

Special thanks belong to my colleagues and friends at the American Enterprise Institute (AEI), including Joe Gates, Olivier Ballou, Gary J. Schmitt, Katie Earle, and above all to Dany Pletka, who hired me and let me run with my ideas. Jon Rodeback, AEI's senior editor, dramatically improved the manuscript—as did James Cunningham, Lauren Duffy, Eleanor O'Neil, Heather Sims, and Sahana Kumar.

Finally, I owe an enormous deal of gratitude to my loving and tolerant wife, Petra Orogványiová.

Washington, DC, February 2016

NOTES

1. Schulz, "Pulling Europe Back from the Brink."
2. Soros and Schmitz, "'The EU Is on the Verge of Collapse'—An Interview."
3. Olterman, "Jürgen Habermas's Verdict on the EU/Greece Debt Deal."
4. Juncker, "State of the Union 2015: Time for Honesty, Unity and Solidarity."
5. Global Agenda Council on Europe, *Europe*, 1.
6. BBC News, "Nigel Farage."

7. Rohac, "Why the EU's Microsoft Fine Is Self-Defeating."
8. Rohac, "Europe Doesn't Need an Alexander Hamilton."
9. Lachman and Rohac, "A European Economic Tsunami?"
10. Rohac, "How the European Union Corrupted Eastern Europe."
11. Rohac, "Is the Common Agricultural Policy sustainable?"
12. Rohac, "The Libertarian Case for the European Union."
13. Rohac, "The Conservative's Case for the European Union."
14. Rohac, "The Dangerous Eurosceptic Myth."
15. Rohac, "Concerns of Brexit Are Not Scaremongering."
16. Rohac, "Ending the Refugee Deadlock."
17. Rohac, "Europe Returns to the 1930s."
18. Rohac, "Playing with Fire."

REFERENCES

BBC News, "Nigel Farage: Referendum a Tipping Point for EU 'Project.'" December 16, 2015. http://www.bbc.com/news/uk-politics-eu-referendum-35111029.

Global Agenda Council on Europe. *Europe: What to Watch Out for in 2016–2017.* World Economic Forum, 2016. http://www3.weforum.org/docs/WEF_White_Paper_Europe_What_Watch_Out_for_2016-2017.pdf.

Juncker, Jean-Claude. "State of the Union 2015: Time for Honesty, Unity and Solidarity." Address to the European Parliament, Strasbourg, September 9, 2015. http://europa.eu/rapid/press-release_SPEECH-15-5614_en.htm.

Lachman, Desmond, and Dalibor Rohac. "A European Economic Tsunami?" *International Herald Tribune*, December 11, 2010. http://www.nytimes.com/2010/12/11/opinion/11iht-edlachman11.html?_r=1.

Olterman, Philip. "Jürgen Habermas's Verdict on the EU/Greece Debt Deal—Full Transcript." *The Guardian*, July 16, 2015. http://www.theguardian.com/commentisfree/2015/jul/16/jurgen-habermas-eu-greece-debt-deal.

Rohac, Dalibor. "Is the Common Agricultural Policy Sustainable?" *L'Anglophone*, March 11, 2011. http://www.langlophone.com/fulleuopinion.php?id=725.

———. "Europe Doesn't Need an Alexander Hamilton—It Needs Leaders Who Will Stand Against Bailouts." *Conservative Home*, August 14, 2012. http://www.conservativehome.com/platform/2012/08/from-dalibor-rohac-europe-doesnt-need-an-alexander-hamilton.html.

———. "Why the EU's Microsoft Fine Is Self-Defeating." *US News & World Report*, March 11, 2013. http://www.usnews.com/opinion/articles/2013/03/11/europes-outdated-self-defeating-competition-policy.

———. "How the European Union Corrupted Eastern Europe." *National Review*, May 26, 2014. http://www.nationalreview.com/agenda/378798/how-european-union-corrupted-eastern-europe-dalibor-rohac.

———. "The Libertarian Case for the European Union." *Reason*, September 9, 2014. http://reason.com/archives/2014/09/09/the-libertarian-case-for-the-european-un.

———. "Concerns of Brexit Are Not Scaremongering." *CapX*, November 11, 2015. http://capx.co/concerns-over-brexit-are-not-scaremongering/.

———. "Ending the Refugee Deadlock." New York Times, January 29, 2016. http://www.nytimes.com/2016/01/30/opinion/ending-the-refugee-deadlock.html?_r=0.

———. "Europe Returns to the 1930s." *Politico*, September 9, 2015. http://www.politico.eu/article/europe-returns-to-the-1930s-revolt-leadeship-nazi/.

————. "Playing with Fire." *American Interest*, June 12, 2015. http://www.the-american-interest.com/2015/06/12/playing-with-fire-2/.

————. "The Conservative's Case for the European Union." *Foreign Policy*, September 17, 2015. http://foreignpolicy.com/2015/09/17/the-conservative-case-for-the-european-union-defending-Eurosceptic-onslaught/.

————. "The Dangerous Eurosceptic Myth." *Wall Street Journal*, September 30, 2015. http://www.wsj.com/articles/the-dangerous-Eurosceptic-myth-1443636967.

Schulz, Martin. "Pulling Europe Back from the Brink." Social Europe, January 21, 2016. https://www.socialeurope.eu/2016/01/pulling-europe-back-from-the-brink/.

Soros, George, and Gregor Peter Schmitz. "'The EU Is on the Verge of Collapse'—An Interview." *New York Review of Books*, February 11, 2016. http://www.nybooks.com/articles/2016/02/11/europe-verge-collapse-interview/.

I

EUROPE'S HUBRIS AND NEMESIS

In 1939, just before the outbreak of the Second World War, the Austrian economist Friedrich von Hayek wrote a powerful defense of the idea of a European federation. Hayek later received the Nobel Prize in economics, made substantial contributions to legal theory and political philosophy, and became the central figure of the free-market movement. In the essay, he called a European federation a "goal in whose value [he] profoundly [believed]"[1] and outlined how it could prevent the recurrence of Europe's destructive waves of nationalism and protectionism. Hayek reiterated his message several years later in his world-famous book *The Road to Serfdom*, which in 2010 achieved a new level of popularity in the United States, including a rise to the top of Amazon's best seller list after Glenn Beck mentioned it on his television program.[2] "What we need," Hayek writes there, "is a superior political power which can hold the economic interests in check and in the conflict between them can truly hold the scales."[3] Europe should therefore create a federal structure with an "international government under which certain strictly defined powers are transferred to an international authority,"[4] while leaving other competences to individual countries. In Hayek's opinion, there is no conflict between the idea of a European federation and the principles of classical liberalism and free enterprise. Quite the contrary, the two are mutually reinforcing, with open markets being a prerequisite of a successful federation and "the abrogation of national sovereignties" being "the logical consummation of the liberal program."[5]

Hayek did not see himself as a political conservative. A self-professed *classical liberal*, he even authored an essay[6] bearing the unambiguous title "Why I am Not a Conservative." However, his work has been central to the historic success of modern conservatism in the United States and the United Kingdom. Also known as fusionism in the United States, it brought together elements of center-right thinking in a coalition that advocated for free markets, robust international leadership of Western democracies, and, to a limited extent, social conservatism. The rise of Ronald Reagan in the United States and Margaret Thatcher in the United Kingdom—both heavily influenced by Hayek's thought—is perhaps the most significant illustration of how consequential his work was for the fusionist movement. Thatcher is reported to have pointed to her copy of *The Constitution of Liberty*—a tome that, paradoxically, includes Hayek's critique of conservatism—declaring "this is what we believe."[7]

The contrast between his enthusiastic embrace of European integration and the scathing criticisms of today's European Union (EU) by Hayek's followers could not be greater. In a famous speech in 1988, Thatcher compared the EU to the Soviet Union, a country "which [has] tried to run everything from the center." In the wake of the financial crisis, a rejection of the EU has almost become one of the defining characteristics of the free-market movements. Barbara Kolm, president of the Hayek Institute in Vienna, Austria, predicts that the European Union will not be able to avoid its social unrest and will eventually collapse.[8] At meetings of the Mont Pèlerin Society, a prestigious scholarly association founded by Hayek in 1947, lambasting the EU, the euro, or even the freedom of movement[9] on the continent has become *de rigueur*. "[N]o matter how much the Eurocrats huff and puff, the European Project no longer is the Europeans' project," writes Doug Bandow, a fellow at the libertarian Cato Institute in Washington, DC,[10] which once featured Hayek as its distinguished senior fellow.[11] Conservatives and advocates of free enterprise are by no means alone in their criticisms. The trust of Europeans in their common political institutions, gradually falling since the 1990s, plummeted in the aftermath of the Great Recession, giving birth to new Eurosceptic parties and empowering old ones.[12]

The central argument of this book is that, although the criticisms directed at the EU are often justified, Hayek's followers are mistaken in their wholesale rejection of the European project. Furthermore, their critique comes at a time when the EU is facing unprecedented stress, created not only by its own institutional deficiencies but also by the rise of extremist politics in Europe, sluggish economic performance, and Russia's resurgence as an aggressive, revisionist power. Instead of being at the forefront of discussions about how Europe's common market and political cooperation can be repaired, strengthened, and defended against their enemies, conservative critics of the EU have become cheerleaders for Europe's disintegration, with potentially catastrophic consequences. True, today's EU is far from being the free-market ideal outlined in Hayek's essay. However, even in its current, flawed form, it represents a momentous achievement, which ought to be celebrated by friends of free enterprise and liberal democracy. It secures the functioning of the European single market, restrains protectionist and authoritarian impulses of politicians, and provides a platform for peaceful collaboration between European states. None of those should be taken for granted.

THE RISE OF EUROPE AND THE ROOTS OF THE EUROPEAN IDEA

The story of the EU's rise and of its current crisis cannot be fully understood without appreciating the horrific experience of the two world wars that ravaged the continent in the first half of the 20th century. Hayek's own life was affected by the turmoil. He was born to a wealthy and cultured Viennese family in 1899—at a time of exuberant optimism and progress across Europe. Hayek's father was a botanist, who lectured at the University of Vienna. His mother, in turn, was related to the parents of the philosopher Ludwig von Wittgenstein. But Europe's self-evidently bright future took a dark turn in 1914. Hayek served in an artillery regiment on the Italian front towards the end of World War I, reportedly suffering damage to his hearing in his left ear.[13] After the war, Austria went through a period of political and economic upheaval, including a period of hyperinflation, and frequent clashes between right-wing and left-wing paramilitary groups. Already established as a respected academic economist, Hayek joined the London School of Economics in 1931 and became one of the world's most influential business cycle theorists. His return home became impossible after Adolf Hitler annexed Austria in 1938. Hayek thus became a British subject, moving to the United States in 1950 and returning to Austria and Germany only in the 1960s.

In popular imagination, of course, the idea of a European federation is associated much more strongly with Winston Churchill's "United States of Europe" speech than with anything Hayek wrote. Delivered in Zurich in 1946, Churchill used the speech to show that Europe's federal state was the only possible solution to "frightful nationalistic quarrels" on the continent. The purpose of such a state is to restrain the individual nation-states and impose a formal equality between European countries:

> Small nations will count as much as large ones and gain their honor by a contribution to the common cause. The ancient states and principalities of Germany, freely joined for mutual convenience in a federal system, might take their individual places among the United States of Europe.[14]

The idea of a common European state predates both Churchill's speech and Hayek's writings. In the early 1920s, while Europe was recovering from the war, Richard Nikolaus von Coudenhove-Kalergi, an Austrian contemporary of Hayek, wrote a book, *Pan-Europa*,[15] which gave birth to the eponymous political movement. Coudenhove-Kalergi, born in 1895 to a Japanese mother, was also the scion of an ancient family, tracing its lineage to Byzantine emperors. His father, an Austrian diplomat, known also for his writings on the origins of anti-Semitism, held numerous postings, including in Argentina and Japan, where he met his future wife, Mitsuko Aoyama, who later became one of the first Japanese citizens to ever emigrate to Europe.[16]

Both in its substance and style, *Pan-Europa* reflected the anxieties of the era, marked by the recent war, hyperinflation, and political extremism. Coudenhove-Kalergi says:

> A fragmented Europe leads to war, oppression, misery; a united Europe to peace, freedom, prosperity! Once this either-or in its full meaning is clear to Europeans—then everyone will choose which of these two paths they want to go down: the path of European an-

archy—or the way towards European organization; the path of
death—or the way of life.[17]

Before 1914, many intellectuals simply assumed that deeper economic
ties among Western nations had made military conflicts obsolete—and
indeed impossible. The British politician Norman Angell, who was later
awarded the Nobel Peace Prize, popularized this view in his 1910 book,
The Great Illusion.[18] The title referred to the purportedly illusory idea
that nations had anything to gain from warfare. However, the book
came to illustrate a very different kind of misguided illusion: namely
that rational arguments about the costs and benefits of warfare could
stop politicians from making foolish choices.[19] Thirteen years later,
Coudenhove-Kalergi understood that economic interdependence was
not in itself enough to prevent conflict, unless accompanied by a system
of political cooperation. Like Hayek, he saw the two as sides of the same
coin. "Without a backup of European permanent peace a European
customs union is impossible. As long as each state lives in constant fear
of its neighbors, it must be prepared to produce all its necessary goods
like a besieged fortress even in the event of war." And, "[c]onversely,
national industries and their protection by the state are a hotbed of
European nationalism and a threat to the European Peace."[20]

The idea of a European federation resonated with many intellectuals, including Thomas Mann, Albert Einstein, and Sigmund Freud.
Hayek's mentor, Ludwig von Mises, who is generally seen as an even
more radical defender of free-market capitalism than his protégé, is
reported to have studied the monetary implications of Coudenhove-
Kalergi's plan[21] and agreed that "the evils that those who champion the
idea of a United States of Europe are trying to combat undoubtedly
exist, and the sooner they are eliminated, the better."[22] However, he
remained critical. Unlike today's conservatives, Mises was not concerned by the risk of undermining the sovereignty of Europe's nation-
states. Quite the contrary, for him, that was a selling point of the whole
project. Instead, his concern was that the United States of Europe
would replace the destructive nationalistic chauvinism that existed in
Europe with its equally damaging, pan-European version, directed
against America or Asia. What was needed instead, he argued, was a
genuinely cosmopolitan, peaceful outlook towards the entire world,

which he did not think could be found in attempts to reconstitute the nation-state on a larger scale.[23]

Mises's worries about the chauvinism of a *united* Europe were purely hypothetical, given the circumstances of the era. The interwar period was hardly an auspicious time to translate European federalism into practice. Only the 1950s saw the emergence of institutions establishing tighter economic and political ties between once-warring countries. The European Coal and Steel Community was created in 1951, followed by the European Atomic Energy Community (Euratom) and the European Economic Community (EEC) in 1957, which later formed the fundamental elements of Europe's political architecture. Its enlargements in the 1970s and 1980s brought the UK, Greece, Spain, and Portugal into the club. Gradually, the project started to take a more state-like form. The European Parliament, for example, originally a purely consultative body, was beginning to appear as a real legislature. The Single European Act of 1987 and the Maastricht Treaty, adopted in 1992, consolidated the numerous components of the project into the "three pillars" of the EU: economic integration, common foreign and security policy, and a common approach towards justice and home affairs.

In the decades that followed the war, also known as the *trente glorieuses* (the 30 glorious [years]) or the *Wirtschaftswunder* (the economic miracle), the European project seemed to have everything going for it. Between 1950 and 1971, the 12 Western European economies grew by an impressive annual rate of 4.7 percent.[24] Even after the oil shocks and the global productivity slowdown of the 1970s, integrated Europe enjoyed unprecedented levels of economic prosperity. The collapse of Soviet communism liberated millions of Europeans who had been living behind the Iron Curtain, and gave a new sense of purpose to European integration: to create a *"Europe whole and free,"* as the US President George H. W. Bush put it in his speech in Mainz, Germany, in May 1989.[25]

The economic success of Europe that facilitated European integration also became its hidden enemy, as it fostered the hubris of European elites.[26] In good times, the deficiencies of the European construction were not clearly visible. Neither were Europe's leaders particularly concerned that the popular support for deeper integration was falling since the early 1990s.[27] The euro, another product of the Maastricht

Treaty, was born out of this hubris as a step towards Europe's future political union. In fact, the single currency would not have come as a shock to Hayek, who in his 1939 essay defended the creation of a single monetary unit to limit the discretion of national central banks.[28] However, the ratification of the Maastricht Treaty exposed the growing gap in opinion between the public and Europe's political elites. In the UK, which had just left—with a degree of bitterness—the European Exchange Rate Mechanism (an early precursor of the euro), the prospect of monetary union led to a rebellion by Conservative MPs when the Parliament considered treaty ratification. In Denmark, voters rejected the Treaty in a referendum. Only after the country was granted a number of exemptions—most importantly a permanent opt-out from the euro—was the treaty put to a popular vote again in 1993 and ratified.

But this was not the last time that Europe's political elites, convinced of the historical importance of what they were doing, asked voters to rectify their choice. In 2001, inspired by America's Founding Fathers, European leaders organized a "European Convention," which was given the task of drafting the EU constitution. The convention was chaired by Valéry Giscard d'Estaing, former president of France (1974–1981). An aristocratic figure already in his late seventies at the time of the convention, Giscard d'Estaing was a former Résistance fighter and a lifelong supporter of the European project, which he defended against attacks from the French "gaullistes." The convention was drawn from members of national parliaments and representatives of national governments, as well as the European Commission and European Parliament.

After two years of deliberations, EU leaders signed the Treaty Establishing a Constitution for Europe.[29] Unlike the Constitution of the United States, written on five parchment pages, the European version had 484 pages and featured an extensive list of positive rights guaranteed by the Union, including the rights to paid leave, maternity leave,[30] and housing assistance.[31] The treaty granted the EU legal personhood and added a number of new shared competencies on matters that were previously managed solely by member states. It created the function of the president of the European Council selected for a term of two and a half years, scrapping the system of a six-month rotational presidency. It introduced the position of the Union Minister for Foreign Affairs and Security Policy, who would also serve as the vice president of the European Commission. In the Council, more decisions would be taken by qualified majority rule. To the ire of many of its critics, the Treaty also contained a "passerelle clause,"[32] which enabled the Council to move certain policy areas to qualified majority rule, as opposed to unanimity. That would create space, the critics feared, for even more majoritarian, nonconsensual decision making in the future.

If European leaders felt that they were writing history, voters were increasingly alienated. Some countries ratified the document in their national parliaments; Luxembourg and Spain held referenda. In Spain, just 42 percent of voters showed up to the polls. But the real shock came in the end of May and beginning of June 2005, when France and the Netherlands held their popular votes. Turnout rates were high—over 60 percent—and in both cases, voters rejected the proposed constitutional arrangement for Europe.

Some leaders, including Giscard d'Estaing, were in denial. "It is not France that has said no. It is 55 percent of the French people—45 percent of the French people said yes," he claimed, adding that he wished that "we [would] have a new chance, a second chance, for the constitutional project." Furthermore, "if we had chosen to have a parliamentary vote last year the constitution would have been easily adopted. It is the *method* that has provoked the rejection."[33] In the aftermath of the referendum, there were rumors that ratification in other member states could still continue, in order to pressure France and the Netherlands to put the treaty to another vote or to rush it through their parliaments. Given France's size and importance, that was a tough sell—unlike similar repetitions in EU-related referenda earlier in Denmark or later in Ireland. After a two-year period of "reflection," a committee was created under the leadership of former Prime Minister of Italy Giuliano Amato, another veteran of European politics, and populated by retired European politicians and such other grandees as Dominique Strauss-Kahn, at the time the managing director of the International Monetary Fund, to create an alternative solution.

Within less than a year, the Amato Group released a document that was essentially a rehashed version of the constitution. If it were shorter, it was only because much of its material was relegated to protocols amending previous treaties. Unlike the Constitution for Europe, the Treaty of Lisbon,[34] as the new document was called, did not replace previous European treaties, but amended them in ways that were largely equivalent to the earlier document. It again created a permanent presidency of the Council and a version of the EU "foreign minister," and extended the number of policy areas that were to be decided by qualified majority. The treaty also contained the controversial "passerelle clause," which would enable European leaders to reduce the scope of decision making by unanimity in the future.[35]

"People have the right to change their opinion. The people might consider they made a mistake,"[36] Giscard d'Estaing said about the unsuccessful referendum in France. But this time around, European politicians were not taking any chances. Only one referendum was held, in Ireland, where it was required by constitution. Elsewhere the text was ratified by parliamentary majorities. But in June 2008 Irish voters rejected the proposal. Toughened by the precedent set by the Danish ratification of the Maastricht Treaty and two earlier Irish referenda on the Treaty of Nice (in 2001 and 2002) Europe's political leaders did not blink. Then-President of the European Parliament Hans-Gert Pöttering alleged supposed irregularities around the funding of the Irish "no" campaign, which was organized by the Libertas movement led by businessman Declan Ganley.[37] To some public outrage,[38] the architects of ever closer Europe decided to ask the Irish again, until they got the answer right. The new pre-referendum campaign was intense, with the EU providing funding to the "yes" side.[39] On October 2, 2009, over 67 percent of Irish voters said yes, at a turnout rate of 59 percent.

EU'S NEMESIS

If the convoluted constitutional changes shoved down the Europeans' throats were a sign of the EU's hubris, its nemesis was just around the corner. Since the onset of the global financial crisis, which triggered a series of debt crises on the Eurozone's periphery, the pendulum of European integration has swung firmly in the opposite direction. Some, including the former President of the European Commission José Manuel Barroso, still believe that a European federation should be "our political horizon,"[40] but the European public and the leaders of European countries display little appetite for deeper integration. At the time when Barroso delivered his 2012 "State of the Union" address that urged for tighter federalization, only 8 percent of Europeans reported that they were "very attached" to the EU. In contrast, as many as 51 percent were very attached to their country, and 49 percent reported the same degree of attachment to their town or village. On the same survey, Europeans also saw EU institutions as largely irrelevant. When asked to name the public authorities with the greatest impact on their lives, 51 percent mentioned the national government, 34 percent their local or regional governments, and only 9 percent mentioned the EU.[41]

Today's crisis of confidence in Europe should not be a surprise. Already in 2002, the eminent Oxford philosopher Larry Siedentop warned that "[b]y allowing an elitist strategy for rapid European integration to shape the image of liberal democracy in Europe, . . . centrist politicians may unwittingly be fostering the things which are the most antithetical to liberal democracy—xenophobic nationalism and economic autarky."[42] It is possible that the dwindling enthusiasm for the EU will serve as an impetus to make the European project more restrained and humble. But there is also the risk that the erosion of support for the project, coupled with centrifugal forces on the continent and in the UK, will recreate political dynamics similar to those witnessed by the contemporaries of Hayek and Coudenhove-Kalergi in the 1930s.

A Rising Russia

The ingredients for a major political and economic calamity are already here. First, as in the 1930s, the European continent is facing a formidable challenge in the form of a rising revisionist power: Vladimir Putin's Russia. Of course, one should not overplay this parallel. Putin is no Adolf Hitler. He does not embrace a murderous ideology that would command him to try to take over the world or annihilate any ethnic groups. However, much like Germany in the 1930s, today's Russia is emerging as a belligerent, revisionist autocracy, bent on challenging the international order. Like Germany's defeat in World War I, the collapse of the Soviet Union has left an imprint on the Russian psyche, which Putin has leveraged masterfully to strengthen his own hold on power.

Following the collapse of USSR, Russia was perceived as just another, albeit somewhat larger and more complicated, postcommunist country. Notwithstanding its various flaws and idiosyncrasies, the eventual integration of Russia into Western political structures was seen as a matter of course. In 1994, Russia joined NATO's Partnership for Peace program. In 2002, the NATO-Russia Council was created to provide a platform for strengthening the ties between Russia and its former Western adversaries. In a move vastly out of proportion to the role that Russia played in the world economy, it joined the G7 in 1997.

But Russia is not just a scaled-up, perhaps more corrupt version of Bulgaria or Slovakia. Its regime is not trying to integrate the country into the international political structures devised by liberal democracies, but to subvert them and to reassert itself in its traditional sphere of influence, through militarism and destabilization of its neighbors, including Moldova, Georgia, and Ukraine.[43] The methods of warfare are different than in the 1930s. Russia's control of energy resources and skillful propaganda have enabled the Kremlin to reach even farther west and to erode the democratic gains made by Central European countries that escaped the bosom of the Soviet Union. Following the end of the First World War, the United States retreated from Europe, leaving European countries to organize their own affairs. Today, in light of its pivot to Asia and of the continuing turmoil in the Middle East, the United States, the long-standing guarantor of security in Europe, can no longer be expected to continue to play the same role that it did throughout the Cold War. But no other liberal democracy is ready to take on the responsibility. The UK is drifting away from the continent and has little appetite to play the role of a great world power again. Germany, the EU's natural leader, lacks the ambition to come across as truly assertive in today's world, perhaps due to the trauma of Second World War.

Economic Pains

Second, just like in Hayek's time, Europe is living through a protracted economic crisis. The world, both in the aftermath of the Great Depression and today, is sluggishly recovering from a deep recession, which has tainted the perceptions of free-market capitalism in the popular imagination and paved the road towards political extremism. Some economists, including Milton Friedman, one of the intellectual leaders of the free-market movement, blamed the severity of the Great Depression on inept monetary policy.[44] In the face of a large shock, central banks let Western economies contract and undergo painful downward price adjustments, instead of aggressively providing them with liquidity. One reason was their commitment to gold convertibility. The euro is today's version of the interwar gold standard. While not anchored to the price of a real commodity and therefore allowing for the conduct of a countercyclical monetary policy, it prevents peripheral Eurozone countries, such as Italy or Greece, from using exchange rate adjustments to alleviate economic pain.

The interwar gold standard eventually disintegrated, probably for the best. Countries that left it first and devalued, such as the United Kingdom and the Nordic countries, experienced more vigorous economic recoveries than those that remained trapped in the "golden fetters" for longer. However, leaving the Eurozone is technically and politically a much riskier enterprise than severing the link to gold, which goes a long way towards explaining the length and severity of the recession in a country like Greece. It does not explain, however, why the European Central Bank (ECB) exacerbated the economic downturn by systematically undershooting its own inflation target and by letting countries on the Eurozone's periphery slip into deflation.

The ECB, I argue in chapter 4, deserves a substantial amount of blame for the lackluster performance of European economies after 2008. But it would be misleading to reduce Europe's economic malaise to a cyclical issue. Already in 2008, Alberto Alesina and Francesco Giavazzi, two of the most prominent Italian economists, published a popular book that argued that because "there [was] a good chance that the twenty-first century will be the century of European decline."[45] Their reasons are not difficult to imagine: the lack of incentives encouraging entrepreneurship, innovation, and hard work (when they work, Europeans work much shorter hours than Americans), falling quality of university education, overregulated labor markets, and bloated welfare states. To illustrate the risk of Europe's absolute economic decline, figure 1.1 depicts the evolution of total factor productivity in the "old" EU countries (i.e., the 15 economies that formed the EU before its 2004 enlargement) and compares it with the United States. Total factor productivity (TFP) is a measure used by economists to capture the underlying dynamism of an economy. It tracks the growth of income (output) that cannot be accounted for by the growth of the underlying factors of production (capital and labor) and needs to be explained by other factors, such as technological innovation and entrepreneurship.

TFP matters because it is what drives modern economic growth. In our era, prosperity does not come from ever-larger numbers of workers or from larger amounts physical capital. Western populations are not growing substantially, and there are limits on how much can be invested into new production capabilities. To a great extent, the improvements in our living standards result from the ability of innovators to come up with new ideas about how to put the available resources to productive uses.

Even prior to the Great Recession, TFP growth in Western Europe was slower than in the United States. The figure deliberately excludes postcommunist countries that joined the EU in the 2000s, because those have seen significant catch-up growth, including improvements in productivity, and the problem of secular stagnation is less relevant there. When the recession hit, the contraction in productivity was much deeper in Europe than in the United States. Whereas TFP growth in the United States has quickly rebounded, it continues to fall in Europe, where it is currently lower than in 2000, suggesting that the continent has in many ways "unlearned" how to combine productive resources in useful ways. This is a result of Europe's lack of pro-growth reforms that would, among other things, improve market flexibility and accelerate the creation and diffusion of new technologies.[46]

Of course, the divergence in productivity between the United States and the EU has been amplified by the greater severity of the Great Recession in Europe relative to the United States. But the underlying problem is a much older one. Spain, for example, has seen a negative TFP growth *every year* since 1995. Similarly catastrophic performances have been witnessed by other countries on the EU's Mediterranean periphery. The risk, as Alesina and Giavazzi warn, is not just of relative decline, but also of absolute economic decline, as observed in Argentina during the 20th century.

If growth accounting sounds abstract, consider another measure of economic health: the labor market outcomes of young people. Figure 1.2 displays the rate of unemployment among young people in the United States and in the "old Europe," alongside the particularly alarming example of Spain. Young people are typically more vulnerable to cyclical fluctuations, as companies will typically hold on to their time-tested, experienced employees in times of crisis, rather than the junior staff. For years prior to the Great Recession, youth unemployment in

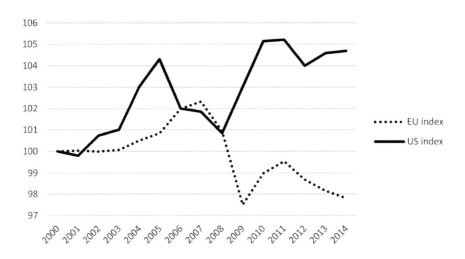

Figure 1.1.   Total factor productivity in the United States and in EU-2004 (2000=100). Data from: Conference Board, Total Economy Database.

the EU had been substantially higher than in the United States, driven by rigidities on its labor markets. In many countries, particularly in the Mediterranean, close to a third of all young people in the labor force were actively seeking employment. The numbers skyrocketed in Greece, Italy, Spain, and Portugal with the onset of the financial crisis and have never returned anywhere near their pre-crisis levels. Although some American commentators and economists deplored "jobless recovery" in their country[47] at a time when US job growth was slow in spite of a vigorous recovery, the situation has been much bleaker in Europe. Again, the Mediterranean countries, such as Spain, where youth unemployment rates have exceeded 50 percent, show a distinctly sad picture. In the aftermath of the crisis, Spain has experienced *net emigration* for the first time since the 1970s, as around 400,000 Spaniards leave each year for Germany, the UK, the United States, and other countries that offer more and better economic opportunities.[48]

Who Is Winning the War of Ideas?

In addition to its social costs, the lack of enticing economic prospects for young people breeds populism and political extremism. Liberal democracy and free enterprise, after all, derive a lot of their popular

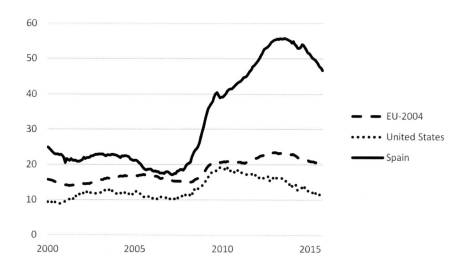

Figure 1.2.   Unemployment under 25 years of age, seasonally adjusted. Data from: Eurostat, Unemployment Statistics.

legitimacy from their ability to deliver tangible economic benefits. That disillusion drives the third worrying parallel with Europe's past: rise of anti-democratic and anti-capitalist thinking.[49] In the aftermath of the Great Depression, many Westerners were convinced of the superiority of the Soviet system, including some leading thinkers. Among economists, the famous "socialist calculation debate" raged between defenders of free enterprise and the mainstream of the economic profession, which concluded, for a period, that planned economies could perform just as well as economies that relied on private ownership and free markets.[50] In all fairness, some pro-Soviet intellectuals, such as André Gide and Arthur Koestler, sobered up after *visiting* the USSR.[51] Neither were fascism and Nazism confined just to Italy and the German-speaking lands. In the UK, Oswald Mosley's British Union of Fascists became a respectable political force, attracting support from a significant portion of the British elite, including figures such as Harold Harmsworth, the publisher of the tabloid *Daily Mail*.

Today, liberal democracies and proponents of free enterprise are doubting themselves again. Notwithstanding China's recent slowdown, the "Beijing Consensus"[52] has gained some currency in the West, suggesting that authoritarianism and a government-dominated economy can be a viable alternative to the model founded on democratic capitalism. In some conservative circles, Putin's authoritarianism is praised for his "defense of traditional values against a so-called tolerance that is genderless and infertile," as Patrick Buchanan, a former US presidential candidate, put it.[53] Much like at the time when Hayek wrote about the prospects for a European federation as an antidote to nationalism, the populist far right and far left are again on the rise. In Poland, the Law and Justice Party secured a parliamentary majority thanks to a virulently xenophobic electoral campaign. In Hungary, the governing Fidesz party of Viktor Orbán has been trying to capture the electorate of Jobbik, a Neo-Nazi group that has grown into the second most popular party in the country. In Greece, the economic crisis brought to power Syriza, a coalition of Marxists, Maoists, and other far-left radicals, some of them with connections to the Kremlin.[54] The UK's Labour Party has elected Jeremy Corbyn, a man with a troubling network of friends[55] and fringe views on matters ranging from economic policy to security matters, as its leader. In political spaces once occupied by mainstream political parties, we increasingly find Front National, Jobbik, Podemos, or Sweden Democrats.

Decay of Trust Among Europe's Nations

The fourth and last echo from the 1930s is the gradual erosion of trust and cooperation between European countries. The interwar period was an era of nationalism and lack of leadership by liberal democracies. Firstly, the United States, the world's leading economy, failed to uphold the principles of free trade by introducing the Smoot-Hawley Tariff in 1931, which was followed by a wave of protectionist measures that disrupted trade in Europe. Secondly, until it was too late, European countries failed to form binding alliances that could have prevented the aggression of Hitler's Germany against its neighbors. Today, Europe lacks leadership again, and seems more divided than ever before.

One such division is over fiscal governance in the Eurozone. When Angela Merkel visited Athens in 2012, in one of many heated moments during Greece's debt crisis, 7,000 police officers, including sharpshooters and navy divers, were dispatched in what had been the biggest security operation in the history of the country since US President Bill Clinton's visit in 1999. The *Wall Street Journal* described "six-foot-high metal barriers outside Parliament, two police helicopters, and 10 extra riot-police units—with a water cannon on standby."[56] The fiscal consolidation programs that have been introduced in Greece—which used to be among the countries where the EU enjoyed the highest levels of support—have been seen by its public as impositions by the Germans and the global financial elites and fueled a violent backlash. On Greece's far right, this backlash is epitomized by the rise of Golden Dawn—a neo-Nazi group, which almost dissolved itself in 2005, only to grow into the third largest political group in the country during the crisis. The far-left Syriza, meanwhile, is Greece's leading political formation and an inspiration for left-wing radicals elsewhere. In the Eurozone's Northern member states, a reciprocal problem has appeared. There, populists are lambasting the rescue packages extended by the Troika to Greece on the grounds of the Greeks' being unreliable, lazy, and undeserving of help. The opposition against the bailouts contributed to the emergence of new Eurosceptic parties in Germany, Finland, and Slovakia, as well as to the rise of nationalism across Europe. Regardless of which side—if any—is right in this debate, the sense of victimhood in Greece combined with the perception of Germans, Slovaks, and the Balts that the Greeks are taking advantage of them will make future cooperation more difficult.

Another division has arisen in response to the influx of asylum-seekers into the EU, which accelerated in 2015. Whereas Germany, Sweden and a number of "old" EU countries expressed an accommodative attitude towards refugees fleeing Syria, Central and Eastern European leaders have been much more reserved. They have rejected, for example, the idea of a common EU response, which would involve the resettlement of fixed quotas of asylum-seekers in their countries. Throughout the EU, the refugee crisis has propelled the resurgence of xenophobic populism and of heated anti-immigration rhetoric, making it increasingly uncertain whether a common European response, which would not jeopardize the freedom of movement of people in the EU, can be found.

Finally, the United Kingdom, one of the EU's most prominent members, is slowly drifting away from the bloc and, depending on the outcome of this year's referendum, might decide to leave it altogether. The Eurozone, the refugee crises, and the possible consequences of Brexit are all discussed later in this book. Unsurprisingly, I argue that the EU's hubris has contributed to some (although not all) of these crises, just as the EU's critics are keen to point out. However, the EU's downfall would be the wrong answer to Europe's problems. Quite the contrary, its unraveling would unleash the political forces of nationalism and protectionism, which can destroy, as they did in Hayek's lifetime, liberal democracy and free enterprise on the continent. It is high time for conservatives and advocates of free markets to stop being cheerleaders for the EU's nemesis, and to become—as they did many times before—a fresh source of reform ideas that will help save the EU from itself.

NOTES

1. Hayek, "The Economic Conditions of Interstate Federalism," 272.
2. "Essential Reading," *The Economist*.
3. Hayek, *The Road to Serfdom*, 238.
4. Ibid., 239.
5. Hayek "The Economic Conditions of Interstate Federalism," 269.
6. Hayek, "Postscript: Why I Am Not a Conservative."
7. Margaret Thatcher Foundation, "Thatcher, Hayek & Friedman."
8. Feine and Manning, "Why the European Union Will Fail."
9. Klaus, "Careless Opening Up of Countries."
10. Bandow, "The European Union: Pretension Without Power."
11. See Cato Institute, "F. A. Hayek (1899–1992)."
12. See Torreblanca and Leonard, "The Continent-Wide Rise of Euroscepticism." It is important to stress the extent to which the erosion of trust in European institutions precedes the crisis. See, e.g., Hix, *What's Wrong with the European Union and How to Fix It*, 50–66.
13. Gordon, "Friedrich Hayek as a Teacher."
14. Churchill, speech at the University of Zurich.
15. Coudenhove-Kalergi, *Pan-Europa*.
16. The idea goes even further back in time. As Simms notes, already in 1871, J. R. Seeley published an article in *Macmillan's Magazine* with the title "United States of Europe." See Simms, "Towards a Mighty Union," 49.
17. Coudenhove-Kalergi, *Pan-Europa*.
18. Angell, *The Great Illusion*.
19. The idea is criticized also in Röpke, *International Economic Disintegration*, 68–70. Wilhelm Röpke was a German economist, a contemporary of Hayek, with whom he shared a number of beliefs, including an appreciation of the need for a system of international political cooperation in Europe.

20. Coudenhove-Kalergi, *Pan-Europa*.

21. Coudenhove-Kalergi, *An Idea Conquers the World*, 247.

22. Mises, *Liberalism*, 143.

23. Mises, *Liberalism*, 143–46.

24. Eichengreen and Vazquez, *Institutions and Economic Growth in Post-war Europe*.

25. Bush, "Remarks to the Citizens in Mainz" (emphasis added).

26. On the disconnect between elites and popular opinion about European integration, see Hooghe, "Europe Divided?"

27. See Mudde, "Three Decades of Populist Radical Right Parties in Western Europe," 12.

28. "[T]he states within the Union will not be able to pursue an independent monetary policy. With a common monetary unit, the latitude given to the national central banks will be restricted as much as it was under a rigid gold standard—and possibly rather more since, even under the traditional gold standard, the fluctuations in exchanges between countries were greater than those between different parts of a single state, or than would be desirable to allow within the Union." Hayek, "The Economic Conditions of Interstate Federalism," 259.

29. Treaty Establishing a Constitution for Europe.

30. Ibid., 54.

31. Ibid., 55.

32. Ibid., art. IV-444, 197.

33. Beunderman, "Giscard Demands Second Chance for EU Constitution."

34. Treaty of Lisbon.

35. Ibid., art. 48 (7).

36. Beunderman, "Giscard Demands Second Chance for EU Constitution."

37. Smyth, "MEPs Transparent in Their Suspicions About Libertas."

38. Collins, "Demonstrators Claim EU Is Trying to Railroad Irish Voters."

39. Waterfields, "EU Intervention in Irish Referendum 'Unlawful.'"

40. Barroso, "2012 State of the Union Address."

41. European Commission, "European Citizenship."

42. Siedentop, *Democracy in Europe*, 219.

43. The kleptocratic nature of the regime is discussed in Dawisha, *Putin's Kleptocracy*. For a discussion of the geopolitical threat posed by Putin's regime, see Lucas, *The New Cold War*. See also Aron, *Putin's Russia*.

44. Friedman and Schwartz, *A Monetary History of the United States*.

45. Alesina and Giavazzi, *The Future of Europe*. Even earlier, the 2004 Sapir report noticed Europe's stagnation and proposed remedies. See Sapir et al., *An Agenda for a Growing Europe*.

46. For a more thorough assessment of the productivity slowdown in Western Europe and its causes, see Crafts, *Western Europe's Growth Prospects*.

47. For an early discussion, see Kolesnikova and Liu, "Jobless Recoveries."

48. See Izquierdo et al., "Spain."

49. Existing research suggests that the financial crises have a significant impact on the rise of political extremism. For historical evidence from the Great Depression, see Bromhead et al., "Political Extremism in the 1920s and 1930s." A more systematic account from a broader view of history is offered by Funke et al., "Going to Extremes."

50. For a history of the debate, see Hoff, *Economic Calculation in the Socialist Society*.

51. Both of them later authored penetrating discussions of the process of their disenchantment with the Soviet regime. See Gide, *Retour de l'U.R.S.S.*. See also, the edited volume by Crossman, *The God That Failed*.

52. Cooper Ramo, *The Beijing Consensus*.

53. Buchanan, "Is Putin One of Us?" For a journalistic take on Putin's reinvention as a defender of "traditional values" and social conservatism, see Matthews, "Vladimir Putin's New Plan for World Domination."

54. Jones et al., "Alarm Bells Ring over Syriza's Russian Links."

55. Rohac, "Jeremy Corbyn and His Sinister Friends."

56. Pangalos and Angelos, "Athens Braces for Visit by Merkel."

REFERENCES

Alesina, Alberto, and Francesco Giavazzi. *The Future of Europe: Reform or Decline*. Cambridge: MIT Press, 2008.

Angell, Norman. *The Great Illusion: A Study of the Relation of Military Power to National Advantage*. New York & London: G. P. Putnam's Sons, 1910.

Aron, Leon, ed. *Putin's Russia: How It Rose, How It Is Maintained, and How It Might End*. Washington DC: American Enterprise Institute, 2015.

Bandow, Doug. "The European Union: Pretension Without Power." *Forbes*, February 7, 2011. http://www.cato.org/publications/commentary/european-union-pretension-without-power.

Barroso, José Manuel. "2012 State of the Union Address." September 12, 2012. http://europa.eu/rapid/press-release_SPEECH-12-596_en.htm.

Beunderman, Mark. "Giscard Demands Second Chance for EU Constitution in France." *EU Observer*, May 23, 2006. https://euobserver.com/institutional/21674.

Bromhead, Alan de, Barry Eichengreen, and Kevin H. O'Rourke. "Political Extremism in the 1920s and 1930s: Do the German Lessons Generalize?" *Journal of Economic History* 73 (2012): 371–406.

Buchanan, Patrick J. "Is Putin One of Us?" Patrick J. Buchanan—Official Website, December 17, 2013. http://buchanan.org/blog/putin-one-us-6071.

Bush, George H. W. "Remarks to the Citizens in Mainz." Mainz, Federal Republic of Germany, May 31, 1989. http://usa.usembassy.de/etexts/ga6-890531.htm.

Cato Institute. "F. A. Hayek (1899–1992)—Distinguished Senior Fellow." http://www.cato.org/people/hayek.html.

Churchill, Winston. Speech at the University of Zurich. September 19, 1946. http://www.coe. int/t/dgal/dit/ilcd/Archives/selection/Churchill/ZurichSpeech_en.asp.

Collins, Sarah. 2008. "Demonstrators Claim EU Is Trying to Railroad Irish Voters." *Irish Times*, December 12, 2008. http://www.irishtimes.com/news/world/europe/demon strators-claim-eu-is-trying-to-railroad-irish-voters-1.922609.

Conference Board. Total Economy Database, May 2015. http://www.conference-board.org/ data/economydatabase/.

Cooper Ramo, Joshua. *The Beijing Consensus*. London: Foreign Policy Centre, 2004.

Coudenhove-Kalergi, Richard Nicolaus. *Das Paneuropäische Manifest*. 1923. http://vv.varzil. de/II-01.PDF.

Coudenhove-Kalergi, Richard Nicolaus. *Pan-Europa*. Vienna: Pan-Europa-Verlag, 1923.

———. *An Idea Conquers the World*. London: Hutchinson, 1953.

Crafts, Nicholas. *Western Europe's Growth Prospects: An Historical Perspective*. Competitive Advantage in the Global Economy Research Centre, University of Warwick, 2011. http://ec.europa.eu/economy_finance/events/2011/2011-11-21-annual-research-confer ence_en/pdf/session012_crafts_en.pdf.

Crossman, Richard, ed. *The God That Failed*. New York: Columbia University Press, 2001.

Dawisha, Karen. *Putin's Kleptocracy: Who Owns Russia?* New York: Simon & Schuster, 2014.

Eichengreen, Barry, and Pablo Vazquez. *Institutions and Economic Growth in Postwar Europe: Evidence and Conjectures*. Mimeo, 1999. http://eml.berkeley.edu/~eichengr/ research/vanark.pdf.

"Essential Reading." *The Economist*, June 24, 2010. http://www.economist.com/node/ 16438630.

European Commission. "European Citizenship." *Standard Eurobarometer* 77 (Spring 2012). http://ec.europa.eu/public_opinion/archives/eb/eb77/eb77_citizen_en.pdf.

Eurostat. Unemployment Statistics. S.v. "Unemployment Rate by Sex and Age—Monthly Average." 2015. http://ec.europa.eu/eurostat/statistics-explained/index.php/Unemploy ment_statistics.

Feine, Paul, and Alex Manning. "Why the European Union Will Fail: Q&A with Austrian Economist Barbara Kolm." *Reason*, April 16, 2013. https://reason.com/reasontv/2013/04/ 16/will-the-european-economy-collapse-qa-wi.

Friedman, Milton, and Anna J. Schwartz. *A Monetary History of the United States, 1867–1960*. Princeton: Princeton University Press, 1963.

Funke, Manuel, Moritz Schularick, and Christoph Trebesch. "Going to Extremes: Politics After Financial Crisis, 1870–2014." *CESifo Working Paper* No. 5553, 2015.

Gide, André. *Retour de l'U.R.S.S.* Paris: Editions Gallimard, 1966.

Gordon, David. "Friedrich Hayek as a Teacher." *Mises Daily*, May 8, 2009. https://mises.org/ library/friedrich-hayek-teacher.

Hayek, Friedrich August von. "The Economic Conditions of Interstate Federalism." In *Individualism and Economic Order*, 255–72, Chicago: University of Chicago Press, 1948.

———. "Postscript: Why I Am Not a Conservative." In *The Constitution of Liberty*, 397–414, London: Routledge, 2009.

———. *The Road to Serfdom*. London: Routledge, 2009.

Hix, Simon. *What's Wrong with the European Union and How to Fix It*. London: Polity, 2008.

Hoff, Trygve J. B. *Economic Calculation in the Socialist Society*. Indianapolis: Liberty Fund, 1981.

Hooghe, Liesbet. "Europe Divided? Elites vs. Public Opinion on European Integration." *European Union Politics* 4 (2003): 281–304.

Izquierdo, Mario Juan F. Jimeno, and Aitor Lacuesta. "Spain: From Immigration to Emigration." *Documento de Trabajo* No. 1503, Banco de España, 2015. http://www.bde.es/f/ webbde/SES/Secciones/Publicaciones/PublicacionesSeriadas/DocumentosTrabajo/15/ Fich/dt1503e.pdf.

Jones, Sam, Kerin Hope, and Courtney Weaver. "Alarm Bells Ring over Syriza's Russian Links." *Financial Times*, January 28, 2015. http://www.ft.com/cms/s/0/a87747de-a713-11e4-b6bd-00144feab7de.html#axzz3veMLITUU.

Klaus, Václav. "Careless Opening Up of Countries (Without Keeping the Anchor of the Nation-State) Leads Either to Anarchy or to Global Governance: Lessons of the European Experience." Speech at the Mont Pèlerin Society General Meeting, September 1, 2014. http://www.klaus.cz/clanky/3623.

Kolesnikova, Natalia A., and Yang Liu. "Jobless Recoveries: Causes and Consequences." *The Regional Economist*, April 2011, 18–19. https://www.stlouisfed.org/~/media/Files/PDFs/publications/pub_assets/pdf/re/2011/b/jobless.pdf.

Lucas, Edward. *The New Cold War: Putin's Russia and the Threat to the West*. New York: St Martin's Press, 2014.

Margaret Thatcher Foundation. "Thatcher, Hayek & Friedman." *Margaret Thatcher Foundation*, 2015. http://www.margaretthatcher.org/archive/Hayek.asp.

Matthews, Owen. "Vladimir Putin's New Plan for World Domination." *The Spectator*, February 22, 2014. http://www.spectator.co.uk/2014/02/putins-masterplan/.

Mises, Ludwig von. *Liberalism*. Irvington-on-Hudson, NY: Foundation for Economic Education, 1985.

Mudde, Cas. "Three Decades of Populist Radical Right Parties in Western Europe: So What?" *European Journal of Political Research* 52 (2013): 1–19.

Pangalos, Philip and James Angelos. "Athens Braces for Visit by Merkel." *Wall Street Journal*, October 9, 2012. http://www.wsj.com/articles/SB10000872396390444024204578044733434528460.

Rohac, Dalibor. "Jeremy Corbyn and His Sinister Friends." *Weekly Standard*, August 20, 2015. http://www.weeklystandard.com/jeremy-corbyn-and-his-sinister-friends/article/1015157.

Röpke, Wilhelm. *International Economic Disintegration*. London: William Hodge & Co, 1942.

Sapir, André, et al. *An Agenda for a Growing Europe*. Oxford: Oxford University Press, 2004.

Siedentop, Larry. *Democracy in Europe*. New York: Columbia University Press, 2001.

Simms, Brendan. "towardss a Mighty Union: How to Create a Democratic European Superpower." *International Affairs* 88 (2012): 49–62.

Smyth, Jamie. "MEPs Transparent in Their Suspicions About Libertas." *Irish Times*, September 30, 2008. http://www.irishtimes.com/news/meps-transparent-in-their-suspicions-about-libertas-1.941575.

Torreblanca, José Ignacio, and Mark Leonard. "The Continent-Wide Rise of Euroscepticism." European Council on Foreign Relations Brief No. 79, 2013. http://www.ecfr.eu/page/-/ECFR79_EUROSCEPTICISM_BRIEF_AW.pdf.

Treaty Establishing a Constitution for Europe, October 29, 2004. http://europa.eu/eu-law/decision-making/treaties/pdf/treaty_establishing_a_constitution_for_europe/treaty_establishing_a_constitution_for_europe_en.pdf.

Treaty of Lisbon Amending the Treaty on European Union and the Treaty Establishing the European Community, December 13, 2007. http://eur-lex.europa.eu/legal-content/EN/TXT/PDF/?uri=OJ:C:2007:306:FULL&from=EN.

Waterfields, Bruno. "EU Intervention in Irish Referendum 'Unlawful.'" *Daily Telegraph*, September 29, 2009. http://www.telegraph.co.uk/news/worldnews/europe/eu/6239933/EU-intervention-in-Irish-referendum-unlawful.html.

2

WHAT HAS THE EU EVER DONE FOR US?

One scene in *Life of Brian*, the much-loved film by the British comedy group Monty Python, depicts a meeting of the People's Front of Judea, an imaginary group fighting occupation by the Roman Empire. "And what have [the Romans] ever given us in return?" a character played by John Cleese asks. There is a muted response. "The aqueduct." "Oh yeah, yeah they gave us that. Yeah. That's true." Somebody else says: "And the sanitation!" The list progressively grows to include roads, irrigation, medicine, education, public health—and wine. "That's something we'd really miss if the Romans left."

It does not require a lot of imagination to picture the EU's critics having similar conversations. Few Eurosceptic politicians complain about the access to European markets that membership provides to businesses and workers in their countries. Poland's government of the Eurosceptic Law and Justice party is not outraged by the fact that 679,000 Poles are living in the UK, providing for themselves and their families back home far better than they could in Poland.[1] Neither do British conservative critics of the EU complain about the fact that over 2 million Britons live in EU countries outside the UK—almost as many as EU nationals living in the UK.[2] And although free-market advocates like to point out the EU's wasteful spending, one does not hear much grumbling from the EU's poorer member states about the transfers that their countries are receiving. Between 2014 and 2020, the EU will spend over €350 billion to narrow economic disparities between its member states.[3] The funding flows through several vehicles: the European Regional Development Fund, which finances infrastructure investment and job creation; the European Social Fund, which purports to help the unemployed and the disadvantaged, mostly by providing training programs; and the Cohesion Fund, which was set up in 1994 to provide funding to the poorest member states.

There is, of course, much to criticize about these funds. The disbursements are typically matched by contributions from national budgets, so instead of boosting investment in infrastructure the funds often crowd out domestic spending.[4] The value of many of the projects is questionable. CEE Bankwatch, a public watchdog group operating in Central and Eastern Europe, keeps a list of dubious infrastructure projects financed by EU funds. Examples include the expensive 19-kilometer highway between Sofia, Bulgaria's capital, and the city of Pernik. In spite of the price tag of nearly €10 million per kilometer, it had very little impact on traffic in the area.[5] In the Czech Republic, EU funds were used to increase the height of a railway bridge in the town of Kolín to make space for largely nonexistent river navigation. The repair was seen widely as unnecessary and expensive. Characteristically, only one company participated in the tender procedure and was awarded the contract.[6] Anecdotes aside, very little evidence indicates that the EU funds do anything to promote economic growth in Europe's poorer regions.[7]

For citizens of former communist countries, EU membership matters at a much deeper level than the supposed free lunch that the EU funds might provide. For one, these countries spent decades in the shackles of totalitarian regimes. For them, liberal democracy, market economy, and mass prosperity cannot be taken for granted. On a symbolic level, their EU membership is an affirmation of the irreversibility of their break with the communist past and their embrace of Western values. However, their accession had an important practical side as well. As Central and Eastern European countries entered into talks about their prospective EU membership, they were asked to pursue deep economic and political reforms. They had to complete their transitions towards the market by privatizing their economies and opening them to competition. They were required to strengthen the independence of their judiciaries and hold themselves to high standards of democratic accountability and the rule of law. Many of these economic and political reforms came at a political cost. Reforms in the energy sector, for example, meant increasing the heavily subsidized prices of electricity and natural gas and establishing independent regulators to make sure that energy prices reflected the costs of production. Without the prospect of EU membership, such reforms would likely be short-lived and reversed by the next populist government. The fact that these and many other reforms succeeded was in part a result of the commitment, shared across the political spectrum, to join the EU.[8] Ivan Mikloš, the former deputy prime minister and finance minister of Slovakia, who spearheaded the program of radical pro-market reforms in his country, refers to this effect as the "integration anchor." Such an anchor, he argues, "was very helpful in passing necessary changes, which would otherwise have encountered [. . .] resistance."[9] Attempts to undo these reforms today, more than 10 years after joining the EU, are legally impossible and would provoke the ire of Brussels—something that even the more populist politicians generally try to avoid. If one has any doubts regarding the role that the prospect of EU membership played in fostering market-friendly policies in the region, it is only necessary to compare Slovakia's experience with that of Ukraine. Ukraine's accession to the EU was long seen as impossible and even today remains extremely remote. Unsurprisingly, the country has seen hardly any economic or institutional reforms. The result is a catastrophic record in terms of economic development and corruption.[10]

The role of EU membership in facilitating pro-market reforms in postcommunist countries illustrates perhaps the most important function performed by the bloc: its role as a *commitment device*. In his epic poem *The Odyssey*, the Greek poet Homer gives us an excellent exposition of the idea. On their journey home after the fall of Troy, Odysseus and his men reach the land of the Sirens, "crying beauty to bewitch men coasting by," who then crash on the rocky coast of their island. In order to resist the temptation, Odysseus instructs his crew to do the following:

> Therefore
> you are to tie me up, tight as a splint,
> erect along the mast, lashed to the mast,
> and if I shout and beg to be untied,
> take more turns of the rope to muffle me.[11]

The purpose of tying Odysseus to the mast, pictured in the famous painting by John William Waterhouse (figure 2.1), is to make it impossible for him to yield to the temptation presented by the Sirens. In other words, it serves as a *commitment device*. In the same way, policy-makers in modern democracies sometimes need to tie their own hands to keep them from yielding to various temptations. Changes in policies, especially those that make societies better off, can be thought of as contracts between policymakers and the population. In exchange for votes, policymakers promise to deliver a certain surplus (for example, savings from eliminating a wasteful spending program) and distribute it among the people. But such promises can be—and often are—broken. Reformers can backtrack in the face of powerful vested interests, or the reforms can be undone by their successors if it becomes politically convenient.[12]

One way of addressing this concern is to delegate some decisions to independent bodies, such as regulators or central banks. That way, electricity prices or interest rates will not follow political whims, but rather the judgment of a civil servant enjoying a degree of insulation from everyday politics. The same objective is also achieved by creating explicit legal rules guiding policy decisions, instead of discretion by politicians or bureaucrats.[13] Of course, none of these methods is perfect. Because the state exercises a monopoly of coercion on a given territory, it cannot effectively constrain itself.[14] A piece of written legislation can be revised, or its interpretation changed by a politicized judiciary. A central bank governor can be replaced by someone with the right political loyalties. But perfection is not the relevant criterion in this context.

Figure 2.1.   John William Waterhouse, *Ulysses and the Sirens.*

What matters is not whether opportunism or yielding to temptation can be eradicated altogether (it cannot), but whether the commitment devices increase the cost of reneging relative to other available arrangements.[15]

International agreements are one type of such commitment devices. The institutional innovation of the EU—and its main strength in comparison to the arrangements that preceded it—lies in the fact that it binds together a relatively large number of countries and commits them to specific courses of action in a broad number of different policy areas. If one government reneges, for example, by introducing discriminatory legislation against imports of a commodity from one of its neighbors, it risks prompting a *collective* response in areas extending far beyond trade. That makes the cost of reneging higher than could be achieved through a bilateral trade agreement.

As a result, some of the complaints about the undemocratic nature of European institutional architecture miss the point.[16] To make sure that governments adhere to the promises that they made to each other in European treaties, the EU needs rules and enforcement mechanisms that constrain national sovereignty and are independent of political pressures. Such *undemocratic* mechanisms are a feature, not a bug, of the European construction. In the same way, independent central banks, independent regulators, and explicit fiscal rules are commonplace and largely uncontroversial features of national politics, even if they impose limits on what popular majorities do. What is more, EU institutions have not been "imposed" on hapless Europeans against their will. It was European leaders, accountable to their electorates, who decided collectively to tie their hands on a number of policy matters. Friedrich von Hayek understood this point better than many of his followers today. He saw the main role of the federal European government as restraining national governments, similar to the role exercised by the federal government in the United States by the constitution and its various amendments. "[T]he federation," Hayek argues, "will have to possess the negative power of preventing individual states from interfering with economic activity in certain ways, although it may not have the positive power of acting in their stead."[17]

In practice, there is not always a clear distinction between ensuring that the member states adhere to agreed rules and acting in their stead. That contributes to a tension in the European construction, which makes it impossible to dismiss all the complaints about the EU's democratic deficit.[18] Whether they consist of explicit rules or delegation of decisions to independent bureaus, commitment devices work best when they have a clear, narrowly defined mandate, like fostering competition on the market for energy, or regulating money supply and interest rates. The broader the scope, the more difficult it is to devise an explicit set of rules that would cover all possible contingencies.[19] As a result, European institutions—the Commission, for example—are often left with the need to make discretionary decisions about questions that are, rightly or wrongly, perceived as political. To complete the single market, the European institutions often *must do more* than just restrain national governments or act as purely technocratic regulators. They need to overturn national legislation that hinders cross-border competition, and put in place common rules to supersede protectionist national regulation. Prior to the financial crisis of 2008, one could argue that the scope and character of EU-level decision making was so limited, and had so little salience in the eyes of the public, that the democratic deficit was only an abstract, theoretical problem.[20] But the crisis in the Eurozone has created a need for common decisions about highly contentious matters, including public finances or labor reforms, in real time. As we will see later, the EU has not always succeeded in delivering on those fronts. And one reason why European institutions have a somewhat problematic record as autonomous decision makers lies in the fact that they do not possess the same democratic mandate as the one enjoyed by national governments.[21]

PEACE AND DEMOCRACY

However, before discussing the details of the EU's construction and its democratic deficit, it is worth going to the basics of what the EU does well. First, its existence has given European countries a formal structure that keeps European countries at peace.[22] The Treaty of Rome commits European countries to "preserve and strengthen peace and liberty,"[23] mirroring Hayek's idea that "the main purpose of interstate federation is to secure peace: to prevent war between the parts of the federation by eliminating causes of friction between them and by providing effective machinery for the settlement of any disputes which may arise between them and prevent war between the federation and any independent states by making the former so strong as to eliminate any danger of attack from without."[24]

Throughout the existence of the European integration project, the participating countries have been indeed at peace. It is not easy to imagine a situation in which an EU member today would wage war against another. Obviously, that does not prove that EU membership deserves sole credit for its role in preventing conflict on the continent. As Marc Plattner, the founder of the *Journal of Democracy*, argued, "the nature of the member states is more important in this regard than the framework that connects them. After all, war is equally unthinkable between an EU member state and a nonmember like Norway, just as it is unthinkable between the United States and Canada or between Australia and New Zealand."[25]

However, the nature of European states as liberal democracies is not independent of the process of European integration. For all the concern about the EU's democratic deficit, European integration has helped to entrench basic norms of democracy, government accountability, and the rule of law in countries that did not have a long tradition of democratic rule. According to the so-called Copenhagen Criteria,[26] adopted in 1993, only stable democracies that respect human rights and protect their minorities can successfully apply to join the EU. Spain and Greece were able to become members only in the 1980s, after dismantling their authoritarian regimes. For Central and Eastern European nations of the former Soviet bloc, the prospect of membership created a strong incentive to build functioning democratic institutions and the rule of law, in some cases from scratch.[27] Of course, the EU has also seen some instances of democratic backsliding: in Austria, where the far-right Austrian Freedom Party (FPÖ) joined a coalition government in 1999, or more recently in Hungary and Poland. However, by and large the membership of European countries in the EU coincides with a historically unique period of democratic governance, rule of law, and peace.[28]

Of course, the United States deserves a large part of the credit for the peaceful and democratic character of today's Europe. First, it acted as a guarantor of security by retaining a large military presence in Europe and building the collective security arrangement that is the North Atlantic Treaty Organization (NATO), which was built to protect Europe from the threat posed by the Soviet Union. Secondly, through the Marshall Plan, the United States set the stage for the postwar economic success of Europe and its economic integration. The Marshall Plan was not significant for the size of the financing it provided to the reconstruction of Europe's infrastructure. Nor did it provide, as some suggest, a sizeable macroeconomic stimulus to European economies. It was far too small to accomplish that. Instead, its main role was in providing the financial resources necessary to overcome the opposition to pro-market reforms that enabled Western European economies to grow in the decades to come.[29]

European integration is part of a bigger geopolitical package that has secured peace and political cooperation among Europe's nation-states. Today, as the focus of US foreign policy shifts elsewhere,[30] the EU will need to play a more active role in securing peace not just within its borders, but also in its neighborhood. Faced with Russia's invasion of Ukraine in 2014—a major challenge to the international legal and political order—the EU mustered enough strength for a common response and imposed a range of economic sanctions on Russia and its political representatives. The terrorist attacks in Paris in November 2015 opened the question of cooperation among EU intelligence services, including perhaps the creation of a common European security service. The refugee crisis that swept across the EU in 2015 is a direct consequence of the war in Syria, which had brewed in Europe's immediate vicinity for years. The resurgence of security and geopolitical matters, in the relative absence of the United States from the continent, means that to keep the continent at peace, the EU and individual European countries will have to step up their game as foreign policy and military actors.[31]

FREEING EUROPE'S MARKETS

With 28 member countries and a total GDP of almost €14 trillion, the EU's single market is the world's largest economy. Instead of being a natural occurrence, its existence is the result of decades of conscious effort to eliminate tariff barriers and other forms of protectionism in Europe. The tariff barriers between founding members of the European Economic Community disappeared in 1968. Meanwhile, in 1960, the United Kingdom, Austria, Denmark, Portugal, Norway, Sweden, and Switzerland formed the European Free Trade Area (EFTA). These two groups of countries concluded a bilateral free-trade agreement in 1974, ushering in an era of free trade throughout Western Europe.

Most economists agree that, as a general rule, free trade is desirable. It opens new opportunities for mutually beneficial exchanges, fosters competition, and deepens the division of labor. It enables producers and consumers to realize greater welfare gains than in the presence of restrictions that make some exchanges impracticable. Free trade also enables entrepreneurs to access larger markets, creating stronger incentives for innovation. Because European integration eliminated only those tariffs that had existed between its members, it was an instance of a *partial* liberalization. As a result, the EU has *destroyed* trade with countries outside the bloc, through an effect that economists call "trade diversion." The favorable conditions for trade within the EU, which resulted from the elimination of tariffs among European countries, have made it less appealing for Europeans to trade with countries outside the bloc.[32] Furthermore, the EU is a customs union, not a free-trade area. This means that while Canada, the United States, and Mexico—signatories to the North American Free Trade Agreement—are free to pursue their own trade policies with regard to third countries and conclude bilateral agreements with third countries, the EU maintains a common external tariff, applied to imports to all EU member states. While generally modest, it does preserve a degree of protection in areas such as agriculture and the automobile industry—a fact the EU's critics have repeatedly raised.[33] The advocates of free markets are fully justified in criticizing these trade barriers and demanding that they be dismantled. However, no evidence suggests that the existence of the EU as a customs union has resulted in substantial trade diversion, or indeed that the destruction of trading opportunities with the outside world has outweighed the welfare gains from trade liberalization within Europe.[34]

According to the EU's critics, the common external tariff prevents deeper liberalization in some EU countries. For example, it is argued that if the UK left the EU, it could pursue a much more aggressive liberalization agenda with its trading partners outside the EU.[35] Assessing the merits of such a hypothetical is difficult, but there is an obvious flipside to it. The common external tariff also *prevents* EU countries from engaging in unilateral acts of protectionism against third countries. Moreover, it is possible to argue that politicians are more often tempted to raise trade barriers than to scrap them. This asymmetry is one of the key insights of public choice theory, developed by Gordon Tullock and the Nobel Prize–winning economist James Buchanan.[36] Because the benefits of protectionism tend to be concentrated in specific industries, and its costs are dispersed among all consumers, pressure groups arguing for trade barriers will tend to have an edge over their uncoordinated opponents in their influence over policymaking.[37] Hence, whereas the customs union existing in Europe may have hindered some attempts at trade liberalization, it likely prevented *many more* attempts to introduce trade barriers in EU member states.

Its critics often choose to disregard the fact that the EU has done much more than just eliminate tariffs between European countries. The ideas of *freedom of movement* and the *single market*, which are embedded in the EU treaties, are much stronger guiding principles than a simple absence of conventional forms of protectionism, such as tariffs or import quotas. These traditional forms of protectionism are becoming less salient as their magnitude is at historical lows after decades of liberalization efforts within the WTO and through various multilateral and bilateral trade arrangements. In 2014, for instance, the EU's average tariff, applied to third countries, was just 1 percent.[38] More importantly, the absence of tariffs is a necessary but not a sufficient condition for the existence of a truly integrated, competitive European market. Regulatory barriers can have the same economic effect as conventional forms of protectionism and can easily exclude producers from nominally open markets. This is why European institutions have moved beyond a mere multilateral tariff arrangement and have focused on removing regulatory barriers to trade.[39]

Supporters of free markets should applaud this "mission creep." In 1974, the ruling of the European Court of Justice (ECJ) in the *Dassonville* case prohibited countries from using regulation that has the same effects as traditional forms of protectionism.[40] The case involved a Belgian legal rule that required importers of Scotch whisky to have certificates authenticating the origin of their product. Gustave Dassonville, a wholesale distributor in France, and his son Benoît were running the Belgian branch of the business and wanted to import Johnnie Walker and Vat 69 whiskies from France to Belgium. Because no certificates of origin were required in France, in order to comply with the Belgian rules the Dassonvilles simply issued the relevant certificates themselves. Belgian authorities saw this as an attempt to get around the existing rules and started legal action. But the ECJ saw the matter differently. Because the product that the Dassonvilles were selling was compliant with French legislation, the attempts of Belgian authorities to stop the whisky from entering Belgium amounted to protectionism, illegal under the rules existing in the EEC. "All trading rules," the Court decided, "enacted by Member States, which are capable of hindering, directly or indirectly, actually or potentially, intra-Community trade are to be considered as measures having an effect equivalent to quantitative restrictions."[41]

A few years later, another famous ECJ decision took the idea one step further. The case again involved alcoholic beverages. This time, Rewe, a German company, decided to import *Crème de cassis de Dijon* to Germany. Crème de cassis is a French liqueur, made with black currants, alcohol, and sugar. It is typically mixed with sparkling wine (or white wine) to prepare *kir*, a popular French aperitif. According to German laws at the time, products marketed as fruit liqueurs had to contain at least 25 percent alcohol, whereas the French drink contains less (typically between 16 and 20 percent). The relevant German agency, with the distinctly charming name *Bundesmonopolverwaltung für Branntwein* (literally meaning the "Federal Monopoly for Brandy") advised the company that while *cassis de Dijon* could be imported, it could not be marketed as a liqueur because of its low alcohol content. The importer challenged that decision at the ECJ, arguing that the German rule was an import restriction in violation of European treaties. In 1979, the ECJ concurred with that view and ruled that for the common market to function, products that were lawfully marketed in one country could not be denied access to other markets on equal terms.[42] In principle, the ruling required the countries of the European Economic Community, or now the EU, to mutually recognize their standards of safety, health, environment, and consumer protection.[43]

The idea of mutual recognition is at the heart of the single market, although its application is not always straightforward. Partly because of a concern about a regulatory "race to the bottom," mutual recognition is conditional on the equivalence of the goals and effects of regulation in the area of consumer protection, safety, health, and the environment in

EU countries. However, determining whether such equivalence holds may be complicated and require tough judgment calls. Individual businesses could then face considerable uncertainty about whether authorities in other EU countries will recognize such equivalence. Conversely, whereas national regulators are in a position to assess the compliance of businesses with rules existing in their own country, they might be unable to evaluate the details of regulatory regimes existing elsewhere in order to determine whether they should be seen as equivalent.

The strictly libertarian answer to this conundrum is to apply the idea of mutual recognition indiscriminately, regardless of the potential for a race to the bottom. A product approved for sale in one member country should be allowed anywhere in the EU, they argue. Although some find such a principled position appealing, an unconditional application of mutual recognition is a political nonstarter and is likely to remain one for the foreseeable future. For a long time, Europe's solution to this problem lay on the other extreme: in rigid regulatory harmonization, which was correctly an object of critiques by free-market Eurosceptics.[44] Up until the 1980s, European authorities were trying to create common, oftentimes very detailed, regulations to supersede those that were applied at the national level. That approach eliminated potentially useful competition that might have existed between different regulatory regimes, forcing a one-size-fits-all solution on the entire EU.

But all that changed in 1985, when the bloc adopted a different approach towards harmonization, friendlier to markets and competition between different regulatory practices.[45] In cases when substantive differences exist between regulations in EU countries, the EU may issue a directive in order to "approximate" the national provisions so that goods can move freely from one country to another, without worrying about compliance with different national rules. Such directives set the essential requirements for, for example, consumer health and safety, typically in very general terms.

The details are then specified in separate technical norms, which are enacted by standardization bodies, such as the European Committee for Standardization (CEN), European Committee for Electrotechnical Standardization (CENELEC), and European Telecommunications Standards Institute (ETSI). Those are common, voluntary standards recognized throughout the EU (and EEA and EFTA) as guarantees of compliance with the essential regulatory provisions. Meeting these standards is a *sufficient*, but not a *necessary* condition for a product to be marketed in other member states. Their existence, however, does not preclude competition between regulatory regimes—an idea that is dear to many free-market critics of the EU, for whom competition of different policies and legal regimes provides an incentive for institutional innovation and curbs the excesses of the state. Producers can decide to follow the technical standards used in their own countries, as long as they are planning to sell their products only there. Furthermore, they might choose to ignore the voluntary standards and still sell anywhere on the single market, as long as they are able and willing to directly demonstrate to national regulators that their products meet the requirements specified in the relevant EU directive. This option may be of particular importance for entrepreneurs who are marketing new products which escape the categories created by authors of common European technical standards. For many companies, however, the existence of the voluntary technical standards created under the EU's auspices is immensely helpful in reducing legal uncertainty and information costs. It enables modestly sized companies to punch above their weight and sell their products in all EU countries, in a way that would not be imaginable if they had to bear the burden of compliance with 28 different regulatory regimes.[46]

But even this relatively mild form of harmonization of regulatory regimes across Europe comes at the cost of creating a layer of common European legislation. It is possible to argue, as I show in chapter 4, that the EU regulates *too much* and that many of the existing directives are unnecessary, or even harmful. The question of political legitimacy of the common European legislation, especially in areas seen as political, lingers in the background too. Not only is there a case for an EU-wide deregulation and for introduction of more stringent rules that would curb future growth of EU legislation, but there is also a need for stronger oversight of the EU by national parliaments and citizens, through a better functioning democracy at the European level. Whatever our preferred solution, it is worth remembering the relevant counterfactual to the status quo is not—as Eurosceptics might be imagining—a Europe free of any unnecessary regulatory burden. Rather, it is a Europe where governments pursue their regulatory agendas independently and erect, inadvertently or deliberately, regulatory barriers that hinder trade on the continent. Much like in the case of tariffs, without the EU, national policymakers would be more often tempted to tighten the screws of economic regulation to protect their domestic industries than to deregulate.[47]

CURBING WASTE

The EU's competition, or "antitrust," policies are another important, albeit controversial, element in the architecture of the single market. As a rule of thumb, free-market economists are suspicious of competition policy, which starts from a static vision of markets still present in textbooks of microeconomics.[48] Such a vision of competition mistakes market *share* for market *power*, and is prone to rely on heavy-handed tools to curb imaginary abuses of dominant position by companies that have grown big by innovating or by creating new markets altogether. However, as we will see later, some markets, such as those in energy, come close to textbook models of imperfect competition and might warrant an active role for a European regulator. The European Commission's role as a competition authority also helps dismantle the barriers to competition imposed by national governments in other industries.

There is another role for competition policy: to limit government aid to politically connected companies or to national champions. Conservatives and friends of free enterprise should be glad to see the EU curb the wasteful spending and protectionism of European governments. In one of its many roles, the European Commission serves as the enforcer of the EU rules on state aid, which prohibit governments from providing financial assistance to businesses—such as in the form of subsidies, loan guarantees, or tax breaks—in a way that would distort competition in the single market.[49] In some countries with long traditions of protecting "national champions," such as France or Italy, the EU's pressure on market liberalization fueled the opposition to the European project. It was thus under a threat of lawsuits from the European Commission that the French government opened its electricity market to competition in 1999 and that Italy closed down its government-subsidized steel mills.[50]

In 2014, the European Commission cancelled sizeable contracts between the state-owned airports in Angoulême, Pau Pyrénées, and Nîmes in France and Ryanair, a low-cost airline. The contracts obliged the airports to purchase expensive advertising space on the airliner's website, and the airline also benefited from significantly reduced air-port service fees, compared with those charged to other airlines.[51] Another recent example involves Cyprus Airways, an ailing state-owned carrier, which received a significant restructuring aid package from the government of Cyprus. Following the EC's investigation, Commissioner for Competition Policy Margrethe Vestager concluded:

> Cyprus Airways has received large quantities of public money since 2007 but was unable to restructure and become viable without continued state support. Therefore, injecting additional public money would only have prolonged the struggle without achieving a turnaround. Companies need to be profitable based on their own merits, and their ability to compete and cannot and should not rely on taxpayer money to stay in the market artificially.[52]

That should be music to the ears of opponents of state interventionism, just like the fact that the decision returned €65 million, plus interest, to the Cypriot public budget. The EC also overturned subsidies worth €265 million given by the Valencia Regional Government in Spain to film studios Ciudad de la Luz,[53] concluding that the investment under such terms would not be undertaken by any private investor. The Commission also stopped state aid totaling around €290 million directed at Portugal's shipyard Estaileros Navais de Viana do Castelo.[54] The importance of these decisions lies not only in saving taxpayers' money and disciplining governments, but also in making sure that that the single market fosters competition based on economic merit, not cronyism. Free-market advocates who want to see the EU gone need to explain how the temptation of European politicians to provide aid to their national champions would be curbed in the absence of a common competition policy.[55]

True, the EU itself is a source of waste. Each year, 40 percent of the EU budget (around €62 billion in 2016)[56] goes to the anachronistic Common Agricultural Policy, in addition to the structural funds channeled to local infrastructure projects of dubious value. The agricultural subsidies are highly distortionary. They benefit landowners, make European produce more expensive, and have a debilitating impact on agricultural producers outside the EU, especially in Latin America.[57] But even if the entire EU budget were completely wasted, it would amount to just 1 percent of EU GDP—a tiny fraction of the public budgets of individual EU countries.[58] That is not to say that we should willingly disregard wasteful spending by the EU—quite the contrary. It does mean, however, that we should retain a sense of proportion. The economic gains created by the existence of the single market and by restraining the power of national government to pursue policies of economic nationalism and protectionism far outweigh any damage inflicted on Europeans by wasteful spending by the EU itself.

THE LONG AND WINDING ROAD TO THE SINGLE MARKET

The EU is still far away from having a genuine single market in several areas, including services. Services matter in part because, in the past decades, their share of GDP has been growing steadily in advanced economies, including in the EU. But service markets also matter because they differ from markets with tangible commodities in a number of important respects. Services do not always "cross borders" in a strict sense, but their providers sometimes do. They often, but not always, require a simultaneity of production and consumption and a physical proximity of the customer and the provider. Licensing and training requirements for numerous professions differ vastly across the EU and may follow very different objectives. Liberalizing service markets thus raises a different set of questions than the physical goods that are crossing European borders.

To take an example that resonated in the debates over the liberalization of services in the EU, if a Polish plumber wants to offer her services in France, she faces the question of compliance with rules existing in Poland and France. In the absence of a single market for services, nothing stops the French government from tweaking its regulations in a way that make it essentially impossible for the Pole to provide her services in France. The authorities could require expensive training and certification, even if the plumber were licensed to exercise her profession in Poland. To address the problem, in January 2004, the EU Commissioner Frits Bolkestein proposed a directive seeking to ensure that member states could not impose discriminatory legislation prohibiting providers of *services*, including Polish plumbers, from offering their services in France. The directive was a somewhat complicated variation on the idea of mutual recognition, embodied in the *Cassis de Dijon* ruling. Service providers would be required to follow a combination of social protection legislation in the country of origin and in the country where the service would be provided. A Polish plumber working outside her home country would be paying her unemployment and pension insurance contributions in Poland, where she would also be entitled to benefits. To prevent a real or imaginary "race to the bottom" of social standards, the directive ensured that the plumber would simultaneously be required to follow the minimum wage law and health and safety regulations of France if she wanted to provide her services there.

Although the proposed directive was more measured than a simple, unqualified application of the principle of mutual recognition, it triggered a wave of protests. In old member states, particularly in France, the opponents of the directive made alarmist claims about social dumping and the erosion of Europe's social model, if the directive were approved,[59] notwithstanding the evidence of sizeable economic benefits that a single market in services would provide.[60] In the European Parliament, a number of revisions to the directive were added, effectively removing the principle of mutual recognition—a key idea behind the directive. The watered-down piece of legislation, applied since the end of 2006,[61] preserves the legal vacuum surrounding the movement of services across the EU and leaves member states, their regulators, and courts to decide on a case-by-case basis the conditions under which foreign providers can offer their services.

It is worth pointing out that the EU's failure to liberalize service markets can be attributed, at least in part, to its democratic deficit and the tension between its role as a "commitment device" and its role as a mover and shaker of public policy. The Services Directive was not just a technical measure but a significant, far-reaching reform, bound to create both winners and losers. Notwithstanding the leadership displayed by Commissioner Frits Bolkestein,[62] who spearheaded the initiative, the European Commission lacked the political mandate to override special interests in the same way reformist, democratically elected politicians could.[63] The failure to liberalize the service sectors across the EU and create a unified regulatory framework has created a paradox, which is seldom acknowledged by the EU's critics, who are always eager to point out to the instances of its growing powers and overreach. Because the economic importance of services, measured relative to

GDP, is growing in advanced economies, their segmentation in Europe de facto means that the EU is not growing, but shrinking, in its influence over the everyday economic lives of Europeans.[64]

The integration of some service markets has seen more progress than others. Following the introduction of the EU "financial passport," banks and other financial institutions legally established in one member state have been allowed to provide their services elsewhere in the EU without the need of further authorization. Similar rules are applied to trucking and bus transport, and to various professional and advisory services. In contrast, many network services—broadcasting, railways, telecom, Internet service providers, and so forth—have proven to be much more immune to cross-border competition.[65] The digital single market is another example of a less-than-stellar job by EU institutions. Whereas a technology startup in the United States has immediate access to an immense integrated market with over 300 million customers, European businesses still must deal with 28 different sets of laws, including telecom regulations, postal service rules, value-added tax, and copyright. As a result, reports *The Economist*, "[o]nly 4% of internet traffic from EU countries goes to online services in another European country, whereas 54% of it goes to services in America."[66] This is unfortunate. Žiga Turk, a Slovenian economist and the country's former minister for growth and minister of education, writes:

> The World Wide Web was invented in Europe's CERN. A Finn developed Linux, disrupting the operating system market and bringing the open source paradigm to a whole new level. A Swede and a Dane invented Skype, shaking up telephony. Nokia, Ericsson and Siemens dominated the early days of the mobile telephony business. Fraunhofer Institute invented the MP3 codec that changed the music industry.[67]

Yet all of these inventions, he notes, became commercial successes in North America. Instead of opening the EU to accommodate an expansion of new technology markets, European institutions are often busy fighting yesterday's battles, trying to regulate roaming charges or break up supposed digital "monopolies," such as Google.[68]

The absence of a truly competitive digital market in Europe has nothing to do with the presence of large corporations holding too much market power. The roots of the problem lie instead in the regulatory barriers in individual countries, sometimes designed explicitly to protect incumbents against potential competitors.[69] Germany and France prohibit book discounts and free shipping,[70] holding back the growth of online commerce. Back in 2008, Amazon was even given a hefty fine by French courts for offering such services.[71] In other areas, the differences between legal regimes are an obstacle to competition, even without an explicit aim of the government to protect the incumbents. In spite of years of efforts to introduce a single electronic registration and value-added tax (VAT) payment mechanism, the member states' different VAT regimes still complicate cross-border transactions online.

Energy is another sector in which the EU plays a beneficial role, but could do much better.[72] In early January 2009, Gazprom, Russia's natural gas monopoly, cut off the flow of natural gas to Ukraine, exacerbating the deep economic crisis facing the country and creating acute energy shortages in Ukraine and other countries dependent on Russian natural gas. In Sarajevo, the capital of Bosnia and Herzegovina, more than 70,000 apartments were left without heating for days in the middle of a freezing winter. Likewise, heating in Chişinău, the capital of Moldova, was turned off. In Bulgaria, already a member state of the EU, major industrial energy consumers were forced to shut down their operations until an agreement was reached.[73]

The episode highlighted the importance of market competition, not only for economic efficiency, but also for national security. Bulgaria, Slovakia, and the Baltic countries—to name just a few—depend almost completely on imports of Russian natural gas. That exposes these countries to serious economic and security risks. Russian natural gas is sold to these countries by Russia's state-owned monopoly provider, Gazprom. In some countries, including Ukraine and Moldova, the Russian regime has openly and repeatedly used gas supplies and pricing policies as a political lever to dissuade their political elites from forging closer ties with the West. Even in its contracts with gas companies in EU member states, the company has commonly insisted on restricting the re-exports of gas, preventing importers from selling gas outside their own country of operation. Gazprom also made gas sales conditional on participation in projects extending Gazprom's infrastructure in Europe, entrenching its incumbent position in the region even further.[74]

In economic terms, the supply of natural gas and of energy more generally count among the most compelling real-world examples of textbook models of natural monopoly. The fixed costs of entering the market are enormous. The provision of electricity or natural gas requires significant infrastructure. To be profitable, such infrastructure must span large geographical areas and serve many customers, making the industry one with "increasing returns to scale," as economists put it. Displacing an incumbent supplier with the needed network infrastructure is an extremely costly enterprise. Energy markets are thus prone to market structures in which the incumbents enjoy a lot of leeway to use their dominant position to their advantage. One canonical solution, applied by regulators worldwide, is to separate the ownership of the transmission network from the production and sales of energy. The two were historically bundled as they formed part of the same state-run monopolies. The separation enables different suppliers to compete without having to build duplicate supply networks. A complementary measure is to ensure interconnectivity of the transmission network, so that the existing supply network, whether gas pipes or an electrical grid, is connected to many potential suppliers, at home and abroad, rather than just one.

European regulators are in a much better position to open up the EU energy market to competition compared to regulators in member states. One reason has to do with the economies of scale present in the energy sector. Connecting electricity grids or gas supply networks across Europe requires coordinated policies—if not some form of *planning*—which can only be provided by a collective platform like the EU. Another reason is related to the idea of the independence of energy regulators, which is typically recommended by economists.[75] Insulating a regulator from political pressures in a small country might be a more challenging task than at the European level, where the European Commission might be in a better position to override the interests of special interests—such as large energy companies—since those are going to be only *one of many* interest groups present at the European level. However, as a 2010 report by the European Center for International Political Economy concludes, the EU authorities have largely left "the gas markets subject to monopolies and, in Central and Eastern Europe, to erratic regulatory supervision, and severe transparency deficits,"[76] creating space for Gazprom to exercise leverage over individual countries dependent on its gas supplies. The EU has also done relatively little to encourage competition between alternative sources of energy, perhaps with the exception of renewables, such as wind or solar. Their deployment has also required investment into "smart grids," which can efficiently connect such intermittent sources of energy with end users, whose demands also vary over time. But much more needs to be done to bring other sources of energy into the mix.[77] In light of the Canadian and US experience, shale gas may be one promising avenue towards unlocking Europe's energy potential. This is why Gazprom and Russian-funded environmental groups have been vigorously campaigning against its exploration in countries such as Poland.[78] According to an estimate by the US Department of Energy, Poland has enough shale gas to meet its energy needs for the next 300 years.[79] While contested, the estimate places Poland alongside Romania, Bulgaria, Germany, and others with potentially large reserves, although considerable uncertainty exists over the precise amounts in each country.

This chapter provided examples of European *public goods* that the EU has been instrumental in providing: peace, democratic governance, and open markets. Throughout this book, I am using the term "public goods" in a deliberately loose way to denote public goods in the traditional sense as well as projects with participation synergies or simply common policies of mutual interest.[80] This chapter does not claim that the EU does a perfect, or even a remotely satisfactory, job in providing these goods. Worse yet, as the critics of the European project are quick to point out, the EU does many other things, which qualify, if anything, as European *public bads*. But as we scrutinize the Union's performance, it is important not to succumb to what the University of Chicago economist Harold Demsetz called the nirvana fallacy[81]—the temptation to compare the actually existing, highly imperfect institutional arrangements with an idealized, yet totally unrealistic alternative. A common trait of many of the EU's most vocal critics introduced in the next chapter—including many who are otherwise conversant in Chicago School economic reasoning—is that they commit this error of judgment. They look at the shortcomings of the EU and conclude that its continuous existence is undesirable, without fully pondering the implications of the arrangement that would likely replace it.

NOTES

1. Whitehead, "Campaign to Lure Poles Back Home amid Fears of Brain Drain to Britain."

2. Rettman, "Two Million British People Emigrated to EU, Figures Show."

3. European Commission, "EU Annual Budget Life-Cycle: Figures."

4. Rosenberg and Sierhej, "Interpreting EU Funds Data for Macroeconomic Analysis."

5. CEE Bankwatch Network, EU Funds in Eastern and Central Europe, s.v. "Bulgaria."

6. Ibid., s.v. "Czech Republic." http://bankwatch.org/billions/country/detail/czech-republic#.

7. An ECB study concludes that "net fiscal transfers, while achieving regional redistribution, seem to impede output growth." Checherita et al., "The Role of Fiscal Transfers," 4. Another paper finds "positive per capita GDP growth effects of Objective 1 transfers, but no employment growth effects." Becker et al., "Going NUTS."

8. Schimmelfennig and Sedelmeier, "Governance by Conditionality."

9. Mikloš "Slovakia: The Latecomer," 132.

10. Åslund, *Ukraine: What Went Wrong.*

11. Homer, *The Odyssey,* 1249–53.

12. For a classic treatment of the problem of policy credibility in the context of reforms, see Rodrik, "Promises, Promises."

13. Much of this literature has been originally developed in the context of monetary policy. See Kydland and Prescott "Rules Rather Than Discretion."

14. The question of constraining the government through constitutional design has been explored by leading free-market thinkers, most notably by the Nobel Prize–winning economist James M. Buchanan. See most prominently Buchanan, *The Limits of Liberty*.

15. For a practical application of the model of credible commitments, including a discussion of the range of available commitment mechanisms, to the issue of enterprise reform in the developing world, see Campos and Esfahani, "Credible Commitment and Success."

16. A similar argument is made by Majone, who shows that as long as the EU's purpose is limited to maintaining and overseeing an integrated European market, its legitimacy cannot be measured by the same standards as a democratic state. Majone, "Europe's 'Democratic Deficit.'" Moravcsik argues that the EU's appearance of being disconnected from everyday politics has to do with the bloc's narrow mandate, focused on issues that rarely are of immediate

salience to voters. Moravcsik, "Reassessing Legitimacy in the European Union."

17. Hayek, "The Economic Conditions of Interstate Federalism," 267.

18. Needless to say, Majone's and Moravcsik's contributions, mentioned above, have attracted controversy. See, e.g., Follesdal and Hix, "Why There Is a Democratic Deficit."

19. This is a corollary of a much more general finding in economic theory, namely that in the real world, contracts are necessarily incomplete because of transaction costs and bounded rationality. For a classic contribution, see Hart and Moore, "Incomplete Contracts and Renegotiation." Among other things, the impossibility of complete contracts helps explain the existence of firms. On that, see Grossman and Hart, "The Costs and Benefits of Ownership."

20. See particularly Moravcsik, "The Myth of Europe's Democratic Deficit."

21. The tension between different facets of the EU, the political mechanisms it relies on, and their inadequacy, are studied by Hix. Hix, "The EU as Polity." For a book-long discussion, see Hix and Høyland, *The Political System of the European Union.*

22. Eilstrup-Sangiovanni and Verdier, "European Integration as a Solution to War."

23. *Treaty Establishing the European Economic Community.*

24. Hayek, "The Economic Conditions of Interstate Federalism," 255.

25. Plattner, "Sovereignty and Democracy."

26. European Council, *Presidency Conclusions.*

27. Flynn and Farrell, "Piecing Together the Democratic Peace." Checkel, "Why Comply?" For some caveats to that generally accurate assessment, see Pridham, "EU Enlargement and Consolidating Democracy."

28. If anything, the puzzle that needs explaining is why there has not been *more* democratic backsliding in countries that have already joined and are therefore not subjected to the same scrutiny as prospective members. See Levitz and Pop-Eleches, "Why No Backsliding?"

29. De Long and Eichengreen, "The Marshall Plan."

30. In 2011, the administration of President Barack Obama announced its famous "pivot to Asia," signaling an end of the Atlantic-centered foreign and security policy that has characterized the postwar era. For a manifesto of that new strategy, see Clinton, "America's Pacific Century."

31. For an overview of the EU's foreign policy, see Smith, *European Union Foreign Policy.*

32. For an assessment of historical significance of trade diversion in the EU's and EFTA's history, see Bayoumi and Eichengreen, "Is Regionalism Simply a Diversion?"

33. Hannan, "The EU Is Not a Free Trade Area but a Customs Union."

34. Evidence from enlargements in Central and Eastern Europe, for example, shows large trade creation effects and only limited trade diversion. See, e.g., Wilhelmsson, *Trade Creation, Diversion and Displacement of the EU Enlargement Process*. Even in the case of the UK, where anecdotal evidence for trade diversion exists, the magnitude of trading opportunities created by the EEC membership outweighed the magnitude of the trade with the outside world, which it hindered. If there were any diversionary effect among the founding members of the EEC, it died out by 1962, argues Eichengreen. Eichengreen, *The European Economy Since 1945*. See also the classic study by Balassa, who arrived at an identical conclusion. Balassa, "Trade Creation and Diversion." However, certain policies existing within the EU, most prominently the Common Agricultural Policy, are sources of distortionary trade diversion.

35. Hannan, "The EU Is Not a Free Trade Area but a Customs Union."

36. For a foundational contribution to this field of research, see Buchanan and Tullock, *The Calculus of Consent*.

37. The origins of the idea are sometimes attributed to Olson. Olson, *The Logic of Collective Action*.

38. World Bank, "Tariff Rate, Applied, Weighted Mean, All Products."

39. For a more general discussion of regulatory protectionism and of the tools curbing it that are available within WTO, EU, and other arrangements, see Sykes, "Regulatory Protectionism and the Law of International Trade," 1–46.

40. A discussion of the political context and the ramifications for policy in the EU is given by Nowak, "Of Garbage Cans and Rulings," 753–69.

41. European Court of Justice, *Procureur du Roi v Benoît and Gustave Dassonville*.

42. European Court of Justice, *Rewe-Zentral AG v Bundesmonopolverwaltung für Branntwein*.

43. See also Alter and Meunier-Aitsahalia, "Judicial Politics in the European Community," 535–61.

44. Salin, "World Regulations and Harmonization."

45. European Council, "A New Approach to Technical Harmonization."

46. Compare with Pelkmans, "Mutual Recognition in Goods and Services."

47. An early public-choice study of regulation is provided by Aranson and Ordeshook. Aranson and Ordeshook, "Regulation, Redistribution, and Public Choice."

48. For a compelling critique of neoclassical view of competition from an "Austrian" perspective, see Salin, *"Competition, Coordination and Diversity."*

49. An overview of the EU's state aid policies can be found in Friederiszick et al. "European State Aid Control."

50. Alesina and Giavazzi *The Future of Europe*, 94.

51. European Commission, "State Aid: Further Details on Commission Decisions."

52. European Commission, "State Aid: Commission Orders Cyprus to Recover."

53. European Commission, "State aid: Commission Asks Spain to Recover €265 Million."

54. European Commission, "State Aid: Commission Finds Portuguese Shipyard Operator."

55. The mechanism through which unrestrained state aid leads to a waste of public funds is described by Dewatripont and Seabright, "'Wasteful' Public Spending State Aid Control."

56. European Commission, *EU Annual Budget Life-Cycle*, s.v. "2016."

57. A 2010 study by economists at the University of Lausanne estimated that the static efficiency gains from eliminating CAP would amount to €38 billion, most of it accruing to the EU. See Boulanger et al., *An Economic Assessment of Removing the Most Distortive Instruments of the Common Agricultural Policy*.

58. Benedetto and Milio provide a detailed look at the budgetary process in the EU. Benedetto and Milio, *European Union Budget Reform*.

59. Grossman and Woll, "The French Debate over the Bolkestein Directive."

60. Sejerøe, et al., "The Copenhagen Economics Study on the Economic Impact of the Services Directive."

61. European Parliament and European Council, Directive 2006/123/EC.

62. Bolkestein's economic and political views can be understood from a book of his conversations with Michel Rocard, the former socialist Prime Minister of France. Bolkestein and Rocard, *Peut-on réformer la France?"*

63. This argument is made also by Hix, *What's Wrong with the European Union and How to Fix It*, 103–4.

64. Majone, "Rethinking European Integration After the Debt Crisis," 5.

65. See European Commission *Single Market Act II: Together for New Growth*, and Pelkmans, "Mutual Recognition in Goods and Services."

66. "Disconnected Continent," *The Economist*.

67. Lisbon Council, *An Action Plan for Europe 2020*, 20.

68. Google's market share, for example, is wrongly interpreted as a sign of its market power. Alarm bells have been rung about the fact that the company bundles different services together, ignoring that fact that unlike in the case of

large utilities or natural monopolies, the barriers to entry are practically non-existent. See, e.g., Garside "From Google to Amazon."

69. Even telecom markets, after their successful liberalization in member states, remain fragmented. See Pelkmans and Renda, "Single eCOMMs Market? No Such Thing."

70. Brito, "Le Stasis: C'est Moi."

71. Albanesius, "France Fines Amazon for Free Shipping."

72. An overview of the efforts to complete the single energy market in Europe can be found in Glachan, *Electricity Reform in Europe.*

73. Kovacevic, *The Impact of the Russia–Ukraine Gas Crisis in South Eastern Europe.*

74. European Commission, "Antitrust: Commission Sends Statement of Objections to Gazprom—Factsheet." See also Ratner et al., "Europe's Energy Security."

75. See, e.g., OECD, *The Governance of Regulator.*

76. Dreyer et al., "The Quest for Gas Market Competition."

77. Kanellakisa et al., "European Energy Policy—A Review."

78. Harvey, "Russia 'Secretly Working with Environmentalists to Oppose Fracking.'"

79. Sobczyk, "U.S. Estimates Poland Has 300 Years' Worth of Shale Gas."

80. The same ambiguity can be found in Alesina et al., "What Does the European Union Do?"

81. Demsetz, "Information and Efficiency: Another Viewpoint."

REFERENCES

Albanesius, Chloe. "France Fines Amazon for Free Shipping." *PC Mag*, January 16, 2008. http://www.pcmag.com/article2/0,2817,2249940,00.asp.

Alesina, Alberto, and Francesco Giavazzi. *The Future of Europe: Reform or Decline*. Cambridge: MIT Press, 2008.

Alesina, Alberto, Ignazio Angeloni, and Ludger Shuknecht. "What Does the European Union Do?" NBER Working Paper No. 8647, December 2001. http://www.nber.org/papers/w8647.

Alter, Karen J., and Sophie Meunier-Aitsahalia. "Judicial Politics in the European Community: European Integration and the Pathbreaking Cassis de Dijon Decision." *Comparative Political Studies* 26 (1994): 535–61.

Aranson, Peter H., and Peter C. Ordeshook. "Regulation, Redistribution, and Public Choice." *Public Choice* 37 (1981): 69–100.

Åslund, Anders. *Ukraine: What Went Wrong and How to Fix It*. Washington DC: Peterson Institute for International Economics, 2015.

Balassa, Bela. "Trade Creation and Diversion in the European Common Market." In *European Economic Integration*, edited by Bela Balassa, 79–118. Amsterdam: North Holland, 1975.

Bayoumi, Tamim, and Barry Eichengreen. "Is Regionalism Simply a Diversion? Evidence from the Evolution of the EC and EFTA." In *Regionalism Versus Multilateral Trade*

Arrangements, edited by Takatoshi Ito and Anne O. Krueger, 141–68. Cambridge: NBER, 1997. http://www.nber.org/chapters/c8599.pdf.

Becker, Sasha O., Peter H. Egger, and Maximilian von Ehrlich. "Going NUTS: The Effect of EU Structural Funds on Regional Performance." *Journal of Public Economics* 94 (2010): 578–90.

Benedetto, Giacomo, and Simona Milio. *European Union Budget Reform: Institutions, Policy and Economic Crisis*. London: Palgrave Macmillan, 2012.

Bolkestein, Frits, and Michel Rocard. *Peut-on réformer la France?* Paris: Autrement, 2007.

Boulanger, Pierre, et al. *An Economic Assessment of Removing the Most Distortive Instruments of the Common Agricultural Policy (CAP)*. Paper presented at the ETSG 2010 Lausanne 12th Annual Conference, September 9–11, 2010. http://www.etsg.org/ETSG2010/papers/Boulanger_Jomini_Zhang_Costa_Osborne.pdf.

Brito, Jerry. "Le Stasis: C'est Moi." *The Umlaut*, February 21, 2013. https://theumlaut.com/2013/02/21/le-stasis-cest-moi/.

Buchanan, James M. *The Limits of Liberty: Between Anarchy and Leviathan*. Vol. 7, in *Collected Works of James M. Buchanan*. Indianapolis IN: Liberty Fund, 2000.

Buchanan, James M., and Gordon Tullock. *The Calculus of Consent: Logical Foundations of Constitutional Democracy*. Ann Arbor: University of Michigan Press, 1962.

Butler, Eamonn. *Public Choice—A Primer*. London: Institute of Economic Affairs, 2012.

Campos, José Edgardo, and Hadi Salehi Esfahani. "Credible Commitment and Success with Public Enterprise Reform." *World Development* 28 (2000): 221–43.

CEE Bankwatch Network. "EU Funds in Eastern and Central Europe." http://bankwatch.org/billions/country/.

Checherita, Cristina, Christiane Nickel, and Philipp Rother. "The Role of Fiscal Transfers for Regional Economic Convergence in Europe." *ECB Working Paper* No. 1029, 2009. https://www.ecb.europa.eu/pub/pdf/scpwps/ecbwp1029.pdf.

Checkel, Jeffrey T. "Why Comply? Social Learning and European Identity Change." *International Organization* 55 (2001): 553–88.

Clinton, Hillary. "America's Pacific Century." *Foreign Policy*, October 11, 2011. http://foreignpolicy.com/2011/10/11/americas-pacific-century/.

De Long, J. Bradford, and Barry Eichengreen. "The Marshall Plan: History's Most Successful Structural Adjustment Program." *NBER Working Paper* No. 3899, 1991. http://www.nber.org/papers/w3899.

Demsetz, Harold. "Information and Efficiency: Another Viewpoint." *Journal of Law and Economics* 12 (1969): 1–22.

Dewatripont, Matthias, and Paul Seabright. "'Wasteful' Public Spending State Aid Control." *Journal of the European Economic Association* 4 (2006): 513–22.

"Disconnected Continent." *The Economist*, May 9, 2015. http://www.economist.com/news/business/21650558-eus-digital-master-plan-all-right-far-it-goes-disconnected-continent.

Dreyer, Iana, Fredrik Erixon, and Robin Winkler. "The Quest for Gas Market Competition: Fighting Europe's Dependency on Russian Gas More Effectively." *ECIPE Occasional Paper* No. 1/2010, 2010. http://www.ecipe.org/app/uploads/2014/12/the-quest-for-gas-market-competition.pdf.

Eichengreen, Barry. *The European Economy Since 1945: Coordinated Capitalism and Beyond*. Princeton NJ: Princeton University Press, 2007.

Eilstrup-Sangiovanni, Mette, and Daniel Verdier. "European Integration as a Solution to War." *European Journal of International Relations* 11 (2005): 99–135.

European Commission. *Single Market Act II: Together for New Growth*. Communication from the Commission to the European Parliament, the Council, the European Economic and Social Committee and the Committee of the Regions, 2012. http://ec.europa.eu/internal_market/smact/docs/single-market-act2_en.pdf.

———. "State Aid: Commission Asks Spain to Recover €265 Million from Ciudad De La Luz Film Studio Complex," May 8, 2012. http://europa.eu/rapid/press-release_IP-12-459_en.htm.

———. "State Aid: Further Details on Commission Decisions Regarding Public Financing of Airports and Airlines in Germany, France and Austria," July 23, 2014. http://europa.eu/rapid/press-release_MEMO-14-498_en.htm.

———. "State Aid: Commission Finds Portuguese Shipyard Operator ENVC Received €290 Million of Incompatible Aid; Orders Recovery from ENVC but Not from New Operator Westsea," May 7, 2015. http://europa.eu/rapid/press-release_IP-15-4940_en.htm.

———. "Antitrust: Commission Sends Statement of Objections to Gazprom—Factsheet." http://europa.eu/rapid/press-release_MEMO-15-4829_en.htm.

———. EU Annual Budget Life-Cycle: Figures. http://ec.europa.eu/budget/annual/index_en.cfm?year=2016.

———. Regional Policy—Available Budget for 2014–2020. http://ec.europa.eu/regional_policy/index.cfm/en/funding/available-budget/.

———. "State Aid: Commission Orders Cyprus to Recover Incompatible Aid from National Air Carrier Cyprus Airways," January 9, 2015. http://europa.eu/rapid/press-release_IP-15-3121_en.htm.

European Council. *Council Resolution 85/C 136/01 on a New Approach to Technical Harmonization and Standards*, May 7, 1985. http://eur-lex.europa.eu/legal-content/EN/TXT/?uri=uriserv:l21001a.

———. *Presidency Conclusions. Copenhagen European Council*, June 22, 1993. http://www.europarl.europa.eu/enlargement/ec/pdf/cop_en.pdf.

European Court of Justice. *Procureur du Roi v Benoît and Gustave Dassonville*. Case 8/74, July 11, 1974. http://eur-lex.europa.eu/legal-content/EN/TXT/?uri=CELEX:61974CJ0008.

———. *Rewe-Zentral AG v Bundesmonopolverwaltung für Branntwein*. Case 120/78, February 20, 1979. http://eur-lex.europa.eu/legal-content/EN/TXT/?uri=CELEX%3A61978CJ0120.

European Parliament and European Council. *Directive 2006/123/EC of the European Parliament and of the Council on Services in the Internal Market*, December 12, 2006. http://eur-lex.europa.eu/legal-content/EN/TXT/?uri=celex:32006L0123.

Flynn, Gregory, and Henry Farrell. "Piecing Together the Democratic Peace: The CSCE, Norms, and the 'Construction' of Security in Post–Cold War Europe." *International Organization* 53 (1999): 505-35.

Follesdal, Andreas, and Simon Hix."Why There Is a Democratic Deficit in the EU: A Response to Majone and Moravcsik." *Journal of Common Market Studies* 44 (2006): 533–62.

Friederiszick, Hans W., Lars-Hendrik Röller, and Vincent Verouden. "European State Aid Control: An Economic Framework." In *Handbook of Antitrust Economics*, edited by Paolo Buccirossi, 625–69. Cambridge: MIT Press, 2007.

Garside, Juliette. "From Google to Amazon: EU Goes to War Against Power of US Digital Giants." *The Guardian*, July 6, 2014. http://www.theguardian.com/technology/2014/jul/06/google-amazon-europe-goes-to-war-power-digital-giants.

Glachan, Jean-Michel. *Electricity Reform in Europe: towardss a Single Energy Market*. Cheltenham: Edward Elgar, 2009.

Grossman, Sanford, and Oliver Hart. "The Costs and Benefits of Ownership: A Theory of Vertical and Lateral Integration." *Journal of Political Economy* 94 (1986): 691–719.

Grossman, Emiliano, and Cornelia Woll. "The French Debate over the Bolkestein Directive." *Comparative European Politics* 9 (2011): 344–66.

Hannan, Daniel. 2012. "The EU Is Not a Free Trade Area but a Customs Union: Until We Understand the Difference, the Debate About Our Membership Is Meaningless." *The Telegraph*, October 23, 2012. http://blogs.telegraph.co.uk/news/danielhannan/100186074/the-eu-is-not-a-free-trade-area-but-a-customs-union-until-we-understand-the-difference-the-debate-about-our-membership-is-meaningless/.

Hart, Oliver, and John Moore. "Incomplete Contracts and Renegotiation." *Econometrica* 56 (1988): 755–85.

Harvey, Fiona. "Russia 'Secretly Working with Environmentalists to Oppose Fracking.'" *The Guardian*, June 19, 2014. http://www.theguardian.com/environment/2014/jun/19/russia-secretly-working-with-environmentalists-to-oppose-fracking.

Hayek, Friedrich A. von. "The Economic Conditions of Interstate Federalism." In *Individualism and Economic Order*, 255–72. Chicago: University of Chicago Press, 1948.

Hix, Simon. "The EU as Polity (I)." In *The SAGE Handbook of European Union Politics*, edited by Knud Erik Jørgensen, Mark Pollack, and Ben Rosamon, 141–58. New York: SAGE, 2007.

Hix, Simon, and Bjørn Høyland. *The Political System of the European Union*, 3rd ed. London: Palgrave Macmillan, 2011.

———. *What's Wrong with the European Union and How to Fix It*. London: Polity, 2008.

Homer. *The Odyssey*. Translated by Robert Fitzgerald. New York: Farrar, Straus and Giroux, 1998.

Kanellakisa, Marinos, Georgios Martinopoulos, and Theodoros Zachariadis. "European Energy Policy—A Review." *Energy Policy* 62 (2013): 1020–30.

Kovacevic, Aleksandar. *The Impact of the Russia–Ukraine Gas Crisis in South Eastern Europe*. Oxford Institute for Energy Studies, 2009. http://www.oxfordenergy.org/wpcms/wp-content/uploads/2010/11/NG29-TheImpactoftheRussiaUkrainianCrisisinSouthEastern Europe-AleksandarKovacevic-2009.pdf.

Kydland, Finn E., and Edward C. Prescott. "Rules Rather Than Discretion: The Inconsistency of Optimal Plans." *Journal of Political Economy* 85 (1977): 473–92.

Levitz, Philip, and Grigore Pop-Eleches. "Why No Backsliding? The EU's Impact on Democracy and Governance Before and After Accession." *Comparative Political Studies* 43 (2010): 457–85.

Lisbon Council. *An Action Plan for Europe 2020: Strategic Advice for the Post-Crisis World*. Lisbon Council Policy Brief, 2011. http://www.lisboncouncil.net/component/downloads/? id=470.

Majone, Giandomenico. "Europe's 'Democratic Deficit': The Question of Standards." *European Law Journal* 4 (1998): 5–28.

———. "Rethinking European Integration After the Debt Crisis." *UCL European Institute Working Paper* No. 3/2012. https://www.ucl.ac.uk/european-institute/analysis-publi cations/publications/WP3.pdf.

Mikloš, Ivan. "Slovakia: The Latecomer That Caught Up." In *The Great Rebirth: Lessons from the Victory of Capitalism over Communism*, edited by Anders Åslund and Simeon Djankov, 113–34. Washington DC: Peterson Institute for International Economics, 2015.

Moravcsik, Andrew. "Reassessing Legitimacy in the European Union." *Journal of Common Market Studies* 40 (2002): 603–24.

———. "The Myth of Europe's Democratic Deficit." *Intereconomics*, November–December 2008: 331–40.

Nowak, Tobias. "Of Garbage Cans and Rulings: Judgments of the European Court of Justice in the EU Legislative Process." *West European Politics* 33 (2010): 753–69.

OECD. *The Governance of Regulators. OECD Best Practice Principles for Regulatory Policy*. Paris: OECD Publishing, 2014. http://dx.doi.org/10.1787/9789264209015-en.

Olson, Mancur. *The Logic of Collective Action*. Cambridge: Harvard University Press, 1965.

Pelkmans, Jacques. "Mutual Recognition in Goods and Services: An Economic Perspective." *ENEPRI Working Paper* No. 16, 2003. http://aei.pitt.edu/1852/1/ENEPRI_WP16.pdf.

Pelkmans, Jacques, and Andrea Renda. "Single eCOMMs Market? No Such Thing." *CEPS Policy Brief* No. 231, 2011.

Plattner, Marc F. "Sovereignty and Democracy." *Policy Review*, December 2003–January 2004. http://www.hoover.org/research/sovereignty-and-democracy.

Pridham, Geoffrey. "EU Enlargement and Consolidating Democracy in Post–Communist States — Formality and Reality." *Journal of Common Market Studies* 40 (2002): 953–73.

Ratner, Michael, et al. "Europe's Energy Security: Options and Challenges to Natural Gas Supply Diversification." *CRS Report for Congress*, August 20, 2013. https://www.fas.org/ sgp/crs/row/R42405.pdf.

Rettman, Andrew. "Two Million British People Emigrated to EU, Figures Show." *EU Observer*, February 10, 2014, https://euobserver.com/social/123066.

Rodrik, Dani. "Promises, Promises: Credible Policy Reform via Signaling." *NBER Working Paper* No. 2600, 1988. http://www.nber.org/papers/w2600.pdf.

Rosenberg, Christoph B., and Robert Sierhej. "Interpreting EU Funds Data for Macroeconomic Analysis in the New Member States." *IMF Working Paper* 07/77, 2007. https://www.imf.org/external/pubs/ft/wp/2007/wp0777.pdf.

Salin, Pascal. "World Regulations and Harmonization." *Independent Review* 6 (2001): 59–80.

————. *Competition, Coordination and Diversity: From the Firm to Economic Integration.* Cheltenham UK: Edward Elgar, 2015.

Schimmelfennig, Frank, and Ulrich Sedelmeier. "Governance by Conditionality: EU Rule Transfer to the Candidate Countries of Central and Eastern Europe." *Journal of European Public Policy* 11 (2004): 661–79.

Sejerøe, Anders, et al. "The Copenhagen Economics Study on the Economic Impact of the Services Directive." *Intereconomics* 40 (2005): 125–29.

Smith, Karen E. *European Union Foreign Policy in a Changing World*, 3rd ed. London: Polity Press, 2014.

Sobczyk, Marcin. "U.S. Estimates Poland Has 300 Years' Worth of Shale Gas." *WSJ Emerging Europe*, April 7, 2011. http://blogs.wsj.com/emergingeurope/2011/04/07/u-s-estimates-poland-has-300-years-worth-of-shale-gas/.

Sykes, Alan O. "Regulatory Protectionism and the Law of International Trade." *University of Chicago Law Review* 66 (1999): 1–46.

Treaty Establishing the European Economic Community, EEC Treaty, 1957. http://eur-lex.europa.eu/legal-content/FR/TXT/PDF/?uri=CELEX:11957E/TXT&from=EN.

Whitehead, Tom. "Campaign to Lure Poles Back Home amid Fears of Brain Drain to Britain." *The Telegraph*, March 6, 2015. http://www.telegraph.co.uk/news/uknews/immigration/11454795/Campaign-to-lure-Poles-back-home-amid-fears-of-brain-drain-to-Britain.html.

Wilhelmsson, Fredrik. *Trade Creation, Diversion and Displacement of the EU Enlargement Process*, Lund University, 2006.

World Bank. "Tariff Rate, Applied, Weighted Mean, All Products (%)." 2015. http://data.worldbank.org/indicator/TM.TAX.MRCH.WM.AR.ZS.

3

MEET THE DISCONTENTS

A few months before the United Kingdom's general election in May 2015, BBC Two aired a documentary about the activists running the campaign of the United Kingdom Independence Party (UKIP) in the constituency of South Thanet, on the Eastern coast of Kent, where UKIP leader Nigel Farage had chosen to run. *Meet the Ukippers*, as the documentary was called, attracted 1.42 million viewers—a large number given its genre. It showcased the chairman of the South Thanet branch of the party, formerly a member of the extremist National Front, which he describes as "a bit of a social club."[1] There is a UKIP member of European Parliament who refers to a Thai constituent as a "ting tong from somewhere" and Rozanne Duncan (since expelled), a local councilor for UKIP, who denies any charges of xenophobia throughout the program—only to add that she had a "real problem with people of negroid [*sic*] features." Rest assured, that is not racism, only "something in [her] psyche" or "karma from a previous life."

It is impossible to ignore the fact that conservative Eurosceptics—at whom this book is primarily directed—find themselves in colorful company. As the example of UKIP's supporters in South Thanet shows, many other political groups reject the idea of European integration, too. Their reasons are different—and not all of them have to do with the cerebral arguments about the EU's lack of accountability, overregulation, or wasteful spending. For some, the European project is seen as a threat to nationhood. Others might believe that national sovereignty, unencumbered by Brussels, is necessary for the existence of a well-governed state. Only the final category encompasses the instrumental concerns,[2] which we often hear from free-market critics of the EU, such as the belief that EU membership is not justified by the benefits that it provides.

The economic crisis has magnified anti-European sentiments.[3] In spring 2007, 52 percent of EU citizens expressed a positive view of the EU, with only 15 percent expressing a negative one. In spring 2013, by contrast, only 30 percent of Europeans held a positive view, and, almost the same number, 29 percent, a negative one.[4] Over the same period, the average unemployment rate across the EU increased by almost 4 percentage points, from around 7 percent to almost 11. Unsurprisingly, the opposition to the European project is concentrated in countries that were hit by the crisis. According to the Eurobarometer survey from fall 2014, 44 percent of Greeks had a negative view of the EU, followed by 38 percent of Cypriots, and 32 percent of Britons, traditionally Eurosceptic. By contrast, only 6 percent of Poles and Lithuanians and 7 percent of Estonians shared such a view.

Eurosceptic politicians striving for mass appeal seek to reconcile nationalist impulses and more polished political or economic criticisms of the EU. In November 2009, Farage gave a talk to the Oxford Libertarian Society, a student group promoting free-market ideas. The lecture theatre at the Manor Road Building, which houses Oxford University's Department of Economics, was packed with young conservatives and libertarians who nodded in agreement as Farage deplored the growth of government in the West and the corruption of the UK's entrenched political class. Farage enumerated the various defects of the European project, the senseless bureaucracy, and the erosion of UK sovereignty. He made a powerful case for Brexit, which, according to him, would not mean the end of economic, social, and cultural ties with the continent—merely a liberation from the diktat of unaccountable European institutions. Similar speeches established Farage's credentials among conservatives and libertarians. Another part of his appeal has to do with his qualities as a passionate and entertaining orator. Some of his performances in the European Parliament have gone viral—most notably the one in which he compared Herman van Rompuy, the lackluster president of the European Council, to a "damp rag."

In the 2015 general election, Nigel Farage lost in South Thanet to a Conservative candidate, Craig Mackinlay. UKIP earned only one seat in the House of Commons, in spite of receiving some 3.8 million votes. This was due more to the first-past-the-post electoral system than to the widespread perception of the party as a bunch of "fruitcakes, loonies and closet racists,"[5] as UK Prime Minister David Cameron once put it. In fact, research into UKIP's support reveals that the group of "core loyalists" of UKIP is formed precisely by politically disaffected voters animated by xenophobic impulses, including women who otherwise tend to reject far-right groups, such as the fascist British National Party. Another large group of UKIP voters are "strategic defectors," whose aim is simply to punish mainstream politicians, without necessarily harboring any deep-seated disdain for the EU.[6]

This chapter introduces five archetypal Eurosceptic narratives, peddled by different critics of the EU. There are, most prominently, the free-market criticisms of a conservative or libertarian variety. The far left offers a different account of the flaws of the EU. There exists, of course, a nationalist version of Euroscepticism. Some of the EU's critics are infatuated with Russia and Vladimir Putin. Finally, a number of conspiracy theories about the EU have gained currency in certain Eurosceptic circles. Although the material covered in this chapter focuses disproportionately on claims made by politicians and on political platforms, it is worth emphasizing that the many critiques of the EU have deeper intellectual foundations, in economics as well as in political philosophy. I discuss the central claims of these intellectual criticisms in the remainder of this book.

The five narratives are not mutually exclusive: many critics of the EU have adopted several of them at once. They are oftentimes simultaneously critical of EU bureaucracy and lack of accountability, pander to nationalistic and xenophobic sentiments, *and* approve of Putin's regime in Russia. Because voters rarely care enough about European issues, critical attitudes towards the EU ("soft Euroscepticism") or its outright rejection ("hard Euroscepticism"), are more salient at the level of elites, politicians, and political parties than at the level of popular discourse.[7] For voters themselves, European themes are typically associated with domestic grievances over immigration or poor economic performance, and the support for the EU also reflects some well-known political cleavages, such as the one existing between the city and the village in Central and Eastern European countries.[8]

EU AS ATTACK ON FREE MARKETS

The archetypal free-market critic of the EU sees it as an unaccountable bureaucratic monstrosity, churning out regulations that destroy Europeans' freedom and erode their democracies. Very often, they will also say that there is no point in reforming the Union, as it was pointless to reform Soviet communism. The EU, in short, is a failed attempt to mastermind and plan economic activity, inimical to free enterprise.

Douglas Carswell is a fine representative of this school of thought. Initially a Conservative Member of Parliament for Clacton, in Essex, he defected to UKIP in August 2014. He won the subsequent by-election and was also the only UKIP candidate elected in the 2015 general election. A son of Wilson Carswell, a famous medical researcher who helped discover HIV/AIDS and served as the inspiration for the main character of the film *Last King of Scotland*,[9] Douglas spent much of his childhood and teenage years in Africa. Besides his work as a Conservative MP, he teamed up with his colleague Steve Baker, a Conservative MP for Wycombe, to establish the Cobden Centre, a think tank focused on somewhat esoteric questions of monetary policy and banking.

Unlike a vast majority of economists, including many prominent free marketeers, Carswell and Baker believe that the key problem behind the financial crisis of 2008, and behind Western economic woes more generally, is the ability of banks to operate under the regime of so-called fractional reserves. The dominant portion of any deposit at a commercial bank is used to extend credit, with only a small fraction going into the bank's reserves. This technique, which also enables banks to offer interest on on-demand deposits, is seen as inherently inflationary as it expands the monetary base and supposedly fosters financial speculation. At the same time, they argue, it benefits a narrow interest group in the financial industry because it enables them to channel money that was created "out of thin air" into new investment projects—many of them too risky or ultimately unprofitable. "Policymakers," Carswell said in the House of Commons, "have had to face the unenviable choice between letting the edifice of crony capitalism come crashing down, with calamitous consequences for the rest of us, or printing more real money to shore up this Ponzi scheme."[10] In 2010, Carswell and Baker proposed a bill that would ban fractional reserve banking, unless bank depositors agreed explicitly that their deposit be lent further.[11]

The proposal would have put an end to the banking industry as we know it, turning banks into warehouses and drastically limiting the tools available to conduct monetary policy.

Carswell's 2012 book, *The End of Politics*[12] —which was praised by Mayor of London Boris Johnson as "a fascinating read from a refreshing and independent Conservative voice"—predicted that big government would be unable to cope with the advent of the digital age. New technologies of communication, he claimed, would soon allow for more personalization, for instant feedback, and ultimately for the introduction of market mechanisms and personal choice into areas that are governed, quite unsatisfactorily, by the political process. The EU and other international bodies thus do not herald the advent of a new age of global governance. Instead, they are relics of an ending era and are bound to wither into irrelevance. The main problem with the EU, according to Carswell, is that the organization is out of control, unresponsive to feedback from member states. It is a drag on countries' economic engagement with the rest of the world, too. "Instead of making it easier to do business, it makes it harder—by undermining the global competitiveness of British companies with pointless regulation."[13] All of that makes it imperative for the UK to get out in order to regain its prosperity.[14]

Among free-market economists, these ideas are hardly new. The eminent German public choice scholar, Roland Vaubel, for example, has long argued that the institutional design of the European Union is biased in favor of unchecked centralization and overregulation.[15] His and similar critiques[16] are not without their merits. However, they tend to ignore the real contribution of European integration in dismantling economic barriers between European nations. Carswell's rejection of the EU is steeped also in a distinctly British version of conservatism. The Euroscepticism that has emerged in the United Kingdom, both of the soft and the hard varieties, reflects in part the country's insular nature and its history of distrust of other European powers. The UK was initially hesitant to join the process of European integration for reasons that had little to do with free-market economics—quite the contrary. The Macmillan government insisted that the UK should retain its preferential trade arrangements with other members of the Commonwealth. That would mean keeping the British market closed to

European agricultural imports, while enjoying the freedom of access to markets on the European continent.

The UK's application for membership in the European Economic Community (EEC) was blocked in 1963 by the French, who feared that the UK would weaken France's leadership position on the continent.[17] The UK's eventual accession, in 1973, led to a controversy at home. In the campaign leading to the 1974 general election, Labour's Harold Wilson promised to hold a referendum about UK membership. When he became prime minister, he honored that promise. A referendum was organized in 1975. It led to a split within the cabinet between support- ers of the "yes" and "no" votes. The Tory opposition was divided as well, with the freshly elected leader of the Conservative Party, Margaret Thatcher, leading the Conservative "yes" camp. In spite of a number of backbenchers from both parties campaigning in favor of Brexit, more than 67 percent of voters wanted the UK to remain a part of the inte- gration project. As prime minister, Thatcher became one of the leading voices behind the Single European Act of 1987, which was an impulse for tighter economic integration and strengthening the position of the competition directorate at the European Commission, pushing for deeper liberalization.[18] Thatcher's government oversaw the institution of a directly elected European Parliament, the creation of common EU- wide passport covers, and the decision to build the Channel Tunnel— all of which have become emblematic of European integration. Her government also increased the contributions to the EEC budget, by some 400 percent.[19]

Paradoxically, Thatcher is now remembered for her role in the UK's drift away from Brussels on issues including agricultural subsidies, which then accounted for a dominant part of the EEC's budget and remain sizeable even today. During this period, subsidies were flowing disproportionately to the "old" EEC countries, most notably France. But the British did not warm up to the European project even after that problem was addressed in 1984 through the permanent rebate that since then returned a significant portion of the UK's annual contribu- tions back to its national budget. In 1988, Thatcher gave a famous speech to the College of Europe in Bruges, which became known as the "Bruges Speech"[20] and has since served as a manifesto of sorts for Eurosceptics in the UK and beyond. It starts by outlining the history of UK ties to continental Europe, going back to the times of the Celts and

Romans, and presents guiding principles for the European policies of the future in order to correct what Thatcher saw as the main flaws of the European integration efforts. Europe, for her, should be a community of sovereign states. She deplores the efforts to "suppress nationhood and concentrate power at the center of a European conglomerate." And, if the European project is to succeed, she adds, the continent will have to open to economic reform, free enterprise, and trade.

A group of Conservatives—including the free-market economist Ralph Harris, who had earlier been among the founders of the Institute of Economic Affairs, the iconic free-market think tank—founded the Bruges Group, an organization dedicated to the promotion of the speech's message. The sentiment shared by many of Thatcher's followers is that, in the decades following the Bruges speech, Europe has ignored her advice and moved in the opposite direction towards greater centralization and away from the economic opening that the Bruges speech called for. That sentiment grew stronger around the time of the ratification of the Maastricht Treaty, which consolidated EU institutions and created the basic infrastructure needed for the introduction of the common currency. As the Maastricht Treaty was about to be ratified, the UK and the European Exchange Rate Mechanism (ERM)—a precursor of the euro—were in the midst of a bitter divorce. ERM was a system of fixed exchange rates that the UK joined in 1990. The system was dubbed the "Eternal Recession Mechanism" because the UK's membership coincided with a protracted economic downturn in the country. When the UK withdrew from the ERM in September 1992, many felt discouraged by the experiment. A group of Conservatives, who became known as the "Maastricht Rebels," refused to vote for the Treaty in Parliament, almost bringing down the government of John Major.

The Bruges Group became a focal point for the Maastricht Rebels and other hard Eurosceptics, both during and after their political careers. It provided them with a platform to articulate their ideas through conferences, meetings, and publications. Numerous Tory backbenchers and Eurosceptic MEPs, such as the libertarian Daniel Hannan and the veteran MP John Redwood, have ties to the organization. Norman Lamont, former Chancellor of the Exchequer, became the honorary chairman of the group. Their opposition against the EU has been driven almost exclusively by free-market impulses, combined with the feeling "that [the UK's] sovereign independence is being gradually whittled away by EU laws and regulations,"[21] as John O'Sullivan, a former speechwriter for Margaret Thatcher and editor-at-large of the US magazine *National Review*, put it.

Many on the continent see the EU as an enemy of free markets, too, such as Václav Klaus, the former president of the Czech Republic. Long a superstar in the American conservative and libertarian circles, he was called "one of the most remarkable political figures of our time" by Margaret Thatcher.[22] He earned his reputation, in part, by leading the Czech transition to democracy and a market economy in the 1990s, although his actual record as a reformer was mixed. While the Czech transition was broadly successful, Klaus's government failed to privatize the banking sector and open it to competition. "Banking socialism," as the situation was dubbed, led to an accumulation of bad debts and to the need to restructure the banking industry later.[23] The main reason for his bona fides among conservatives and libertarians lies in his free-market rhetoric, rather than in the actual track record as a politician.

Over time, Klaus's intellectual interests converged on two issues: climate change, or "global warming alarmism"[24] as he called it, and the European Union, which he compared to the Soviet Union in his famous speech to the European Parliament in February 2009.[25] The core of Klaus's argument is that the process of European integration is an attack on the Europe of democratic nation-states. He deplores living "in a system based on the ideology of Europeism which prefers supranational institutions with their post-democracy to the good old democratic institutions in a well-defined constitutional sovereign state." For Klaus, the problem was not just about governance but also about ideology. "Europeism," he claims, has implications for other areas of life, as it hides in itself also "multiculturalism, humanrightism, and political correctness."[26]

As president, Klaus kept a circle of young economic advisers. One of them, Petr Mach, left the president's office in 2009 to start his own political movement: the Party of Free Citizens. An unapologetic hard Eurosceptic and libertarian, Mach struggled to gain wider recognition until the European election in 2014, when he was elected to the European Parliament as one of 21 Czech MEPs. He joined Europe of Freedom and Direct Democracy, a parliamentary group led by Nigel Farage. In neighboring Slovakia, which joined the EU in 2004 and became a Eurozone member in January 2009, Eurosceptic ideas came to prominence after the debt crisis erupted on the Eurozone's Mediterranean periphery. Slovaks were unpleasantly surprised to see that they were expected to contribute to the bailout package for Greece, as well as to the new lending facilities created by the EU to increase its resilience to future financial crises. In October 2011, the disagreement over boosting the EU's temporary lending tool, the European Financial Stability Facility (EFSF), led to the fall of the government of Iveta Radičová. The Freedom and Solidarity Party (SaS), a junior coalition partner led by Richard Sulík, a businessman-turned-politician, refused to acquiesce to what was a minor change to the EU financial infrastructure. Sulík objected to the unfairness of a situation in which poorer member states were supposed to chip in to provide financial assistance to wealthier European economies, such as Greece and Spain.

Sulík has since then become the leading soft Eurosceptic voice in Slovakia. In addition to opposing bailouts in the Eurozone, he has spoken against EU aid to Ukraine, which he compared—like Greece—to a bottomless barrel,[27] as well as against Germany's open-door policy towards Syrian asylum-seekers. The SaS thus resembles the Alternative for Germany (AfD), Germany's main Eurosceptic force. The AfD was founded in 2012 by Bernd Lucke, a macroeconomist teaching at the University of Hamburg; Alexander Gauland, a lawyer and civil servant; and Konrad Adam, a former editor of *Frankfurter Allgemeine Zeitung*. The three authored a manifesto opposing the common currency in Europe, which they blamed for the economic crisis on the periphery. Their economic argument was straightforward: imposing a single currency on the continent eliminated the possibility of interest and exchange rate adjustments in individual countries. For southern Europe, the common currency is overvalued; for Germany and other northern European nations, the euro is undervalued, propping up exports at the expense of domestic consumption.

The document, which led to the creation of a political party, was endorsed by a number of conservative academics and intellectuals, giving the group the nickname of the "professors' party." Although no AfD candidate made it to the Bundestag in the parliamentary election in 2013, the party received over 7 percent of all votes in the 2014 European election and seven seats in the European Parliament. According to its electoral manifesto, "[t]he AfD calls for the dissolution of the euro currency zone, or at least a complete reorganization of its current poli-cy,"[28] giving each country the right to leave the Eurozone without leav-ing the EU. What put the AfD on the political map was its opposition to fiscal assistance to Eurozone countries. Not only is the AfD asking for abolition of the European Stability Mechanism (ESM), the permanent lending facility created to help Eurozone countries in distress, it also demands an overhaul of the European Central Bank (ECB) to prevent it from financing public-sector debt in the Eurozone. As the English version of the manifesto puts it, the "ECB is to be prohibited on princi-ple from purchasing government bonds."[29] As one would expect, the AfD is also critical of the lack of democratic accountability in the EU and demands more direct citizen participation in the common deci-sions—including more referenda and citizens' initiatives—as well as genuine subsidiarity—devolving more decisions from the level of the EU down to the level of nation-states and below. The AfD also wants to end "the superfluous daylight-saving time."[30]

I concur with many of the critiques of the EU coming from the conservative camp. Free enterprise is, of course, the most important engine of economic prosperity in Europe and elsewhere. Many ele-ments of the EU's current architecture are inimical to free markets. Where I depart from the conservative Eurosceptic orthodoxy is in maintaining that integrated markets in Europe are unlikely to survive with a functioning system of international governance, such as the one provided by the EU.

EU AS "NEOLIBERAL" CABAL

A different group of Eurosceptics do not believe that the EU is a drag on markets. Instead, they claim, there is *too much* unregulated free-market capitalism in the bloc, actively encouraged by the Union's insti-tutions. For example, the EU has forced its member states into painful austerity programs, cutting welfare for those who need it. It unleashes unrestrained economic competition, erodes Europe's social standards, and ultimately impoverishes the most vulnerable—supposedly for the benefit of large corporations and a narrow elite.

Many left-leaning economists—just as the right-leaning ones—long harbored suspicions about the flaws in the design of the Eurozone. Paul

Krugman's and Joseph Stiglitz's writings about the euro closely mirror the arguments made by the early conservative critics of the common currency, such as Milton Friedman and Martin Feldstein. At the height of the political standoff between Greece's Syriza-led government and the EU in summer 2015, Krugman noted that "the creation of the euro was a terrible mistake" and his advice to the Greek government was "if necessary, to leave the euro."[31] Stiglitz, in turn, claimed that "concern for popular legitimacy is incompatible with the politics of the Eurozone, which was never a very democratic project," hoping that "Greece, with its strong democratic tradition, might grasp its destiny in its own hands," by escaping the diktat of Brussels.[32]

Stiglitz and Krugman lack the commitment to European integration shared by many of their counterparts on the intellectual left in Europe. But even that commitment can be no longer taken for granted in the aftermath of the financial crisis in Greece. Syriza's electoral platform in Greece's parliamentary election in January 2015 may not have been distinctly Eurosceptic, but it involved a rejection of the existing austerity program under the auspices of the EU and IMF, and essentially a return to the pre-2010 economic status quo. The intention—which enjoyed significant popular support—of going against a joint EU decision represented a significant break with the past, as Greece traditionally counted among the most pro-EU countries of all the Union.[33]

Syriza's anti-austerity agenda was a political no-go with Greece's partners, who were unwilling to make further concession unless Greece demonstrated material progress in implementing economic reforms. The conflict between the intentions of a democratically elected Greek government and the EU, imposing a program of fiscal consolidation and reforms, resonated on the European left outside Greece as well. *The Guardian*'s commentator Owen Jones described Greece as "a society that has been progressively dismantled by EU-dictated austerity."[34] The sentiment that the EU's insistence on fiscal consolidation amounted to a political coup by an unelected clique was echoed by numerous left-wing Twitteratis, particularly under the hashtag #ThisIsACoup during the night of the negotiations between the government of Alexis Tsipras and its European creditors after the Greek referendum that had rejected austerity in July 2015.

Many on Europe's left, some of them within Syriza, are embracing the Eurosceptic label. By dismissing some of the foundational principles of the EU as "neoliberal" dogmas and proposing to rebuild the EU without such principles, they blur the traditional distinction between soft and hard Euroscepticism. For example, Costas Lapavitsas, a professor at London's School of Oriental and African Studies and an MP from Syriza, deplores "the conservative mechanisms at the heart of the EU"[35] and hopes that the left would succeed in "sending a clear anti-capitalist message that combines radical policies with progressive Euroscepticism."[36] He wants the current EU "dismantled and replaced"[37] by a system of managed exchange rates and controlled capital flows, putting an end to one (if not more) of the EU's fundamental freedoms. These ideas are also echoed by the Podemos party, founded in 2014 by Pablo Iglesias, a young Spanish political scientist, with the explicit purpose of challenging mainstream European politics from the left. Ending austerity, introducing basic income for everyone, and imposing public control over much of the economy formed the core of the Podemos economic program, alongside a revision of the Lisbon Treaty to exempt public services from any cross-border competition and impose levies on capital within the EU (as well in third countries), in line with Lapavitsas's intention of ending the freedom of the movement of capital.[38]

The far-left Euroscepticism that has resurged in response to the economic crisis in Greece is not new. Heterodox, left-leaning economists have been long critical of the liberalization that European integration has brought about, particularly in the area of capital flows, as well as of its overall reliance on markets as opposed to state control.[39] The *political*, as opposed to purely intellectual, opposition to the EU on the left is not without its antecedents, either. In the 1970s, as the UK was facing a deep economic crisis because of its own legacy of statism and profligate spending, a large part of the Labour Party blamed the IMF and EEC for preventing the adoption of unspecified policies that would somehow preserve high social standards and shield the country from foreign competition, without sacrificing economic prosperity. For those, the EEC meant surrendering to the anonymous forces of international capitalism, abetted by a foreign bureaucracy.

I do not provide a direct rebuttal to those who deplore the supposedly excessive reliance of the EU on unregulated markets in this book. Instead, its premise is that free enterprise and democratic capitalism are highly desirable and that much of what the progressives present as their fundamental flaws are in reality outcomes of ill-conceived economic policies, both at the national and the international level. However, left-leaning Eurosceptics deserve a fair hearing when they point to the democratic deficit that exists in the EU, in areas that are political by their very nature. Fiscal restraint and market-friendly reforms, for example, are unlikely to be effective, and might even be harmful, if they are simply imposed, the way they were imposed by the Troika on Greece. For the Eurozone to prosper, the advocates of free enterprise and responsible budgeting must prevail in an open and democratic discussion, perceived as legitimate by most, if not all, Europeans.

EU AS ANATHEMA OF NATIONAL GREATNESS

Nationalist critics of the EU see the organization as an affront to national greatness. They argue that the membership limits national sovereignty and prevents the government from pursuing desirable policies, protecting domestic industries, and defending legitimate national interest. Free movement of people within the EU, a nationalist would claim, has opened the gates to a deluge of immigrants who free-ride on welfare and social services or, alternatively, undercut local wages and slowly erode the character of European countries.

UKIP's closeted racists aside, the issues of national identity, economic nationalism, and social conservatism resonate more strongly on the European continent than in the Anglo-Saxon world. One prominent example is France's Front National (FN), founded in the 1970s by Jean-Marie Le Pen. Le Pen was a veteran of the French wars in Indochina and Algeria, as well as the Suez Crisis, and was long active in nationalist politics. He worked, for example, in the 1965 presidential campaign of Jean-Louis Tixier-Vignancour, the well-known apologist of Maréchal Petain's regime. Since its early days, the FN has undergone a significant transformation. Under the direction of Marine, Le Pen's daughter, it has been striving to become a part of mainstream French politics, distancing itself from the excesses of the past. That prompted, in turn, Le Pen Senior to speak out against the current direction of the party. "I am ashamed that she bears my name," he said about Marine Le Pen, after his membership in the party was suspended.[40]

Under Marine Le Pen's leadership, the FN is no longer universally shunned. It has been allowed, for example, to form a student association at the Paris Institute of Political Studies (Sciences Po), one of the most prestigious institutions of higher learning in the country.[41] The FN proposes a renegotiation of EU treaties to make a "break with the dogmatic and totally failed European construction,"[42] making it unclear whether it seeks, like soft Eurosceptic groups, to reform the EU or to end it altogether. Perhaps most significantly, the ability to control immigration should be returned, the FN argues, into the hands of the nation-states. Le Pen's party is also very critical of the euro and is advocating a reintroduction of the franc, nationalization of banks, and capital controls to limit "speculation." Needless to say, this would represent the end of the freedom of movement of capital in the EU, one of the key components of the single market. The party's proposal to prioritize the employment of French citizens in certain professions, as well as the obligation of the government to use only domestic, French firms in public procurement tenders would likely also run against existing European norms. Yet it is worth noting that the departure of the party's economic program from the European orthodoxy follows a very different logic from conservatives in the Anglosphere. For the latter, the problem resides with market-distorting subsidies and regulations coming from an unaccountable bureaucratic body in Brussels. The likes of Le Pen aim to restore France's full sovereignty and empower the French government to pursue policies that are essentially incompatible with the existence of free markets in the EU, including protectionist measures and activist industrial policy. The FN calls, for example, for "strategic planning of re-industrialization"[43] under the auspices of the prime minister, using the insights of leading academics, representatives of business, and the government, which is "to take place in parallel with the introduction of reasonable border protection against unfair international competition (targeted tariffs and quotas)."[44] Other policy ideas include the regulation of banking fees, unspecific policies aiming to "establish an equilibrium between independent business and large retailers," and a ban on financial derivatives.[45] In short, Le Pen's is an agenda that ought to make every free marketeer deeply uncomfortable.

Hungary, with its nationalist Prime Minister Viktor Orbán and his party, Fidesz, have taken Eurosceptic nationalism from the realm of rhetoric into practice. To the outside world, Orbán long portrayed himself as a center-right leader who wanted his country to make a break with its communist heritage. As a Soros Scholar, he spent four months at Pembroke College, Oxford, in 1989. Nine years, later he became the second youngest prime minister in the history of the country and established himself as a firmly pro-Western, reformist leader. Since then, much has changed in Hungary, including Viktor Orbán. What was initially a Hungarian brand of center-right conservatism has slowly morphed into populist nationalism. In spring 2015, for example, he covered Budapest with posters addressed to incoming asylum-seekers, warning them not to take the jobs of Hungarians and asking them to respect Hungary's culture and laws. Written in Hungarian, their true audience was, quite obviously, Hungarian nationalist voters, not immigrants.[46]

From a staunch "euro-atlanticist," Orbán morphed into a soft Euro-sceptic. His response to the financial crisis that hit Hungary was a smorgasbord of unorthodox measures, including the nationalization of pension assets and levies targeted at specific industries and foreign investors, many of which triggered a pushback from the European Commission (EC).[47] The Commission also raised red flags about the constitution passed by the Fidesz-dominated parliament in 2012.[48] In his frequent disputes with the EC, Orbán presents himself as a defender of Hungarian national interests. In his widely cited July 2014 speech about "illiberal democracy," he highlighted the EU as "an obstacle of reorganizing the state" in the desired, illiberal direction—although not an obstacle that would be impossible to overcome.[49]

Other critics of the EU flirt with nationalist ideas, too. In May 2015, Marine Le Pen visited Prague to give a talk at a conference of anti-EU parties from around Europe. The night before the conference, she met with Václav Klaus, former President of the Czech Republic, at a local pub. A photo of the two appeared on the Facebook page of the Václav Klaus Institute shortly thereafter,[50] with a caption saying "modern leftist politicians would have taken a selfie—Marine Le Pen and I had a beer instead," followed by Klaus's glowing endorsement of Le Pen as a "rational politician, with an intrinsically open and friendly mindset."[51]

To think that the French nationalist and the Czech free marketeer would make an awkward political couple is to misunderstand the nationalist undercurrent of some of Klaus's rhetoric. Several months before their meeting, at a conference of the classical liberal Mont Pèlerin Society, he delivered a speech that lambasted the "careless opening up" that had eroded nation-states and called for "responsible citizens anchored in domestic realities, not cosmopolitan, selfish individuals 'float-ing' at the surface and searching for short-term pleasures and advan-tages—without roots and responsibility."[52] Even in 2009, as Klaus kept Europe's elites on tenterhooks before he signed the Lisbon Treaty into law, his declared motives had as much to do with his opposition to Brussels' overreach as they had with the fears of some Czech national-ists that the treaty would open the door to a legal challenge to the controversial Beneš decrees, through which Czechoslovakia's sizeable German population was expropriated and expelled from the country after World War II. Klaus decided to sign the document only after the Czech Republic was granted an exception from the EU Charter of Fundamental Rights, which would prevent any legal challenge to the decrees.[53] Likewise, the party of Mr. Mach, Klaus's former adviser, has not attracted only libertarian activists. In 2014, Petr Hampl, a sociolo-gist, created a self-styled "November Initiative" within Mach's party to promote "patriotic" views. Hampl has virulently anti-Muslim views and argued in favor of sinking boats with refugees crossing the Mediterra-nean Sea and shooting the illegal immigrants once they arrive ashore[54] —much to the dismay of his colleagues, who have so far failed in their efforts to expel him from the party.

Striving to come across as a demure, nonpopulist force, Germany's AfD repeatedly distanced itself from the more radical Eurosceptic groups in Germany, particularly the far-right movement Patriotic Euro-peans Against the Islamization of the West (PEGIDA), whose leader Lutz Bachmann famously posed for a photo styled as Adolf Hitler.[55] In spite of these efforts, there is overlap between the supporters of the two, especially in the wake of the 2015 refugee crisis. The AfD's voters are also concerned about the "Islamization" of the West and support PEGIDA's mass demonstrations.[56] Thilo Sarrazin, a former board member of the Bundesbank and author of the bestselling book *Germa-ny Is Abolishing Itself*,[57] has been a frequent guest speaker at AfD events. While critical of the euro, his main concern is the alleged corro-sive effect of immigration from Muslim-majority countries on Western societies—a subject that the leadership of AfD has mostly tried to avoid.

The EU is a subject that places many well-intentioned conservatives and free-market advocates into the company of nationalists and xeno-phobes. This does not allow us to dismiss their own criticisms of the EU through "guilt by association." However, this alignment does raise questions about the strategic prowess, if not the wisdom, of conservatives and free marketeers, and about the impact that such alliances have on their own ideas, and about the legitimation that they provide to some of the least savory undercurrents of European political thinking.

EUROPE IS DECADENT, LET'S TURN EAST

A "Putinist" critic of the EU might start from any of the previous three lines of thought—free-market, leftist, or nationalist—and make the additional assumption that the enemy of one's enemy is one's friend. Because the EU is irreparably flawed and because the EU and Putin's Russia have found themselves repeatedly in disagreement, for instance over the future of Ukraine, some Eurosceptics are inclined to believe that Vladimir Putin must be in the right, and the EU in the wrong.

Václav Klaus, for example, described the annexation of Crimea using the chess term "forced move," which refers to a move that has no viable alternative and is therefore "forced" by the opponent—insinuating that the Kremlin was merely reacting to the events in Ukraine, which had unfolded without its prior interference. Nigel Farage famously said that he admired Vladimir Putin,[58] although only "as an operator, but not as a human being." At a discussion at the Heritage Foundation in July 2015 in Washington, Farage also channeled the Kremlin's interpretation of events in Ukraine: "There was a democratically elected leader of the Ukraine that was brought down by a street-staged coup d'état by people waving European Union flags."[59] Some critics of the EU, such as the British Conservative MEP Daniel Hannan, lambasted Putinist Eurosceptics. His own perspective, he says, "leaves no place for Putin" and argues that "Putinism is, in Britain at any rate, a minority Eurosceptic pursuit."[60]

The subject of Russia divides Eurosceptics in Germany too. In the summer of 2014, a number of MEPs for AfD, including AfD leader Bernd Lucke, voted for the extension of EU sanctions against Russia, adopted in response to the annexation of Crimea. The vote triggered a backlash from their colleagues, particularly from Alexander Gauland, one of the party's cofounders. "Lucke admitted that it was wrong not to inform the executive committee about the vote," Gauland claimed after a meeting of the leadership of the party,[61] referring to a party resolution opposing sanctions that was adopted in March 2014. Later that year, in an interview for the Russian propagandist outlet Radio Stimme Russland (an earlier version of Sputnik News, in German), Gauland called sanctions "superfluous" and suggested that they "create basically only new conflicts."[62] In the same interview, he called Vladimir Putin a leader rooted deeply in Russia's traditions and committed to restoring Russia's honor. In Gauland's interpretation, Crimea was a distinctly Russian territory at least since its conquest by Catherine the Great. In July 2015, following protracted conflicts within the party, Lucke and a number of his colleagues left the AfD to form a new political party, the Alliance for Progress and Renewal (Alfa), which tries to distance itself from the pro-Putinist stream of thinking as well as from latent xenophobia that unites some members of AfD and PEGIDA.

Marine Le Pen famously called Vladimir Putin "a patriot." "He is attached to the sovereignty of his people," she says, and "understands that we are defending common values—those of the European civilization."[63] Le Pen has been a frequent visitor to Moscow, receiving a red carpet treatment in 2014, only weeks after the annexation of Crimea. The FN also received a loan of €9 million from the First Czech-Russian Bank, a small financial institution created originally to service trade between the Czech Republic and Russia, which may have represented only one tranche in a series of payments totaling €40 million, according to some reports.[64] Needless to say, the theme of Russia as a bulwark against the decadence of the West is underlined by the Kremlin's posture against Russia's gays and by Russia's military intervention in Syria, ostentatiously juxtaposed by the regime against the Western inability to tackle the problem.

Those in positions of influence are not assisting the Kremlin just rhetorically, but also in practical terms. In the European Parliament a diverse coalition of Vladimir Putin's supporters has formed, trying to effectively block the Union's moves against Russia's aggressive posture in Eastern Europe.[65] In August 2014, Hungary's Prime Minister Orbán compared the sanctions against Russia to "shooting oneself in the foot,"[66] and a couple of months later, he hosted Putin for a one-day working visit to Budapest, the first to any EU country since the shooting down of Flight MH17 over Donetsk, in occupied Ukraine. In the midst of the crisis in Ukraine, Orbán also signed, without going through a competitive public tender, a secret €12 billion nuclear deal with Ros-atom, which will tie Hungary to Russian sources of nuclear fuel for decades to come. Euratom Supply Agency, which oversees the supply of nuclear fuels to EU users, initially refused to cosign the fuel supply contract for the Paks power plant. According to Zoltán Illés, a former MP from Orbán's own party, Fidesz, "[t]his [was] a financial transaction, and for the Russians this [was] buying influence."[67] Whatever one thinks of such charges, the leniency of the Hungarian nationalist leader towards Russia is difficult to square with the historical experience of the Hungarian nation, particularly with the Soviet repression that followed the revolution in 1956.

The explicit or hidden sympathies of some of the EU's opponents to the Kremlin are more than just intellectual quirks. As has been documented by many organizations, Europe's Putinism goes hand in hand with the Kremlin's deliberate campaign of propaganda and misinformation, and with efforts to co-opt parts of Europe's political class, aiming to destabilize the West.[68] Regardless of one's position on the future of the EU is, it is important to remain cognizant of the *security threat* that the close links between the Eurosceptic right and the aggressive regime in Europe's neighborhood can pose.

BILDERBERGERS AND REPTILIANS

Finally, like many other ideas that seek to challenge conventional wisdom, the Eurosceptic cause has attracted a rich array of conspiracy theorists and cranks. For these, the EU is a part of a bigger, more or less secret project of global governance, to be imposed on the world's nations by a narrow clique of Bilderbergers, American neoconservatives, or perhaps Jews. In some ways, the opacity of the European project, its abstract nature, and its seeming disconnect from national political debates are an invitation for wild speculation and conspiratorial thinking. Some of it owes its origins to the 1997 book by British conservative commentator John Laughland, *The Tainted Source*, which alleged through a very selective reading of history that the intellectual origins of the integration project had been already laid by Nazis and their sympathizers.

Gerard Batten, an MEP for UKIP, quizzed in all seriousness the President of the European Commission in 2011 about the meeting of the Bilderberg Group in St. Moritz earlier that year. He suggested that the lack of media coverage that the meeting received was a result of a "conspiracy between the organizers and the media" and said that it confirmed the suspicion that "the hidden agenda and purpose of the Bilderberg Group [was] to bring about undemocratic world government."[69]

Then there is the chain-smoking Petr Hájek, who served as Václav Klaus's press secretary and deputy head of the Office of the President. Like Klaus, Hájek has nothing but disdain for the EU. But his contrarianism far eclipses that of his boss. Besides the EU, Hájek rejects the theory of evolution, claiming that he is "no descendant of monkeys."[70] At a public event moderated by Klaus in 2009—who was then a European head of state—he compared Darwinism to Marxism.[71] In a 2012 book, which was praised by Klaus,[72] Hájek argued that the attacks on 9/11 "never happened in the form that [had] been presented to us by the media" and that Osama Bin Laden "never existed."[73] "There is a real possibility," he argued, "that 9/11 [was] orchestrated by American intelligence agencies."[74] According to his boss, the book should be "mandatory reading."[75] After Klaus's second term ended, Hájek started his own Internet magazine, *Protiproud* ("Against the Current," reminiscent of the American neo-Fascist and racist *Counter Currents*), which publishes articles by Klaus,[76] alongside paleoconservative content,[77] glowing citations of and references to openly Neo-Fascist thinkers such as Aleksandr Dugin,[78] and conspiracy theories[79] as well as frequent articles by Petr Hampl, the anti-Muslim member of Petr Mach's Party of Free Citizens.[80]

Janusz Korwin-Mikke, a Polish MEP and serial presidential candidate, believes that the "European Union is trying to uniformize everything following the example of the Third Reich"[81] and confesses to "[hating] all the socialists—Vladimir Ulyanov (alias "Lenin"), Barack Hussein Obama, Pol-pot [*sic*], Olaf Palme, Adolf Hitler, Francis [*sic*] Hollande, Ze-Dong Mao."[82] Márton Gyöngyösi, deputy leader of Hungary's Jobbik party, demanded the creation of lists of publicly active Jews who might pose a security threat to Hungary[83] and sees the EU as a form of economic colonization of the Hungarian nation. The fact that Euroscepticism has attracted to its side those whose contrarianism extends far beyond their views of Europe's political institutions is certainly an embarrassment for the more credible critics of European integration. Again, it should not serve as a reason for a blanket dismissal of all Eurosceptic arguments. Instead, it should be a wake-up call for conservative critics of the EU, so that they assess the nature of the intellectual alliances they have formed in their onslaught against European integration.

The opposition to the European project springs from different sources.[84] Understanding its underlying motives and effects on European politics constitutes a worthwhile research agenda in its own right. However, such a study goes beyond the scope of this book, which is not an exercise in empirical political research. Instead, its purpose is to identify and respond to those criticisms of the EU that have a basis in serious, thoughtful arguments, which are based in an appreciation for free enterprise, market competition, and accountable, democratic government. By focusing on those, the following chapters leave unanswered a whole range of charges against the EU, including those that are based on the assumption that markets are inherently unstable or unjust and those that are concerned about national greatness or the erosion of Europe's ethnic homogeneity. Neither do we debunk the claims about the EU's supposed entanglements with democratic revolutions in countries such as Ukraine or countries of the Middle East and North Africa, or the notion that the Union is only a part of a broader effort to subjugate the world to a totalitarian globalist government. Neither does this book, on its own, try to convince those who do not feel any political allegiance to Europe that they *ought to feel* as European citizens.

This is not to say that these issues are unimportant. Quite the contrary, it is possible that the future of Europe will be decided by prejudice and by how people *feel* about being European citizens, instead of a measured discussion of the costs and benefits of membership. But visceral, gut-level Euroscepticism is largely impervious to reasoned argument. In contrast, the idea that the EU is a hindrance to economic development in Europe deserves a rigorous assessment. Likewise, the institutional design of the Union and its democratic accountability should also be subject to careful scrutiny. On these fronts, the critics of the European project are making valid points, worthy of serious consideration. Where they are mistaken, as we shall see, is in the solutions that they propose.

NOTES

1. Owen, "Pictured During His National Front Days."
2. Lubbers and Scheepers, "Divergent Trends of Euroscepticism." See also McLaren, "Public Support for the European Union."
3. Serricchio, et al., "Euroscepticism and the Global Financial Crisis."
4. European Commission, *Standard Eurobarometer*.
5. Cameron, interview with Nick Ferrari.
6. Ford et al., "Strategic Eurosceptics and Polite Xenophobes."
7. Mudde, "The Comparative Study of Party-Based Euroscepticism." See also earlier work by Taggart and Szczerbiak, "The Party Politics of Euroscepticism."
8. Mudde, "EU Accession and a New Populist Center-Periphery Cleavage."
9. "Profile: Dougless Carswell MP."
10. Dyson, "Douglass Carswell MP Introduces Bill to Stop Factionary Reserve Banking."
11. Carswell and Baker, Financial Services (Regulation of Deposits and Lending) Bill.
12. Carswell, *The End of Politics*.
13. Carswell, "The Future's Bright, the Future's Global."
14. Carswell, "Why I'm Backing Vote Leave in the EU Referendum."
15. Vaubel, "The Public Choice Analysis of European Integration."
16. Salin, for example, makes the argument for competition among different regulatory regimes in Europe as a means of keeping overreach in check and as a way of discovering those that work best. Salin, "Pour une Europe Non-Harmonisée."
17. See, e.g., Eichengreen, *The European Economy Since 1945*, 175–78.
18. Gillingham, *European Integration, 1950–2003*, 6–7.
19. MacShane, *Brexit*, 64.
20. Thatcher, "Speech to the College of Europe."
21. O'Sullivan, "Britain Will Decide on the EU for Itself, Mr. Obama."
22. Quoted in Cato Institute, "Up from Communism," 3.
23. Kreuzbergová, "Dismantling Banking Socialism in the Czech Republic."
24. Klaus, "The Other Side of Global Warming Alarmism."
25. "The present decision-making system of the European Union is different from a classic parliamentary democracy, tested and proven by history. In a

normal parliamentary system, part of the MPs support the government and part support the opposition. In the European Parliament, this arrangement has been missing. Here, only one single alternative is being promoted, and those who dare think about a different option are labelled as enemies of European integration. Not so long ago, in our part of Europe we lived in a political system that permitted no alternatives and therefore also no parliamentary opposition. It was through this experience that we learned the bitter lesson that with no opposition, there is no freedom." Klaus, "Projev prezidenta republiky v Evropském parlamentu."

26. Klaus, "Dvě cesty do dvou velmi odlišných zemí."

27. Sulík, "Ukrajina bude druhé Grécko."

28. Alternative für Deutschland, "Courage to Stand Up for Germany," 5.

29. Ibid., 6.

30. Ibid., 10.

31. Krugman, "Greece over the Brink."

32. Stiglitz, "Europe's Attack on Greek Democracy."

33. Llamazares and Gramacho, "Eurosceptics Among Euroenthusiasts."

34. Jones, "Syriza's victory."

35. Lapavitas, "The Left Needs a Progressive Euroscepticism." For a book-long discussion of the Eurozone crisis by the same author, see Lapavitsas, *Crisis in the Eurozone*.

36. Ibid.

37. Ibid.

38. Open Europe, "Meet Podemos."

39. For a recent compendium of heterodox views of the crisis, see Bitzenis et al., *Europe in Crisis*.

40. Hausalter, "Jean-Marie Le Pen repudie sa fille Marine."

41. Chassany, French National Front Secures Status at Sciences Po."

42. Le Pen, "Mon projet pour la France et les Français," 15.

43. Front National, Le projet du Front national.

44. Ibid.

45. Ibid.

46. "Hungarian Official Admits Campaign to Generate Hate Against Migrants."

47. Byrne and Shubber, "Hungary Threatens Foreign Companies in Tax Dispute."

48. Westervelt, "Hungary Faces EU Action over New Constitution."

49. Tóth, "Full Text of Viktor Orbán's Speech at Baile Tusnad."

50. Václav Klaus Institute, Facebook.

51. Klaus, "Odpovědi Václava Klause na otázku severu Parlamentní listy."

52. Klaus, "Careless Opening Up of Countries."

53. Mahony, "EU Treaty Closer to Ratification After Czech Deal Agreed."

54. Hampl, "To je děsivá amorálnost, nemá obdoby."

55. Connolly, "Germany's Pegida Leader Steps Down over Adolf Hitler Photo."

56. According to a 2014 poll, 71 percent of AfD supporters could consider joining a PEGIDA demonstration, compared with a population average of just 13 percent. See Mathes, "13 Prozent der Deutschen wurden fur Pegida marschieren."

57. Sarrazin, *Deutschland schafft sich ab*.

58. "Nigel Farage: I Admire Vladimir Putin."

59. Heritage Foundation, "Patriotic Voices from Europe."

60. Hannan, "Why Eurosceptics Should Back Ukraine."

61. Sagener, "Russia-Ukraine Conflict Divides Germany's Eurosceptics."

62. Siebert, "Gauland: Putin findet modernen Weg zu traditionellen Werten."

63. "Marine Le Pen salue Vladimir Poutine," *Le Monde*.

64. Rettman, "Mediapart: National Front's Kremlin Loan Is Worth 40mn."

65. See Krekó et al., "Europe's New Pro-Putin Coalition: The Parties of 'No.'"

66. Szakacs, "Europe 'Shot Itself in Foot' with Russia Sanctions."

67. Than, "Inside Hungary's $10.8 Billion Nuclear Deal with Russia."

68. Pomerantsev and Weiss, "The Menace of Unreality."

69. Batten, speech before European Parliament.

70. Hájek, "Já z opice nepocházím."

71. Prokop, "Klausův muž Hájek odmítl evoluci a útočil na darwinisty."

72. "Klaus: Hájkova kniha je téměř povinné čtení," *Lidové noviny*.

73. "Bin Ládin je pohádka pro dospělé," *MF Dnes*.

74. Ibid.

75. "Klaus: Hájkova kniha je téměř povinné čtení," *Lidové noviny*.

76. Klaus, Přišel jsem o významného spojence."

77. Čejka, "Depilovaní muži a kácení posvátných hájů."

78. Zemánek, "Předpověď, která se naplnila."

79. " Trilaterála," *Protiproud*.

80. "Author's Profile: Petr Hampl."

81. Janusz Korwin-Mikke, an email message to author.

82. Ibid.

83. Dunai, "Anger as Hungary Far-Right Leader Demands Lists of Jews."

84. For an account of how difficult the measurement of Eurosceptic attitudes is, see Boomgaarden et al., "Mapping EU Attitudes."

REFERENCES

Alternative für Deutschland. *Courage to Stand Up for Germany. For European Diversity. Party Program of the Alternative für Deutschland for the election to the European Parliament on May 25, 2014.* Berlin: Alternative für Deutschland.

Batten, Gerard. Speech before European Parliament, September 12, 2011. https://www.youtube.com/watch?v=L0Dr96s34r0.

BBC News. "Profile: Douglas Carswell MP," October 14, 2014. http://www.bbc.com/news/uk-politics-28967101.

"Bin Ládin je pohádka pro dospělé, tvrdí prezidentův poradce Hájek." MF Dnes, May 2, 2011. http://zpravy.idnes.cz/bin-ladin-je-pohadka-pro-dospele-tvrdi-prezidentuv-poradce-hajek-p8r-/domaci.aspx?c=A110502_190744_domaci_vel.

Bitzenis, Aristidis, Nikolaos Karagiannis, and John Marangos, eds., *Europe in Crisis: Problems, Challenges, and Alternative Perspectives.* London: Palgrave Macmillan, 2015.

Boomgaarden, Hajo G., et al. "Mapping EU Attitudes: Conceptual and Empirical Dimensions of Euroscepticism and EU Support." *European Union Politics* 12 (2011): 241–66.

Byrne, Andrew, and Kadhim Shubber. "Hungary Threatens Foreign Companies in Tax Dispute." *Financial Times*, July 19, 2015. http://www.ft.com/cms/s/0/b86018ca-2c7d-11e5-acfb-cbd2e1c81cca.html#axzz3ge6OILOX.

Cameron David. Interview with Nick Ferrari. LBC 97.3, April 4, 2006. http://www.lbc.co.uk/david-cameron-ukip-fruitcakes-and-loonies-63456.

Carswell, Douglas. *The End of Politics: And the Rebirth of iDemocracy.* London: Biteback Publishing, 2012.

———. "The Future's Bright, the Future's Global." Douglas Carswell's Blog, September 25, 2015. http://www.talkcarswell.com/home/the-futures-bright-the-futures-global/2874.

———. "Why I'm Backing Vote Leave in the EU Referendum." *The Telegraph*, October 9, 2015. http://www.telegraph.co.uk/news/newstopics/eureferendum/11922172/Douglas-Carswell-Why-Im-backing-Vote-Leave-in-the-EU-referendum.html.

Carswell, Douglas, and Steve Barker. Financial Services (Regulation of Deposits and Lending) Bill. U.K. House of Commons, September 15, 2010. http://www.publications.parliament.uk/pa/cm201011/cmbills/071/2011071.pdf.

Cato Institute. "Up from Communism." Cato Policy Report 19 (May/June 1997): 3. http://object.cato.org/sites/cato.org/files/serials/files/policy-report/1997/6/cpr-19n3.pdf.

Čejka, Martin. "Depilovaní muži a kácení posvátných hájů." *Protiproud*, March 1, 2013. http://protiproud.parlamentnilisty.cz/stopy/pamet/hodnoty/73-depilovani-muzi-a-kaceni-posvatnych-haju.htm.

Chassany, Anne-Sylvaine. "French National Front Secures Status at Sciences Po." *Financial Times*, October 2, 2015. http://www.ft.com/cms/s/0/2ccc1184-6912-11e5-97d0-1456a776a4f5.html#axzz3nvEMELsF.

Connolly, Kate. "Germany's Pegida Leader Steps Down over Adolf Hitler Photo." *The Guardian*, January 21, 2015. http://www.theguardian.com/world/2015/jan/21/germany-pegida-adolf-hitler-lutz-bachmann.

Dunai, Marton. "Anger as Hungary Far-Right Leader Demands Lists of Jews." Reuters, November 27, 2014. http://www.reuters.com/article/2012/11/27/us-hungary-antisemitism-idUSBRE8AQ0L920121127.

Dyson, Ben. "Douglas Carswell MP Introduces Bill to Stop Fractionary Reserve Banking." *Positive Money*, September 15, 2010. http://positivemoney.org/2010/09/douglas-carswell-mp-introduces-bill-to-stop-fractional-reserve-banking/.

Eichengreen, Barry. *The European Economy Since 1945: Coordinated Capitalism and Beyond.* Princeton NJ: Princeton University Press, 2007.

European Commission. *Standard Eurobarometer* 82 (2014). http://ec.europa.eu/public_opinion/archives/eb/eb82/eb82_en.htm.

Ford, Robert, Matthew J. Goodwin, and David Cutts. "Strategic Eurosceptics and Polite Xenophobes: Support for the United Kingdom Independence Party (UKIP) in the 2009 European Parliament Elections." *European Journal of Political Research* 51 (2012): 204–34.

Front National. *Le projet du Front national.* Website, 2016. http://www.frontnational.com/le-projet-de-marine-le-pen/.

Gillingham, John. *European Integration, 1950–2003: Superstate or New Market Economy?* Cambridge: Cambridge University Press, 2003.

Hájek, Petr. *Já z opice nepocházím.* Speech delivered at "Darwin a darwinismus—věda, nebo ideologie?" seminar, Center for Economics and Politics, Prague, April 20, 2009. http://cepin.cz/cze/clanek.php?ID=896.

Hampl, Petr. "To je děsivá amorálnost, nemá obdoby. Čeští občané to zaplatí životy. Darmošlapové žijící z našich daní otevírají dveře drancujícím hordám, jež nás zotročí." *Parlamentní Listy,* June 4, 2015. http://www.parlamentnilisty.cz/arena/rozhovory/Petr-Hampl-To-je-desiva-amoralnost-nema-obdoby-Cesti-obcane-to-zaplati-zivoty-Darmoslapove-zijici-z-nasich-dani-oteviraji-dvere-drancujicim-hordam-jez-nas-zotroci-378166.

Hannan, Daniel. "Why Eurosceptics Should Back Ukraine." *Telegraph,* September 25, 2014. http://blogs.telegraph.co.uk/news/danielhannan/100287639/Eurosceptics-should-support-ukrainian-sovereignty/.

Hausalter, Louis. "Jean-Marie Le Pen répudie sa fille Marine: 'J'ai honte qu'elle porte mon nom.'" *Europe 1,* May 5, 2015. http://www.europe1.fr/politique/jean-marie-le-pen-sur-sa-fille-jai-honte-quelle-porte-mon-nom-938662.

Heritage Foundation. "Patriotic Voices from Europe." July 15, 2015. http://www.heritage.org/events/2015/07/patriotic-voices-from-europe

"Hungarian Official Admits Campaign to Generate Hate Against Migrants." *Euractiv,* September 7, 2015. http://www.euractiv.com/sections/justice-home-affairs/hungarian-official-admits-campaign-generate-hate-against-migrants.

Jones, Owen. "Syriza's Victory: This Is What the Politics of Hope Looks Like." *Guardian,* January 26, 2015. http://www.theguardian.com/commentisfree/2015/jan/26/syriza-victory-lifted-greek-politics-cynicism-hope.

Klaus, Václav. "The Other Side of Global Warming Alarmism." Speech at Chatham House, London, November 7, 2007. http://www.klaus.cz/clanky/266.

———. *Projev prezidenta republiky v Evropském parlamentu.* Speech before the European Parliament, February 19, 2009. http://www.klaus.cz/clanky/229.

———. "Přišel jsem o významného spojence. Pozvání na schůzku, která se už nikdy neuskuteční. Slavný český rodák, který doma nebyl prorokem." *Protiproud,* June 3, 2014. http://protiproud.parlamentnilisty.cz/svet/obcan/osobnosti/1047-vaclav-klaus-prisel-jsem-o-vyznamneho-spojence-pozvani-na-schuzku-ktera-se-uz-nikdy-neuskutecni-slavny-cesky-rodak-ktery-doma-nebyl-prorokem.htm.

———. "Careless Opening Up of Countries (Without Keeping the Anchor of the Nation-State) Leads Either to Anarchy or to Global Governance: Lessons of the European Experience." Speech at the Mont Pelerin Society General Meeting, Hong Kong, September 1, 2014. http://www.klaus.cz/clanky/3623.

———. "Dvě cesty do dvou velmi odlišných zemí—Rusko a USA." Official Website of Vaclav Klaus, June 30, 2015. http://www.klaus.cz/clanky/3773.

———. "Odpovědi Václava Klause na otázky serveru Parlamentnílisty.cz o Marine Le Penové." Website, June 5, 2015. http://www.klaus.cz/clanky/3745.

Korwin-Mikke, Janusz. An email message to the author, September 19, 2015.

Krekó, Péter, et al. "Europe's New Pro-Putin Coalition: The Parties of 'No.'" Institute of Modern Russia, August 3, 2015. http://imrussia.org/en/analysis/world/2368-europes-new-pro-putin-coalition-the-parties-of-no.

Kreuzbergová, Eva. "Dismantling Banking Socialism in the Czech Republic." *Public Policy and Forward Studies* 006 (2006). http://publication.fsv.cuni.cz/attachments/112_006_Kreuzbergova_aj.pdf.

Krugman, Paul. "Greece over the Brink." *New York Times,* June 29, 2015. http://www.nytimes.com/2015/06/29/opinion/paul-krugman-greece-over-the-brink.html.

Lapavitsas, Costas. *Crisis in the Eurozone.* London: Verso, 2012.

————. "The Left Needs a Progressive Euroscepticism to Counter the EU's Ills." *Guardian*, May 7, 2014. http://www.theguardian.com/commentisfree/2014/may/07/left-progressive-euroscepticism-eu-ills.

Laughland, John. *The Tainted Source: The Undemocratic Origins of the European Idea*. London: Little Brown, 1997.

Le Pen, Marine. *Mon projet pour la France et les Français*. Nanterre: Comité de soutien de Marine Le Pen, 2012.

"Klaus: Hájkova kniha je téměř povinnou četbou, kritiku Havla sdílím." *Lidové noviny*, December 11, 2012. http://www.lidovky.cz/klaus-hajkova-kniha-je-temer-povinnou-cetbou-kritiku-havla-sdilim-p9y-/zpravy-domov.aspx?c=A121211_111252_ln_domov_ase.

Llamazares, Iván, and Wladimir Gramacho. "Eurosceptics Among Euroenthusiasts: An Analysis of Southern European Public Opinions." *Acta Politica* 42 (2007): 211–32.

Lubbers, Marcel, and Peer Scheepers. "Divergent Trends of Euroscepticism in Countries and Regions of the European Union." *European Journal of Political Research* 49 (2010): 787–817.

MacShane, Denis. *Brexit: How Britain Will Leave Europe*. London: I.B. Tauris, 2014.

Mahony, Honor. "EU Treaty Closer to Ratification After Czech Deal Agreed." *EU Observer*, October 30, 2009. https://euobserver.com/institutional/28913.

"Marine Le Pen salue Vladimir Poutine avec qui elle défend des 'valeurs communes.'" *Le Monde*, May 18, 2014. http://www.lemonde.fr/europeennes-2014/article/2014/05/18/marine-le-pen-salue-vladimir-poutine-avec-qui-elle-defend-des-valeurs-communes_4420810_4350146.html.

Mathes, Werner. "13 Prozent der Deutschen würden für Pegida marschieren." *Stern*, January 1, 2015. http://www.stern.de/politik/deutschland/fuer-pegida-auf-die-strasse—13-prozent-der-deutschen-wuerden-mitmarschieren-3458070.html.

McLaren, Lauren M. "Public Support for the European Union: Cost/Benefit Analysis or Perceived Cultural Threat?" *Journal of Politics* 64 (2003): 551–66.

Mudde, Cas. "EU Accession and a New Populist Center-Periphery Cleavage in Central and Eastern Europe." University of Antwerp, Center for European Studies Working Paper No. 62, 2003.

————. "The Comparative Study of Party-Based Euroscepticism: The Sussex versus the North Carolina School." *East European Politics* 28 (2012): 193–202.

"Nigel Farage: I Admire Vladimir Putin." *Guardian*, March 31, 2014. http://www.theguardian.com/politics/2014/mar/31/farage-i-admire-putin.

O'Sullivan, John. "Britain Will Decide on the EU for Itself, Mr. Obama." *National Review Online*, June 19, 2015. http://www.nationalreview.com/article/420023/britain-will-decide-eu-itself-mr-obama-john-osullivan.

Open Europe. "Meet Podemos, the Great Newcomer of the European Elections." Open Europe Blog, May 27, 2014. http://openeuropeblog.blogspot.com/2014/05/meet-podemos-great-newcomer-of-european.html.

Owen, Glen. "Pictured During His National Front Days: The Man Behind Ukip's Nigel Farage Ran Group of Far-Right Racists." *Daily Mail*, May 2, 2015. http://www.dailymail.co.uk/news/article-3065674/Pictured-National-days-man-Ukip-s-Nigel-Farage-ran-group-far-right-racists.html.

Pomerantsev, Peter, and Michael Weiss. "The Menace of Unreality: How the Kremlin Weaponizes Information, Culture and Money." Institute of Modern Russia and *Interpreter*, 2015. http://www.interpretermag.com/wp-content/uploads/2014/11/The_Menace_of_Unreality_Final.pdf.

Prokop, Dan. "Klausův muž Hájek odmítl evoluci a útočil na darwinisty. Vědci se zlobí" *MF Dnes*, May 11, 2009. http://zpravy.idnes.cz/klausuv-muz-hajek-odmitl-evoluci-a-utocil-na-darwinisty-vedci-se-zlobi-1zt-/domaci.aspx?c=A090511_140432_domaci_dp.

Protiproud. "Author's Profile: Petr Hampl." http://protiproud.parlamentnilisty.cz/autor/petr-hampl.htm.

Rettman, Andrew. "Mediapart: National Front's Kremlin Loan Is Worth €40mn." *EU Observer*, November 27, 2014. https://euobserver.com/foreign/126693.

Sagener, Nicole. "Russia-Ukraine Conflict Divides Germany's Eurosceptics." *EurActiv*, August 22, 2014. http://www.euractiv.com/sections/global-europe/russia-ukraine-conflict-divides-germanys-Eurosceptics-307920.

Salin, Pascal. "Pour une Europe Non-Harmonisée." *Journal des Economistes et des Etudes Humaines* 1 (1990): 504–6.

Sarrazin, Thilo. *Deutschland schafft sich ab: Wie wir unser Land aufs Spiel setzen.* Munich: Deutsche Verlags-Anstalt, 2010.

Serricchio, Fabio, Myrto Tsakatika, and Lucia Quaglia. "Euroscepticism and the Global Financial Crisis." *Journal of Common Market Studies* 51 (2013): 51–64.

Siebert, Armin. "Gauland: Putin findet modernen Weg zu traditionellen Werten." Radio Stimme Russland, November 27, 2014. http://de.sputniknews.com/german.ruvr.ru/2014_11_27/Gauland-Putin-findet-modernen-Weg-zu-traditionellen-Werten-7852/.

Stiglitz, Joseph. "Europe's Attack on Greek Democracy." *Project Syndicate*, June 29, 2015. http://www.project-syndicate.org/commentary/greece-referendum-troika-eurozone-by-joseph-e—stiglitz-2015-06.

Sulík, Richard. "Ukrajina bude druhé Grécko." *Hospodárske noviny*, January 19, 2015. http://komentare.hnonline.sk/dnes-pise-150/ukrajina-bude-druhe-grecko-641447.

Szakacs, Gergely. "Europe 'Shot Itself in Foot' with Russia Sanctions: Hungary PM." Reuters, August 15, 2014. http://www.reuters.com/article/2014/08/15/us-ukraine-crisis-sanctions-hungary-idUSKBN0GF0ES20140815.

Taggart, Paul, and Aleks Szczerbiak. "The Party Politics of Euroscepticism in EU Member and Candidate States." Sussex European Institute Working Paper No. 51, 2002.

Than, Krisztina. "Inside Hungary's $10.8 Billion Nuclear Deal with Russia." Reuters, March 30, 2015. http://www.reuters.com/article/2015/03/30/us-russia-europe-hungary-specialreport-idUSKBN0MQ0MP20150330.

Thatcher, Margaret. "Speech to the College of Europe ('The Bruges Speech')," September 20, 1988. http://www.margaretthatcher.org/document/107332.

"Trilaterála: Prodloužená ruka Bilderbergu, který se o víkendu sešel v Kodani. Zatkli české odpůrce NWO. Dojemná péče o naše soukromí, které již není. Bude hůř." *Protiproud*, June 1, 2014. http://protiproud.parlamentnilisty.cz/svet/politika/komentare/1043-trilaterala-prodlouzena-ruka-bilderbergu-ktery-se-o-vikendu-sesel-v-kodani-zatkli-ceske-odpurce-nwo-dojemna-pece-o-nase-soukromi-ktere-jiz-neni-bude-hur.htm.

Tóth, Csaba. "Full Text of Viktor Orbán's Speech at Băile Tuşnad (Tusnádfürdő) of 26 July 2014." *Budapest Beacon*, July 29, 2014. http://budapestbeacon.com/public-policy/full-text-of-viktor-orbans-speech-at-baile-tusnad-tusnadfurdo-of-26-july-2014/10592.

Václav Klaus Institute. Facebook, 2015. https://www.facebook.com/institutvk/photos/pb.503333556470978.-2207520000.1437776133./621405367997129/?type=1&theater.

Vaubel, Roland. "The Public Choice Analysis of European Integration: A Survey." *European Journal of Political Economy* 10 (1994): 227–49.

Westervelt, Eric. "Hungary Faces EU Action over New Constitution." NPR, January 18, 2012. http://www.npr.org/2012/01/18/145370167/in-hungary-fears-government-limiting-democracy.

Zemánek, Ladislav. "Předpověď, která se naplnila: 'Plán Majdan' a proamerická nacionalistická diktatura na Ukrajině nepochází z EU. Je to boj USA za zachování světové dominance." *Protiproud*, April 10, 2014. http://protiproud.parlamentnilisty.cz/svet/stat/planeta/945-predpoved-ktera-se-naplnila-plan-majdan-a-proamericka-nacionalisticka-diktatura-na-ukrajine-nepochazeji-z-eu-je-to-boj-usa-za-zachovani-svetove-dominance.htm.

4

EUROPE'S PRESSURE POINTS

According to its critics, the main problem with European integration is that it has gone too far.[1] There is nothing wrong with a platform for cooperation between European countries. What is wrong, they argue, is to create a source of political authority in Brussels, independent of the will of individual nation-states. Indeed, the EU does *too much* in areas where there is little compelling ground for joint European action. Simultaneously, however, many of Europe's most pressing problems result from the fact that the EU does *too little* in areas that matter for the entire continent.[2] Whether it is asylum policy or economic governance in the Eurozone, there is a gap between the EU's mandate and the institutional and political mechanisms available to pursue it. For example, it is impossible to sustain free movement of people within the Schengen area without having a common border protection and immigration policy. Neither can the common currency survive without mechanisms that allow for macroeconomic adjustments, which are otherwise made through changes in exchange rates.

Worse yet, when the EU does act, its decisions are detached from the will of popular majorities across the continent. In some areas, particularly in those where the EU is given the task of restraining the ability of national politicians to interfere with the single market, such a "democratic deficit" plays a helpful role. But the EU makes decisions about other subjects, many of which are political, including labor legislation and asylum and immigration policy. In purely formalistic terms, one could claim that the EU is democratic. It has been built by democratically elected governments through treaties that have been duly ratified, but Europeans do not always see the EU as such. Such perceptions matter for its popular legitimacy—its "claim to a culturally accepted principle or value that shores up the right of that political authority to rule."[3] The EU's legitimacy depends on the consent of those who are governed, not necessarily with the specific political decisions, but rather with the overarching framework within which its decisions are reached.

While hard Eurosceptics are wrong to argue that such legitimacy is completely missing,[4] it cannot be taken for granted, either. This chapter shows, with three concrete examples that have been at the forefront of European discussions, that there is a spectrum of options between making decisions by national majorities and delegating them to international bureaucracies. Furthermore, there are many shades of grey between a Europe of completely sovereign nation-states and a fully centralized European state, run from Brussels. For the EU to function well and be perceived as legitimate, it cannot be shoehorned into a binary choice between these extremes. The EU's critics are making valid arguments about its dysfunctions and its democratic deficit in areas where European institutions are making decisions about public policy. They seldom offer helpful solutions, other than a wholesale rejection of the project.

IMMIGRATION OMNISHAMBLES

In June 2015, two Slovak journalists traveled to the border of Hungary and Serbia, to report on the stories of migrants who were trying to cross into the EU and claim asylum. Among others, they met with Arnahmmad Rahmani, who was badly scarred on his legs and arm from bullet wounds inflicted by the Taliban. Rahmani, who had traveled for more than 40 days from Afghanistan, mostly on foot, was accompanied by his wife—seven months pregnant at the time—and three children. Their hope was to start a new life in Germany. But first, they had to go through Hungary,[5] circumventing the EU regulations on asylum, which would require them to register and remain in the first EU country that they reached.

Since most of the refugees that the two journalists met were young and tech-savvy, the journalists were able to follow their progress on

Facebook and learn that they often eventually made it to Germany, where they applied for asylum. However, Rahmani was older, had a limp, spoke little English, and did not have a smartphone. We may never learn whether he made it with his family across the EU border. What we do know, however, is that after letting hundreds of thousands of asylum-seekers into the EU, the Hungarian government reinvented itself as a defender of the Schengen border. In September, it completed a fence along this border to keep people like Rahmani out,[6] rerouting the influx through the neighboring countries, namely Croatia and Slovenia. In Slovakia, in turn, citizens of the town of Gabčíkovo held a local referendum that rejected the establishment of a temporary refugee facility for 500 asylum-seekers housed at the time in Austria.[7] (The government placed them there anyway.[8]) Farther west, thousands of asylum-seekers congregated in the French port of Calais in the summer of 2015, hoping to cross into Britain. The French police stopped numerous attempts to enter the Channel Tunnel freight terminal by refugees hoping to go to England.[9]

The scale of the refugee crisis was unprecedented. In 2014, more than 283,000 people crossed the EU's Schengen border illegally—more than two and half times the number in 2013. In the first 11 months of 2015, more than 1.5 million illegal crossings of the Schengen border were detected. The number of actual asylum-seekers was lower, since thousands crossed the border multiple times, such as to Greece, and then to Hungary.[10] More than 2,000 people died in the first eight months of 2015 trying to cross the Mediterranean Sea on overcrowded vessels, according to the International Organization for Migration.[11] Italy and Greece, neither the best-resourced nor best-governed countries in the EU, are carrying out the bulk of the rescue operations, sometimes close to the coast of Libya. The terrorist attacks in Paris in November 2015 also raised concerns about the potential security implications of large numbers of refugees entering the EU.

More than any other event to date, the refugee crisis shows the vulnerability of the EU's fundamental freedom of movement of people, long taken for granted. This freedom traces back to 1985, when the Schengen Agreement abolished internal border checks between most EEC countries. Rightly celebrated as a major achievement, it led to the creation of a common visa policy, but it left, for the most part, the protection of the EU common border to its members.[12] The situation is as if, instead of a federally run Customs and Border Protection agency patrolling the US border with Mexico, the US government gave the task to Texas, Arizona, and neighboring states, while Montana, New York, and other northern states were responsible for guarding the northern border. Taxpayers in the affected areas would probably complain that they were being unfairly burdened. Meanwhile, states far from the two borders, such as Kentucky or Missouri, would have little incentive to pitch in and help.

When Syrian refugees, for example, arrive on Greece's shores, it is largely Greece's problem. But rescue operations are expensive, as is resettling refugees. The EU provides some funding for border protection and processing of asylum requests, but not nearly enough. A study commissioned by the European Parliament in 2010 estimated that the amount disbursed from 2008 to 2013 by the European Refugee Fund covered only 14 percent of the asylum costs in the EU for just one year.[13] Neither is there, in spite of efforts to harmonize the asylum system in the EU,[14] a common legal framework for determining eligibility for asylum, in part because of the vagueness of the existing norms.[15]

The EU also has Frontex, an agency that coordinates the work of the economic bloc's border protection agencies. Frontex, in fact, led the emergency response to the crisis in the Mediterranean, with some EU funding and modest voluntary contributions from countries such as Finland, Sweden, Germany, the Netherlands, Poland, and even nonmembers, including Norway and Iceland.[16] But with its current resources, Frontex is nowhere near able to supersede national border protection services or even take on the task of processing asylum requests. The EC has tried to ease the burden on countries such as Greece and Germany, which have become target destinations for refugees, by proposing quotas that would allocate asylum-seekers to different EU member states for processing of their claims. That decision, however, led to pushback from countries that had been largely free-riding on other countries' efforts to secure the Schengen border. In one way, the refugee crisis is a result of an insufficient degree of European integration. To be sustainable, the free movement of people in the EU must go hand in hand with the recognition that securing the Schengen border is the EU's common problem—an EU-wide *public good*.

Immigration did not become a source of controversy just because of the refugee crisis of 2015. Populists have long thrived on overblown stories about "benefit scroungers" of foreign descent or, alternatively, of foreigners "stealing" the jobs of the natives.[17] Even free-market conservatives have expressed concerns about welfare tourism, the capacity of European societies to integrate large numbers of culturally distant immigrants, and the impact that mass migratory inflows might have on the quality of public services. These concerns are not altogether surprising, although migration also carries substantial economic gains: eliminating all legal barriers to movement of people would *double* the world's GDP.[18] The world's population is becoming more mobile, and Europe now has more migrants than at any other point in its history. Germany, the UK, Italy, and France have seen the largest net immigration inflows, both from within the EU and from overseas.[19] In 2013, 1.7 percent of the UK population was born in the eight Central and Eastern European countries that joined the EU in 2004, and 8.2 percent was born outside the EU.[20] Ahead of the 2015 general election, Nigel Farage turned immigration into UKIP's main theme. The inflow of immigrants, according to him, has led to a "change in our communities that has left many people in our towns and cities frankly finding it difficult to recognize the place being the same as it was 10 to 15 years ago."[21]

The fear of Eastern European immigration is almost completely misplaced. Christian Dustmann and Tommaso Frattini, academics at the Centre for Research and Analysis of Migration at University College London, studied the fiscal effects of immigration on the UK's public finances. They found that, in fiscal terms, immigrants from the postcommunist Central and East Europe contribute 12 percent more than they receive from public budgets.[22] The benefit of workers from the "old" EU countries is even greater: they contributed 64 percent to public budgets more than they received.[23] The overwhelming majority of EU migrants in the UK are young, productive, and more eager to work than to take advantage of welfare benefits or health care. Neither is there much evidence that immigration into the UK has negatively affected employment[24] or wages.[25] If there is a small negative effect, it is confined to the bottom of the income distribution. One study found that a 1 percent increase in the share of migrants among the UK-born working-age population leads to a 0.6 percent decline in the wages of workers in the bottom quintile,[26] while increasing wages of workers in the upper echelons of the distribution.

Whereas free movement of people within the EU is a genuine European public good, national welfare systems are *not*. There might be an argument for providing a minimum EU-wide social safety net for those workers who move from one country to another. That aside, individual countries are perfectly justified in limiting, through their internal political decisions, the extent to which migration can be used to exploit the differences in generosity of health care systems, social benefits, or pensions across European countries. Member states are equally justified in deciding how generously they want to treat incoming migrants or refugee seekers from third countries. Actual incidence of "welfare tourism" is very limited, but the EU rulings that encouraged it did more than their fair share to stir up populism. The "[European Court of Justice] jurisprudence incrementally broadens EU citizens' opportunities to claim social benefits abroad while narrowing member states' scope to regulate and restrict access to national welfare systems," found Michael Blauberger and Susanne K. Schmidt, political scientists at the University of Salzburg and the University of Bremen.[27]

But that may be changing now, in part under the threat of UK's exit from the EU, but also because of a shift in the interpretation of European standards of social policy by courts. In a case concerning the Alimanovic family, a Swedish family of Bosnian descent who were seeking welfare benefits in Germany, the European Court of Justice ruled that the German authorities were justified in denying the right to access such social assistance, given that the Alimanovic family moved to Germany not to work but only to seek access to benefits. "Where an EU citizen has not yet worked in the host Member State [for more than six months] . . . , the host Member State may refuse to grant any social assistance," the court decided.[28]

The integration of non-European immigrants, particularly those from Muslim-majority countries, counts among the most contentious issues of European politics, especially in the aftermath of the terrorist attacks in Paris. It divides European societies into the supporters of populist and xenophobic political groups, such as PEGIDA in Germany or Front National in France, and the political mainstream, which thrives on lofty moralization but is uncomfortable talking about the possible shortcomings of the EU's integration strategies.[29] Large cultural divides persist between mainstream societies in Europe and their Muslim minorities. If we are to believe the existing survey data, European Muslims tend, on average, to be more intolerant and more anti-Semitic than mainstream European societies.[30] In 2009, for example, a Gallup survey of British Muslims found that, among 500 respondents, not one was tolerant of homosexual acts.[31] In the past years, thousands of healthy young Muslim men have left prosperous Western societies to fight for the Islamic State of Iraq and Syria (ISIS), the world's most horrendous terrorist organization. Their European countrymen and oftentimes their own mothers cannot grasp the logic behind their decisions.[32]

There are no easy fixes that would bridge the gap between European Muslims and their countrymen. Neither are there any easy solutions to the real or perceived discrimination against Muslim minorities in the EU. Researchers Claire L. Adida, David D. Laitin, and Marie-Anne Valfort, respectively from University of California at San Diego, Stanford, and Paris School of Economics, designed an experiment through which they identified the existence of anti-Muslim discrimination in France. They sent an identical, fictitious resume, under the names of Khadija Diouf (a Muslim Senegalese name) and Marie Ménard (a French Catholic name) to different recruiters. Somewhat unsurprisingly, in spite of identical credentials, Khadija was 2.5 times less likely to receive an interview than Marie.[33] The result might have been driven by statistical discrimination, if recruiters were merely taking into account differences in work ethic or ability existing *on average* between the French Senegalese and the rest of France's population. Alternatively, it could have been a result of willful, bigoted prejudice.[34] Either way, the experiment confirms a widely shared suspicion that French Muslims are often fighting an uphill battle when they are trying to make it in their new homeland.

Of course, the histories of immigration from Muslim-majority countries are different across Europe, as are their Muslim communities. Only a process of experimentation, trial and error, and gradual learning will enable European policymakers to find satisfactory response to this challenge, which involves not just economics but also questions of social capital and cultural norms. There need to be some common European decisions about border protection and immigration policy. At the same time, the EU has to preserve and expand the space for competition and experimentation with integration strategies and indeed in the generosity of welfare systems across Europe, in order to find solutions that work and that also keep native populations on board, instead of fueling xenophobia.

DIVIDED BY A COMMON CURRENCY

Since 2008, Greece has lost over a quarter of its nominal GDP.[35] Its rate of unemployment has gone up from 7.3 percent in May 2008 to 25 percent throughout most of 2015.[36] But the story of the Eurozone's economic crisis is not just about Greece. Figure 4.1 provides the level of nominal GDP in the Eurozone countries. The dotted line shows the trend between 1995 and the onset of the crisis in 2008. Nominal GDP, also known as nominal income or nominal spending, is an important variable, which at the same time captures economic health *and* the stance of monetary policy.[37] Shocks to nominal income matter because debt and labor contracts are written in nominal terms. A contraction in nominal income—or an expectation of its slow growth—makes the burden of debts heavier and leads firms and individuals to deleverage, sometimes in painful ways. If wages are sticky, firms will react to a fall in nominal income by cutting their staff instead of reducing their salaries. During the Great Recession, the Eurozone experienced a decline in nominal GDP, which has never recovered and remains firmly below its pre-crisis trend.

Many economists—including Milton Friedman, the Nobel Laureate and a leading figure of the Chicago School of Economics, and Harvard's Martin Feldstein—foresaw the troubles that the euro was susceptible to creating.[38] Of course, there are advantages to having a common currency too, such as the reduced transaction costs. But those have to be weighed, economists argue, against the costs of losing exchange rate flexibility. Consider Greece, a country with a large tourism industry. It is possible to imagine an economic shock that reduces the inflow of tourists into the country, without necessarily triggering economic problems elsewhere in the Eurozone. Hotels would have to reduce their capacity, and many Greeks would likely end up unemployed. If Greece had kept its former currency, the drachma, there would have been a monetary antidote to such a shock. Greece's central bank could let its

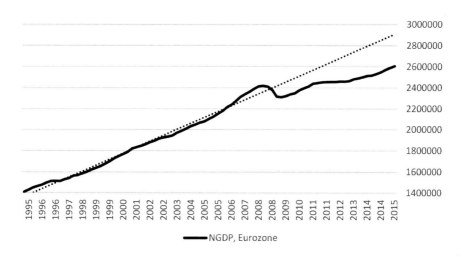

Figure 4.1.   Nominal GDP in the Eurozone, 1995–2015, millions of Euros. Data from: European Central Bank, Gross Domestic Product at Market Prices—Euro Area 19.

currency depreciate to soften the blow. The downside of currency depreciation is that Greeks would have to pay more for their imports and would end up poorer as a result, but that might still be better than being unemployed. However, as a Eurozone member, Greece cannot let its currency depreciate if an "economic shock" arrives. What could the Greeks do instead? For one, tourism is a sector where salaries constitute an important part of the total costs of businesses. If Greeks accepted lower salaries, many of them would be able to keep their jobs. Alternatively, unemployed Greeks could leave for countries with more abundant employment opportunities, such as Germany or the UK. Perhaps, the EU could provide them with financial assistance paid from the EU common budget. In the eyes of most economists, these three criteria—wage flexibility, labor mobility, and fiscal transfers—determine whether a group of countries should be using the same currency or not.

Alas, in most Eurozone countries, wages are far from flexible. Salary cuts are bad for workers' morale[39] and, in many cases, impossible because of unionization. While workers often move from one European country to another—indeed, more than 200,000 mostly young, Greeks have left their homeland since the beginning of the crisis[40]—they face barriers in doing so. Languages spoken across European countries are as different as their cultures, labor laws, and tax systems. In the United States, people share the same language and cultural references, and face only minimal administrative burdens in moving from one state to another. Survey data also reveal that migrants in Europe often perceive being discriminated against.[41] Not surprisingly, a recent study by economists at the International Monetary Fund found that, although labor mobility in the EU has increased, it remains at much lower levels than in the United States. Of 10 people who lose their jobs in the EU, only three seek employment in another country. In the United States, as many as six of 10 move to another state in search of a job.[42]

With minor exceptions, such as EU structural funds, the Eurozone lacks an economically significant system of *fiscal transfers* to its economically depressed areas. In the United States, federal government spending, which includes spending on Social Security, Medicaid, and Medicare, is much larger than the spending of individual states. That helps to mitigate the uneven impact of economic downturns. The crisis in the Eurozone led to the creation of de facto fiscal transfers in the form of the emergency loans provided at below-market interest rates to Greece and other affected countries, but the magnitude of such transfers is trivial compared with spending by member states.

Some critics of the common currency blame the Eurozone's current woes on the lack of a strict enforcement of fiscal rules—and on the admission of countries like Greece to the club.[43] When the euro was devised, it was accompanied by the creation of the so-called Stability and Growth Pact, which imposed restrictions on the size of public deficits and debt levels. But the rules were not credible. For years, key Eurozone countries, including France, openly violated the criteria without any sanctions.[44] Not only did the Stability and Growth Pact lack any explicit provisions for sanctioning noncompliance, but just raising the issue was a political nonstarter given the weight the countries in question commanded in the Eurozone. As for Greece, "[a]ccepting Greece into the euro area should not have been approved given the concrete situation at the time, which could not have been hidden from anyone who looked closer,"[45] said former German Chancellor Helmut Kohl, who once sold the idea of the euro to the German public. Greece's Eurozone membership was approved based on data provided by Greece's statistical office, which claimed the country was meeting the

Maastricht Criteria. Yet when Eurostat, the EU statistical office, re-viewed Greek fiscal statistics in 2002 and 2004, it found major discrep-ancies. The Greek government systematically underreported the size of public expenditures and overreported its revenue. Even when the dis-crepancies were discovered by European authorities, they were not always corrected—in spite of assurances by Greek authorities.[46] In oth-er words, either on purpose or through negligence, the Greek govern-ment—which had a long history of fiscal profligacy—faked its way into the Eurozone. According to Kohl, it was not "easy to resist pressure from a country in such a situation."[47] When the discrepancies were discovered, the Eurozone was doing reasonably well, and EU political elites had little to gain from ruffling feathers by trying to bring fiscal governance in Greece under control.

Today, the Eurozone displays similarities to the system of exchange rates among advanced Western countries during the interwar period.[48] The system was an attempt to restore the pre–World War I gold stan-dard. It relied on fixed exchange rates, which were in some cases artifi-cially overvalued. Like the euro, it offered little in terms of structural or institutional underpinnings that could make it a workable monetary arrangement. There were no fiscal transfers among member countries. Travel was expensive, and labor mobility was much smaller than today. By the 1920s, even wage flexibility that people intuitively associate with an era of Dickensian capitalism was long gone. As economic historians Barry Eichengreen and Peter Temin note in their study of the gold standard and the Great Depression, "in the increasingly structured and politicized labor markets, wages lacked the flexibility they once pos-sessed. The fluidity of labor costs was limited by the spread of union-ism, the growth of internal labor markets and personnel departments in the United States, and the general preoccupation with the relationship of one's wage to that of other workers."[49] There is clear evidence that countries that left the system of fixed exchange rates early recovered more rapidly than those that lingered, like Greece in today's Eurozone. Eichengreen, together with Jeffrey Sachs, showed that the countries that pursued the deepest devaluations—such as the UK and the Nordic countries—reaped the greatest benefits in terms of a speedy economic recovery.[50] On the other end of the spectrum were countries such as France and Czechoslovakia, which tried to defend the gold price of their currency at all cost.

These devaluations are sometimes cited as an example of "beggar-thy-neighbor" policies. In reality, they were a positive-sum game and helped the West recover from the Depression.[51] Regrettably, the demise of the gold standard went hand in hand with a surge in protectionism and a rise in political extremism. One of the motives behind the monetary union in Europe—and perhaps a reason why EU leaders have been clinging so firmly to it—is to prevent another similar tragedy. "The drive for the Euro has been motivated by politics, not economics,"[52] Friedman observed in 1997.

There is one fundamental difference between the gold standard and the euro. In the face of the Great Depression, the hands of central bankers were tied. Instead of pursuing stabilization policies, they had to defend the gold parity. The European Central Bank (ECB), in contrast, has a broad mandate to protect price stability and other economic objectives, including employment and economic growth.[53] However, throughout the crisis, monetary policy in the Eurozone has been extremely tight, as illustrated by the collapse of nominal spending in figure 4.1. Inflation in the Eurozone has mostly stayed below the 2 percent target, and the bloc has even repeatedly fallen into deflation. The deflationary pressures were much more severe on the Eurozone's periphery, which was hit the hardest by the crisis. Unlike in the United Kingdom or the United States, the European Central Bank (ECB) has been reluctant to embark on larger programs of asset purchases, known as quantitative easing. In 2011, as the Eurozone was in turmoil, the ECB raised interest rates.[54] This is commonly attributed to the intellectual and cultural heritage that the ECB received from the Bundesbank, which had built its popular legitimacy among the German public on its hawkish attitude towards inflation.[55]

The Danish economist Lars Christensen dubbed the euro a "Monetary Strangulation Mechanism," referring to the extent to which deflationary monetary policy stifled economic growth in the Eurozone, particularly when compared with other parts of the world. As figure 4.1 shows, the ECB let nominal GDP collapse, but central banks outside the Eurozone did not. As a result, a drastic difference can be seen in economic performance of those European countries that had adopted the euro or pegged their currency to it ("peggers") and those that had not ("floaters"), such as the United Kingdom and Sweden. "If we look at a simple median of the growth rates of real GDP from 2007 until 2015,"

Christensen says, "the floaters have significantly outgrown the euro countries by a factor of five (7.9 percent versus 1.5 percent). Even if we disregard the three fastest floaters (Turkey, Romania and Poland), the floaters still massively outperform the euro countries (6.5 percent versus 1.5 percent)."[56]

Higher inflation rates could not have acted as a substitute for the Eurozone's lack of flexibility, labor mobility, or the overarching system of transfers. However, as recent research suggests, in difficult economic times, structural reforms and looser monetary policy are highly complementary. Without a monetary stimulus, even the best designed structural reforms are politically impossible or deeply contractionary.[57] But whether one believes that the main culprit for the crisis is the lack of fiscal discipline, tight monetary policy, or a lack of adjustment mechanisms that could replace movements of exchange rates, for the common currency to survive the next crisis Eurozone members will have to, sooner or later, rethink the bloc's governance. An important part of the backlash against the EU response to the crisis in Greece had to do with the perception that European elites were making decisions without any regard for the preferences of European citizens. Because questions of employment, taxation, and government spending are inherently political, common governance will have to come hand in hand with stronger democratic mechanisms used to reach decisions about these questions in the Eurozone. Throughout the crisis, the responsibility for supervising economic policies of member states has been left to the European Commission, a body with only very limited claim to popular legitimacy. The meetings of the Eurogroup (finance ministers of the Eurozone) do not take place in the public. Instead, hapless European populations in Greece, Portugal, and elsewhere are simply presented with far-reaching decisions about their public finances, detached from the will of popular majorities.[58]

In 1997, Harvard University economist Martin Feldstein, one of the most prominent critics of the euro, wrote that the common European currency, which would lead to "a much more centralized determination of what are currently nationally determined economic and social policies," is "often advocated as a way to reduce conflict within Europe." In reality, however, "it may well have the opposite effect. Uniform monetary policy and inflexible exchange rates will create conflicts whenever cyclical conditions differ among the member countries. Imposing a single foreign and military policy on countries with very different national traditions and geographic circumstances will exacerbate these economic conflicts."[59] If the Eurozone is to survive in some form, it will have to move past the traditional divides in Europe and create a political and fiscal arrangement that resolves Feldstein's conundrum by producing shared decisions about spending, transfers, taxes, and deficits, which will be perceived as legitimate by European electorates.

REGULATED TO DEATH

Remember the "bent banana" rule—the regulation that supposedly banned the sale of curved bananas in the EU? Although in reality the regulation did not actually "ban" curved bananas, with the help of some eager journalists, it became the epitome of the Brussels bureaucratic apparatus gone mad. But there is more. "If barmy Brussels bureaucrats get their way, baffled Brits will have to ask for hippoglossus instead of plain halibut. . . . Takeaways, restaurants, fishmongers and supermarkets are all set to be banned from using names that have been around for centuries," the *Sun* reported in 2001.[60] The *Daily Express*, in turn, warned that "Britain's lorry drivers' traditional diet of a full English breakfast is under threat from EU bureaucracy."[61] In 2014, a *Daily Mail* headline asked: "Enjoy a yogurt at school? Hard cheese, says EU. Eurocrats want to ban snacks in healthy eating campaign."[62] Even the conservative broadsheet *Daily Telegraph* misleadingly reported that "[t]he acre, one of Britain's historic imperial measurements, is to be banned under a new European directive."[63]

The reality, as always, was more complicated. The EU did not prescribe the use of Latin names of fish in restaurants or shops but only introduced labeling standards that required disclosing the exact name of the fish, how it was produced, and where it was caught. Neither did the EU ban English breakfasts for truck drivers; it only mandated standards for safety training, including information about food, alcohol and drugs, stress, and the importance of rest for drivers. The story about the supposed "ban on snacks" was in fact about a change in the policies of a modest fund of £8 million, supplied by the EU to breakfast clubs at British schools—not about a ban on yogurts as such. And while the UK Land Registry was indeed scrapping the use of acres in its official records, this was done to reflect the practice that had existed in the UK since 1995.

Still, many European regulations, including the "bent banana" rule,[64] appear patently absurd. The purpose of that particular piece of legislation was to "ensure that the market is supplied with products of uniform and satisfactory quality, in particular in the case of bananas harvested in the Community." It acknowledges that member countries might already have their own quality standards for bananas. Those will "continue to apply," but "only at stages subsequent to unripened green bananas, provided those rules are not in conflict with the Community standards and do not impede the free circulation of bananas in the Community."[65] Bananas in the EU must be "free from malformation or abnormal curvature of the fingers."[66] While this has been commonly interpreted as banning the sale of curved bananas, the curvature requirement fully applies only to the top-quality, "Extra Class" bananas. Class I and Class II bananas, which are also sold in the EU, can have "defects in shape." It is not specified how significant those defects can be, but across the three quality categories "the minimum length permitted is 14 cm and the minimum grade permitted is 27 mm."[67]

Anecdotes aside, how much EU regulation is there and how much harm has it done? One way of finding out is by simply counting the pages of relevant legislation. Open Europe, a British think tank, went through the exercise of counting the pages in the Official Journal "L" (legislation) series up to 2005 and found that the EU had passed 666,879 pages of law since its inception in 1957,[68] of which 170,000 were still active in 2005. The EU's own estimate of the amount of active legislation at the time was about 80,000, compared with around 2,500 in 1973.[69] Between 2005 and 2009, the EU produced between 900 and 2,300 new pieces of legislation each year.[70]

Some of this legislation is necessary to support the functioning of the single market and to prevent member states from imposing regulatory barriers to trade. Until Europeans are comfortable with unrestricted competition of regulatory standards across the continent, potentially leading to a race to the bottom, common minimum rules for consumer health safety, for example, or environmental protection, are a price that free-market conservatives have to pay in order for the single market to exist. But it would be disingenuous to try to justify all of the *acquis communautaire* on these grounds. European legislation is typically adopted through the "co-decision procedure," which requires the assent of both the European Parliament and the Council, representing governments of member states. Europe's overregulation is not necessarily a by-product of the organization's democratic deficit, just as overregulation by the federal government in the United States is not somehow an attribute of its undemocratic character. In the EU's case it is rather a result of a lack of checks on new legislative activity by the European Commission. It reflects a culture, shared by policymakers in Brussels *and* in the national capitals, that fears creative destruction and uncertainty and tries to instead instill in Europeans a comforting, albeit stifling, sense of security and permanence.[71]

The burden that EU regulation imposes on the economy is greater than the sum of the costs of its individual parts. Looking at the American context, Steve Teles, a political scientist at Johns Hopkins University, captured this problem through an apt metaphor.[72] He argues that the American policy landscape is plagued by "kludgeocracy":

> The term comes out of the world of computer programming, where a kludge is an inelegant patch put in place to solve an unexpected problem and designed to be backward-compatible with the rest of an existing system. When you add up enough kludges, you get a very complicated program that has no clear organizing principle, is exceedingly difficult to understand, and is subject to crashes. Any user of Microsoft Windows will immediately grasp the concept.[73]

This metaphor resonates powerfully in the European context. Much of the EU regulatory landscape consists of kludges, each aimed at remedying a particular social ill—and perhaps most of them justifiable on their individual merits—but all adding up to a regulatory landscape in which compliance by individual businesses is extremely costly. In 2010, Open Europe looked at 2,300 impact assessments conducted by the UK government and found that EU regulations have cost the UK economy £124 billion since 1998, or 71 percent of the total regulatory costs in the economy.[74] The European Commission itself assessed the annual compliance costs of the EU regulation to be between 3 and 3.5 percent of GDP.[75]

For economists, social costs and benefits are the preferred metric for evaluating new regulation. But European policymakers rarely rely exclusively, or dominantly, on that benchmark. In the area of health and the environment, for example, the EU often uses the so-called precautionary principle. The principle states that in the case of uncertainty over the damage done by a particular product or technology, the burden of proof is on those who want to demonstrate that the technology or product is safe—not the other way around. But that is oftentimes very difficult, particularly in the case of new methods and technologies that have yet to see their commercial deployment. That means that some activities are effectively regulated out of existence by the EU—genetically modified crops come to mind as perhaps the most prominent example—even though by the EU's own admission they have never been shown to be culpable of causing any harm, either to humans or to the environment.[76] Most of the time, the precautionary principle steers policymakers in the direction of extreme risk aversion, preemptively banning anything new and unknown. But a ban on a new technology is itself a source of risks of unknown magnitudes. As Cass Sunstein, President Obama's "regulatory czar" and a prominent legal theorist, argued:

> [T]he principle should be rejected, not because it leads in bad directions, but because it leads to no directions at all. The principle is literally paralyzing—forbidding inaction, stringent regulation, and everything in between. The reason is that in the relevant cases, every step, including inaction, creates a risk to health, the environment, or both.[77]

With special interests and a culture of aversion to risk, it is hardly a surprise that EU regulatory infrastructure can be a drag on innovation. Whereas the precautionary principle hinders the growth of the biotechnology sector, digital markets are being held back by the EU's strict privacy laws, the excessive diversity of regulatory regimes in individual member states that persist in spite of efforts to establish a single digital market, and an obsolete regulatory mindset that treats digital markets the same way it treats natural monopolies.

Any credible case for the European project needs to grapple with these criticisms seriously. The burden of EU regulation is real and goes beyond the exaggerated stories published in the likes of the *Daily Mail* or the *Sun*. Whether one likes it or not, Europe is not the economic powerhouse it would like to be, and the excess of complex regulation—much of it originating at the EU level—bears a significant portion of the blame. What is the solution, however? Eurosceptics believe that an exit from the Union and a unilateral repeal of EU legislation is the way to go. As chapter 6 argues, if a state that seceded still remained economically integrated with the EU, its economy would remain largely burdened by the same regulation. The only difference would be that the country would have no longer any say in it. As the Norwegian political scientist Erik O. Eriksen wrote about his country, which is part of the European Economic Area, but not of the EU, "Norway has become deeply entangled in the European integration project and is, for all intents and purposes, part of the EU, but without any influence."[78] Short of dissolving the bloc, a deregulation in Europe will require—much like deregulation seen in other parts of the world—political leadership in Brussels, with the democratic mandate to override special interests and a shared commitment to limit the growth of economically harmful regulation.

All these examples—dysfunctional asylum policies and fear of immigrants, the Eurozone's economic woes, and the EU's excessive regulatory burden—reveal flaws in the EU's construction. All three also reflect a dated European social contract that stifles economic dynamism. Under the status quo, living in Europe gives one not just an opportunity to pursue economic success, but also an entitlement to receive handouts. As a result, foreigners, it seems to Europeans, are not coming to create new wealth but only to divert available resources away from native populations. One reason why the Eurozone is in disarray is because a number of its member economies are notoriously inflexible and resist reforms that would open them to competition and innovation. And, instead of being a force for economic freedom, European institutions themselves encouraged the growth of an unnecessary regulatory burden.

That is not a recipe for mass prosperity but for economic stagnation. Updating this social contract and reversing the culture of stasis is primarily in the hands of policymakers at the national level who need to explain to their voters that the European economy, built through reindustrialization and investment in the aftermath of World War II, has to be adapted to the realities of the 21st century and of an increasingly globalized, complex, and fluid world. Europe's welfare states need to address their long-term fiscal challenges, which have to do with the anticipated demographic changes in European societies, without leaving behind people in need. European labor markets and educational institutions need to adapt to an economy that places growing demands on individuals' cognitive skills and ability to solve complex problems.

A reform of European institutions is a necessary component of that package. The EU needs both *more* and *less* political integration. Most importantly, it needs a set of institutions, at the national and European levels, that foster peace and shared prosperity and that are accepted as legitimate by the European population. The contours of possible reforms and the likelihood of their occurrence are discussed in chapter 7. First, however, we have to dispense with the idea that eliminating the EU would make Europe more prosperous, more economically dynamic, or more democratic.

NOTES

1. For one formulation of many, see Kay, "Imperial Ambitions Have Pushed Europe to Its Limits." A formal, theoretical discussion is provided by Alesina and Wacziarg, "Is Europe Going Too Far?"

2. A version of this claim is also made by Alesina and Wacziarg, *The Future of Europe*, 3.

3. McNamara, *The Politics of Everyday Europe*, 5.

4. See, e.g., Hannan, "The End of Europe's Fantasy Is Now in Sight."

5. Becková, "Cez hranicu sa šprintuje."

6. Szakacs, "Hungary Expects to Complete Serbian Border Fence by November."

7. "Referendum: Gabcikovo Inhabitants Do Not Want Refugees There."

8. "Mayor: No Problems with Refugees in Slovak Town."

9. Boyle et al., "Calais Migrants."

10. Frontex, "Number of Migrants Arriving in Greece Dropped by Half in November."

11. International Organization for Migration, "Deadly Milestone as Mediterranean Migrant Deaths Pass 2,000."

12. Hobbing, "Integrated Border Management at the EU Level."

13. Matrix Insight et al., "What System of Burden-Sharing Between Member States," 47.

14. See in particular European Union, Convention Determining the State Responsible for Examining Applications. See also European Council, Council Regulation (EC) No 343/2003.

15. Moraga and Rapoport, "Tradable Refugee-Admission Quotas," 6–7. For more detail, see Jaillard et al., *Setting up a Common European Asylum System*.

16. Frontex, "Frontex Expands Its Operation Triton."

17. For a discussion of the links between immigration and populism, see Veenkamp, "The Rise of Anti-Immigration Populism in Europe."

18. Clemens, "Economics and Emigration."

19. Hawkins, "Migration Statistics,"18.

20. Ibid., 16.

21. Mason, "Nigel Farage."

22. University College London, "Positive Economic Impact of UK Immigration from the EU."

23. Ibid.

24. See Migration Advisory Committee, *Analysis of the Impacts of Migration*; and Lucchino et al., "Examining the Relationship Between Immigration and Unemployment."

25. Wadsworth, "Immigration and the UK Labour Market."

26. Dustmann et al., "The Effect of Immigration Along the Distribution of Wages."

27. Blauberger and Schmidt, "Welfare Migration?" 1.

28. Court of Justice of the European Union, "A Member State May Exclude Union Citizens." For full judgment, see Court of Justice of the European Union, "Judgment of the Court (Grand Chamber) of 15 September 2015."

29. An overview of the existing research on the integration strategies used by European countries can be found in Givens, "Immigrant Integration in Europe."

30. Koopmans, "Fundamentalism and Out-Group Hostility."

31. Butt, "Muslims in Britain Have Zero Tolerance of Homosexuality, Say Poll."

32. Ioffe, "Mothers of ISIS."

33. Adida et al., "Identifying Barriers to Muslim Integration in France."

34. Evidence suggesting the existence of systematic anti-Muslim prejudice can be found in Strabac and Listhaug, "Anti-Muslim Prejudice in Europe."

35. Eurostat, "Gross Domestic Product at Market Prices."

36. Eurostat. "Unemployment Rate by Sex and Age—Monthly Average, %."

37. See Sumner, "Why Nominal GDP Matters."

38. Friedman, "The Euro"; and Feldstein, "The Political Economy of the European Economic and Monetary Union."

39. Bewley, "Why Not Cut Pay?"

40. Smith, "Young, Gifted and Greek."

41. Constant et al., "Attitudes Towards Immigrants."

42. Dao et al., "Regional labor Market Adjustments in the United States and Europe."

43. Frankel, "The ECB's Three Mistakes in the Greek Crisis." See also Sinn, *The Euro Trap*.

44. In November 2003, the legal proceedings against France and Germany for their excessive deficits were suspended. The 2005 reform of the Pact then removed its automatic character, turning it into a matter of political decision making. See Majone, "Rethinking European Integration After the Debt Crisis," 3. See also Grauwe, "The Politics of the Maastricht Convergence Criteria."

45. Scally, "Helmut Kohl Blames Gerhard Schroder for Euro Woes."

46. See the letter by Eurostat's head, Hanreich, "Eurostat Takes Issue with Former Greek PM."

47. Scally, "Helmut Kohl Blames Gerhard Schroder for Euro Woes."

48. For a book-long discussion of the parallels and the differences between the Great Depression and the Great Recession, see Eichengreen, *Hall of Mirrors*.

49. Eichengreen and Temin, "The Gold Standard and the Great Depression," 3.

50. Eichengreen and Sachs, "Exchange Rates and Economic Recovery in the 1930s."

51. For a more extensive discussion of the role of the gold standard in the Depression, see Eichengreen, *Golden Fetters*.

52. Friedman, "The Euro."

53. See Consolidated Versions of the Treaty on European Union, art. 127.

54. European Central Bank, "Monetary Policy Decisions."

55. Majone, "Rethinking European Integration After the Debt Crisis," 15–18.

56. Christensen, "The Euro."

57. See Eggertsson et al., "Can Structural Reforms Help Europe?"; and Cacciatore et al., "Market Deregulation and Optimal Monetary Policy in a Monetary Union." For a nontechnical overview and related literature, see Pesenti, "Structural Reforms and Monetary Policy Revisited."

58. As a result, the self-reported satisfaction of Europeans with how they democracies operate declined during the crisis. See Armingeon and Guthmann, "Democracy in Crisis?"

59. Feldstein, "The Political Economy of the European Economic and Monetary Union," 41.

60. European Commission in the United Kingdom, "Cod No Longer to Be Called Cod Thanks to EU."

61. European Commission in the United Kingdom, "EU Bans Lorry Drivers' British Breakfast."

62. "Enjoy a Yogurt at School?" *Daily Mail*.

63. European Commission in the United Kingdom, "Acres Outlawed by Brussels."

64. European Commission, Commission Regulation (EC) No 2257/94.

65. Ibid.

66. Ibid.

67. Ibid.

68. See Miller, "How Much Legislation Comes from Europe?"

69. Ibid., 8.

70. Ibid., 15. for evidence of a dramatic acceleration of the EU's legislative and regulatory activity, including in areas unrelated to the single market, see Alesina et al., "What Does the European Union Do?"

71. An excellent discussion of the problem of Europe's outdated culture of regulation can be found in Alesina and Giavazzi, *The Future of Europe: Reform or Decline*, 57–64 and 101–108.

72. Teles, "Kludgeocracy in America."

73. Ibid.

74. Gaskell and Persson, *Still out of Control?* 1.

75. Ibid., 37.

76. See the conclusions of European Commission, "A Decade of EU-Funded GMO Research."

77. Sunstein, "Beyond the Precautionary Principle," 1.

78. Eriksen, "Norway's Rejection of EU Membership Has Given the Country Less."

REFERENCES

Adida, Claire L., David D. Laitin, and Marie-Anne Valfort. "Identifying Barriers to Muslim Integration in France." *Proceedings of the National Academy of Sciences* 107 (2010): 22384–90.

Alesina, Alberto, and Francesco Giavazzi. *The Future of Europe: Reform or Decline.* Cambridge: MIT Press, 2008.

Alesina, Alberto, and Romain Wacziarg. "Is Europe Going Too Far?" NBER Working Paper No. 6883, January 1999. http://www.nber.org/papers/w6883.

Alesina, Alberto, Ignazio Angeloni, and Ludger Schuknecht. "What Does the European Union Do?" NBER Working Paper No. 8647, December 2001.

Armingeon, Klaus, and Kai Guthmann. "Democracy in Crisis? The Declining Support for National Democracy in European Countries, 2007–2011." *European Journal of Political Research* 53 (2014): 423–42.

Becková, Timea. "Cez hranicu sa šprintuje. Reportáž z miesta, kde zakrátko vypukla vzbura utečencov." *Denník N*, June 26, 2015. https://dennikn.sk/170865/boli-sme-za-utecencami-utekam-lebo-doma-mam-na-ranajky-bomby/.

Bewley, Truman F. "Why Not Cut Pay?" *European Economic Review* 42 (1998): 459–90.

Blauberger, Michael, and Susanne K Schmidt. "Welfare Migration? Free Movement of EU Citizens and Access to Social Benefits." *Research and Politics* 1 (2014): 1–7.

Boyle, Danny, et al. "Calais Migrants: David Cameron Warns Crisis to Last All Summer as Striking French Workers Block Port." *Telegraph*, July 31, 2015. http://www.telegraph.co.uk/news/uknews/immigration/11774895/Calais-illigal-immigrants-crisis-Army-on-standby-live.html.

Butt, Riazat. "Muslims in Britain Have Zero Tolerance of Homosexuality, Says Poll." *Guardian*, May 7, 2009. http://www.theguardian.com/uk/2009/may/07/muslims-britain-france-germany-homosexuality.

Cacciatore, Matteo, Giuseppe Fiori, and Fabio Ghironi. "Market Deregulation and Optimal Monetary Policy in a Monetary Union." NBER Working Paper No. 19025, 2013. http://www.nber.org/papers/w19025.

Christensen, Lars. "The Euro—A Monetary Strangulation Mechanism." *The Market Monetarist*, July 14, 2015. http://marketmonetarist.com/2015/07/14/the-euro-a-monetary-strangulation-mechanism/.

Clemens, Michael A. "Economics and Emigration: Trillion-Dollar Bills on the Sidewalk?" *Journal of Economic Perspectives* 25 (2011): 83–106.

Consolidated Versions of the Treaty on European Union and the Treaty on the Functioning of the European Union. *Official Journal*, December 13, 2007. http://eur-lex.europa.eu/legal-content/EN/TXT/?uri=celex%3A12012E%2FTXT.

Constant, Amelie F., Martin Kahanec, and Klaus F. Zimmerman. "Attitudes Towards Immigrants, Other Integration Barriers and Their Veracity." IZA Discussion Paper No. 3650, 2008.

Court of Justice of the European Union, "A Member State May Exclude Union Citizens Who Go to That State to Find Work from Certain Non-Contributory Social Security Benefits." Press Release No. 101/15, September 15, 2015. http://curia.europa.eu/jcms/upload/docs/application/pdf/2015-09/cp150101en.pdf.

———. *Jobcenter Berlin Neukölln v. Nazifa Alimanovic and Others.* Judgment of the Court (Grand Chamber), September 15, 2015. http://curia.europa.eu/juris/liste.jsf?num=C-67/14.

Dao, Mai, Davide Furceri, and Prakash Loungani. "Regional Labor Market Adjustments in the United States and Europe." IMF Working Paper 14/26, 2014. https://www.imf.org/external/pubs/ft/wp/2014/wp1426.pdf.

Dustmann, Christian, Tommaso Frattini, and Ian P. Preston. "The Effect of Immigration Along the Distribution of Wages." *Review of Economic Studies* 80 (2013): 145–73.

Eggertsson, Gauti, Andrea Ferrero, and Andrea Raffo. "Can Structural Reforms Help Europe?" *Journal of Monetary Economics* 61 (2014): 2–22.

Eichengreen, Barry. *Golden Fetters: The Gold Standard and the Great Depression, 1919–1939.* Oxford: Oxford University Press, 1992.

———. *Hall of Mirrors: The Great Depression, The Great Recession, and the Uses—and Misuses—of History.* Oxford: Oxford University Press, 2014.

Eichengreen, Barry, and Jeffrey Sachs. "Exchange Rates and Economic Recovery in the 1930s." *Journal of Economic History* 45 (1985): 925–46.

Eichengreen, Barry, and Peter Temin. "The Gold Standard and the Great Depression." NBER Working Paper No. 6060, June 1997. http://www.nber.org/papers/w6060.pdf.

"Enjoy a Yogurt at School? Hard Cheese, Says EU: Eurocrats Want to Ban Snacks in 'Healthy Eating' Campaign." *Daily Mail*, February 8, 2014. http://www.dailymail.co.uk/news/article-2554924/Enjoy-yogurt-school-Hadr-cheese-says-EU-Eurocrats-want-ban-snacks-healthy-eating-campaign.html.

Eriksen, Erik O. "Norway's Rejection of EU Membership Has Given the Country Less Self-Determination, Not More." *LSE European Politics & Policy Blog*, April 22, 2014. http://blogs.lse.ac.uk/europpblog/2014/04/22/norways-rejection-of-eu-membership-has-given-the-country-less-self-determination-not-more/.

European Central Bank. "Monetary Policy Decisions," July 7, 2011. https://www.ecb.europa.eu/press/pr/date/2011/html/pr110707.en.html.

European Commission. Commission Regulation (EC) No 2257/94 of 16 September 1994 laying down quality standards for bananas. *Official Journal L* 245 (September 20, 1994), 0006–0010. http://eur-lex.europa.eu/LexUriServ/LexUriServ.do?uri=CELEX:31994R 2257:EN:HTML.

———. "A Decade of EU-Funded GMO Research (2001–2010)." Luxembourg: Publications Office of the European Union, 2014. https://ec.europa.eu/research/biosociety/pdf/a_decade_of_eu-funded_gmo_research.pdf.

European Commission in the United Kingdom. "Cod No Longer to Be Called Cod Thanks to EU." EC in the UK Blog, September 5, 2001. http://blogs.ec.europa.eu/ECintheUK/cod-no-longer-to-be-called-cod-thanks-to-eu/.

———. "EU Bans Lorry Drivers' British Breakfast." EC in the UK Blog, September 21, 2001. http://blogs.ec.europa.eu/ECintheUK/eu-bans-lorry-drivers%E2%80%99-british-breakfast/.

———. "Acres Outlawed by Brussels." EC in the UK Blog, July 21, 2008. http://blogs.ec.europa.eu/ECintheUK/acres-outlawed-by-brussels-2/.

European Council. Council Regulation (EC) No 343/2003 of 18 February 2003 establishing the criteria and mechanisms for determining the Member State responsible for examining an asylum application lodged in one of the Member States by a third-country national. *Official Journal L* 50 (January 23, 2003). http://eur-lex.europa.eu/legal-content/EN/TXT/?uri=celex:32003R0343.

European Union. Convention Determining the State Responsible for Examining Applications for Asylum Lodged in One of the Member States of the European Communities—Dublin Convention. *Official Journal C* 254 (August 19, 1997). http://eur-lex.europa.eu/legal-content/EN/ALL/?uri=CELEX%3A41997A0819(01).

Eurostat. "Gross Domestic Product at Market Prices." September 28, 2015. http://ec.europa.eu/eurostat/tgm/table.do?tab=table&plugin=1&language=en&pcode=tec00001.

———. "Unemployment Rate by Sex and Age—Monthly Average, %." September 28, 2015. http://appsso.eurostat.ec.europa.eu/nui/submitViewTableAction.do.

Feldstein, Martin. "The Political Economy of the European Economic and Monetary Union: Political Sources of an Economic Liability." *Journal of Economic Perspectives* 11 (1997): 23–42.

Frankel, Jeffrey. "The ECB's Three Mistakes in the Greek Crisis and How to Get Sovereign Debt Right in the Future." *VoxEU*, May 16, 2011. http://www.voxeu.org/article/greek-debt-crisis-ecb-s-three-big-mistakes.

Friedman, Milton. "The Euro: Monetary Unity to Political Disunity?" *Project Syndicate*, August 28, 1997. http://www.project-syndicate.org/commentary/the-euro—monetary-unity-to-political-disunity.

Frontex. "Frontex Expands Its Operation Triton." May 26, 2015. http://frontex.europa.eu/news/frontex-expands-its-joint-operation-triton-udpbHP.

———. "Number of Migrants Arriving in Greece Dropped by Half in November." December 15, 2015. http://frontex.europa.eu/news/number-of-migrants-arriving-in-greece-dropped-by-half-in-november-cITv3V.

Gaskell, Sarah, and Mats Persson. *Still out of Control? Measuring Eleven Years of EU Regulation*. London: Open Europe, 2010. http://archive.openeurope.org.uk/Content/Documents/PDFs/stilloutofcontrol.pdf.

Givens, Terry E. "Immigrant Integration in Europe: Empirical Research." *Annual Review of Political Science* 10 (2007): 67–83.

Grauwe, Paul de. "The Politics of the Maastricht Convergence Criteria." *VoxEU*, April 15, 2009. http://www.voxeu.org/article/politics-maastricht-convergence-criteria.

Hannan, Daniel. "The End of Europe's Fantasy Is Now in Sight." *Standpoint*, October 2011. http://www.standpointmag.co.uk/node/4105/full.

Hanreich, Günther. "Eurostat Takes Issue with Former Greek PM on Reasons for the Revision of Economic Data." *Financial Times*, December 28, 2004. http://www.ft.com/cms/s/0/745b2b44-5874-11d9-9940-00000e2511c8.html.

Hawkins, Oliver. "Migration Statistics." Briefing Paper SN06077. London: UK House of Commons, 2015. http://www.parliament.uk/briefing-papers/sn06077.pdf.

Hobbing, Peter. "Integrated Border Management at the EU Level." CEPS Working Documents No. 227, 2005. http://aei.pitt.edu/6672/1/1254_227.pdf.

International Organization for Migration. "Deadly Milestone as Mediterranean Migrant Deaths Pass 2,000." August 4, 2015. http://www.iom.int/news/deadly-milestone-mediterranean-migrant-deaths-pass-2000.

Ioffe, Julia. "Mothers of ISIS." *Huffington Post*, August 12, 2015. http://highline.huffingtonpost.com/articles/en/mothers-of-isis/.

Jaillard, Marion et al. *Setting Up a Common European Asylum System: Report on the Application of Existing Instruments and Proposal for the New System.* Luxembourg: Publications Office of the European Union, 2010. http://www.europarl.europa.eu/meetdocs/2009_2014/documents/libe/dv/pe425622_/pe425622_en.pdf.

Kay, John. "Imperial Ambitions Have Pushed Europe to Its Limits." *Financial Times*, July 14, 2015. http://www.ft.com/cms/s/0/b9c616e0-29ff-11e5-acfb-cbd2e1c81cca.html#axzz3yMSQdonM.

Koopmans, Ruud. "Fundamentalism and Out-Group Hostility. Muslim Immigrants and Christian Natives in Western Europe." *WZB Mitteilungen*, Berlin Social Science Center, December 2013. https://www.wzb.eu/en/press-release/islamic-fundamentalism-is-widely-spread.

Lucchino, Paolo, Chiara Rosazza-Bondibene, and Jonathan Portes. "Examining the Relationship Between Immigration and Unemployment Using National Insurance Number Registration Data." NIESR Discussion Paper 386. London: National Institute of Economic and Social Research, 2012. http://www.niesr.ac.uk/sites/default/files/publications/090112_163827.pdf.

Majone, Giandomenico. "Rethinking European Integration After the Debt Crisis." UCL European Institute Working Paper No. 3/2012, 2012. https://www.ucl.ac.uk/european-institute/analysis-publications/publications/WP3.pdf.

Mason, Rowena. "Nigel Farage: Immigration Has Left Britain Almost Unrecognizable." *Guardian*, March 31, 2015. http://www.theguardian.com/politics/2015/mar/31/nigel-farage-ukip-immigration-britain-unrecognisable-general-election-poster.

Matrix Insight Ltd, et al. *What System of Burden-Sharing Between Member States for the Reception of asylum-seekers?* Document requested by the European Parliament's Committee on Civil Liberties, Justice and Home Affairs, Brussels: European Parliament, 47. http://www.europarl.europa.eu/RegData/etudes/etudes/join/2010/419620/IPOL-LIBE_ET(2010)419620_EN.pdf.

"Mayor: No Problems with Refugees in Slovak Town." *Prague Post*, October 16, 2015. http://www.praguepost.com/eu-news/50277-mayor-no-problems-with-refugees-in-slovak-town#ixzz3wJRv0ilS.

McNamara, Kathleen. *The Politics of Everyday Europe. Constructing Authority in the European Union.* Oxford: Oxford University Press, 2015.

Migration Advisory Committee. *Analysis of the Impacts of Migration.* London: Home Office, 2012.

Miller, Vaughne. "How Much Legislation Comes from Europe?" Research Paper 10/62, UK House of Commons, 2010.

Moraga, Jesús Fernández-Huertas, and Hillel Rapoport. "Tradable Refugee-Admission Quotas and EU Asylum Policy." CESifo Working Paper Series No. 5072, 2014.

Pesenti, Paolo. "Structural Reforms and Monetary Policy Revisited." *VoxEU*, September 7, 2015. http://www.voxeu.org/article/structural-reforms-and-monetary-policy-revisited.

"Referendum: Gabčíkovo Inhabitants Do Not Want Refugees There." *Slovak Spectator*, August 3, 2015. http://spectator.sme.sk/c/20059217/referendum-gabcikovo-inhabitants-do-not-want-refugees-there.html.

Scally, Derek. "Helmut Kohl Blames Gerhard Schröder for Euro Woes." *Irish Times*, November 3, 2014. http://www.irishtimes.com/news/world/europe/helmut-kohl-blames-gerhard-schr%C3%B6der-for-euro-woes-1.1986707.

Sinn, Hans-Werner. *The Euro Trap: On Bursting Bubbles, Budgets, and Beliefs.* Oxford: Oxford University Press, 2014.

Smith, Helena. "Young, Gifted and Greek: Generation G—The World's Biggest Brain Drain." *The Guardian*, January 19, 2015. http://www.theguardian.com/world/2015/jan/19/young-talented-greek-generation-g-worlds-biggest-brain-drain.

Strabac, Zan, and Ola Listhaug. "Anti-Muslim Prejudice in Europe: A Multilevel Analysis of Survey Data from 30 Countries." *Social Science Research* 37 (2008): 268–86.

Sumner, Scott. "Why Nominal GDP Matters." *The Money Illusion*, November 8, 2009. http://www.themoneyillusion.com/?p=2822.

Sunstein, Cass R. "Beyond the Precautionary Principle." *Public Law and Legal Theory Working Paper* No. 38, Chicago: University of Chicago, 2009.

Szakacs, Gergely. "Hungary Expects to Complete Serbian Border Fence by November: Lawmaker." Reuters, July 24, 2015. http://www.reuters.com/article/2015/07/24/us-europe-migrants-hungary-fence-idUSKCN0PY0VX20150724.

Teles, Steven M. "Kludgeocracy in America." *National Affairs*, 17, 2015. http://www.nationalaffairs.com/publications/detail/kludgeocracy-in-america.

University College London. "Positive Economic Impact of UK Immigration from the European Union: New Evidence." *UCL News*, November 5, 2014. https://www.ucl.ac.uk/news/news-articles/1114/051114-economic-impact-EU-immigration.

Veenkamp, Theo. "The Rise of Anti-Immigration Populism in Europe and the Future of European Capitalist Democratic Society: An Exploration." In *Transatlantic 2020: A Tale of Four Futures*, edited by Daniel S. Hamilton and Kurt Volker, 183–214. Washington, DC: Center for Transatlantic Relations, 2011.

Wadsworth, Jonathan. "Immigration and the UK Labour Market." *Centre for Economic Performance 2015 Election Analysis*. London School of Economics, Paper EA019, 2015. http://cep.lse.ac.uk/pubs/download/ea019.pdf.

5

THE MYTH OF THE NATION-STATE

Nostalgia for the past is seldom a good guide to action. Yet it is common, both among intellectuals and laypeople, particularly if a historical episode aligns with their ideological priors. America's left, for example, often indulges in the myth of the 1950s as the golden era of the US economy, which combined, through astute economic policies, high rates of economic growth and social cohesion. Nobel Prize–winning economist Paul Krugman wrote that, in the 1950s, America "made the rich pay their fair share; it gave workers the power to bargain for decent wages and benefits; yet contrary to right-wing propaganda then and now, it prospered. And we can do that again."[1] Krugman's mistake is to assume that the rapid economic growth of the 1950s was a result of the policies adopted during that period that indeed included high marginal tax rates, strong unions, and industrial planning. In reality, the prosperity of the 1950s resulted from a cluster of technological innovations dating back to the prewar era, which started revolutionizing American economic life as soon as the war was over.[2] The idea that transplanting the economic policies of the time into today's world would lead to similar economic outcomes completely disregards how much the US economy has changed in the meantime.

The free-market critics of the EU are by no means immune to their own versions of such a historical nostalgia. Most Eurosceptics acknowledge that European integration has been associated with some tangible benefits, particularly in the form of the single market. But they also claim that free movement of goods, services, and capital once existed without the EU's cumbersome regulatory apparatus. They imagine that scaling the EU back, or eliminating it altogether, would be a boon to democracy on the continent, which, they allege, cannot function outside the nation-state. These two ideas, implicit in most arguments offered by conservative and free-market critics of the EU, rely on a selective and distorted view of Europe's history. To be sure, we can find episodes of relative economic openness and political freedom prior to the EU's inception. However, pre-EU Europe was no free-trade paradise. And, notwithstanding the gradual extension of suffrage that the continent saw in the second half of the 19th century, it would be naïve to equate a Europe of fully sovereign nation-states with a flourishing of liberal democracy. Even the genuine economic and political achievements prior to European integration ended up being disappointingly short-lived.[3] The main reason for this failure, furthermore, can be traced to the absence of international political institutions that would bind European nations together.

Different political arrangements, including the EU or the nation-state, cannot be evaluated by only how well they fare under favorable conditions but also how they cope with distress. It is telling that the Europe of sovereign nation-states has repeatedly led to geopolitical disasters, most significantly in the first half of the 20th century. It is equally telling that both economic openness and liberal democracy started to set more lasting roots in Western Europe only after World War II, when European leaders laid the foundations of Europe's common political institutions. But even then, the progress was slow. Through much of the 1960s, tariff barriers still divided Western European economies. During the same period, Spain and Portugal, at the time not members of the EEC, were ruled by brutal, authoritarian regimes. In 1967, a military junta took power in Greece.[4] If nothing else, the fragility of open markets and liberal democracy even in those early days of European integration should give pause to the claims of those who believe that today's EU can be scaled back to a dramatically more modest form, known in the 1950s or 1960s, without triggering any unintended consequences.

Unlike today's free marketeers, Hayek understood the perils of an international system relying solely on the existence of sovereign nation-states. Indeed, he believed that "it was one of the main deficiencies of nineteenth-century liberalism that its advocates did not sufficiently re-

alize that the achievement of a recognized harmony of interests between inhabitants of the different states was only possible within the
framework of international security."[5] He realized that such a framework, in the form of an international federation, would mean an abrogation of state sovereignty. For him, that was not an unfortunate side
effect but an essential component of a federal system. In fact, "the
abrogation of national sovereignties and the creation of an effective
international order of law is a necessary complement and the logical
consummation of the liberal program."[6] But there is no need to rely on
Hayek's authority to see that the growth of common European institutions has gone hand in hand with the advancement of markets and
democracy. The historical record speaks largely for itself.

EUROPE'S NOT-SO-FREE TRADE

In July 1968, 18 months ahead of the original schedule stipulated in the
Treaty of Rome, customs duties among member countries of the European Economic Community (EEC) were abolished.[7] The customs union did not turn the continent into a free-market utopia. The EU still
imposes tariffs on imports from overseas. Still, it was a historically unprecedented achievement. For centuries, protectionism, not free trade,
had been the norm among European countries. Unlike previous attempts to liberalize trade, the EEC has proved to be surprisingly long-
lasting and stable. None of the initial signatories has yet decided to
leave this trade arrangement, and many others have joined since, typically by becoming members of the EEC or, later, the EU.[8]

In *The Wealth of Nations*, even Adam Smith dismisses as politically
unrealistic the possibility of free trade in his home country. "To expect,"
he writes, "that the freedom of trade should ever be entirely restored in
Great Britain is as absurd as to expect that an Oceana or Utopia should
ever be established in it."[9] Smith, of course, was living at a time when
public discussions about trade were dominated by mercantilism—the
notion that increasing net exports was a worthwhile policy goal, as it led
to the inflow of precious metals into the country.[10] Mercantilism is one
of the ideas that economists have not been able to eradicate, in spite of
its obvious falsity. It has made a recent comeback with the presidential
campaign of Donald Trump, who believes that his country is "losing in

trade" to China, as if the excess of Chinese exports to the United States over American exports to China was impoverishing the American public.

Of course, mercantilist thought varied in its sophistication, and the works of leading mercantilists of the era, such as Thomas Mun,[11] display a much higher degree of economic literacy than Mr. Trump's rhetoric. Its general advice consisted of erecting trade barriers to limit imports and providing support to exporting industries. European states heeded the advice, imposing large import duties and encouraging exports, particularly of high value-added products. Mercantilism was not just an intellectual doctrine but also a method of governing the state in a world where governments had only a peripheral interest in the welfare of the public and were justified in seeing trade as a zero-sum game. The mercantile regulations and trade restrictions benefited a small number of politically connected monopolists and cartels. Those, in turn, provided the revenue that the state needed to finance wars.[12]

In the second half of the 17th century, Britain had a relatively simple system of tariffs, amounting to a tax of 5 percent on most imports and exports, calculated from an officially set value of goods that were crossing the border. On top of that, additional duties were added discretionarily, either for political reasons or with the aim of raising government revenue. The late 17th century saw various attempts to prohibit imports of all French goods, followed by prohibitive duties imposed in 1693–1696, which remained until the Eden Treaty of 1786.[13] Through a series of gradual increases of tariff rates on a broad range of goods, including practically all industrial products, Britain ended up with a baseline tariff of 25 percent on most imported goods by 1759.[14] In addition to some of the obvious consequences of European protectionism, such as high prices of imported commodities and rents for politically connected monopolists, mercantilism left a long-lasting imprint on the consumer habits of Europeans. Britons, for example, became a nation of beer drinkers, only as a result of protectionist measures aimed at keeping French wine out of British markets. Tariffs also stimulated wine production in Portugal, where the local wine industry would not have otherwise been competitive.[15] Trade within Europe and in the world was further disrupted by the Napoleonic wars, which acted as a long-term hindrance to trade and economic integration well into the 19th century.[16] European countries also imposed numerous restrictions on trade with their colonies. For two centuries since 1651, the Brits enforced the Navigation Acts, which prevented foreign ships from engaging in trade between Britain and its colonies. Furthermore, the laws banned businesses in the colonies, including those in North America, from trading directly with other European countries. The motivation was to prevent unwanted imports and to keep Britain at the receiving end of monetary flows.

Under Smith's intellectual influence, as well as that of the Physiocrats in France, mercantilism gradually fell into intellectual disrepute. More importantly, with the advent of modern economic growth, governments and special interests had more to gain from trade openness than from the zero-sum mercantile protectionism. As a result, a reform movement aiming to free up trade started to gain traction in Britain and on the continent. In the 19th century, trade was liberalized by a number of European countries, including England and France.[17] In the UK, the repeal of the Corn Laws in 1846 was heralded as a significant milestone on the way to free trade on the continent. The Corn Laws had imposed import duties on grain imports to the UK to keep grain prices high. As a result, they benefited landowners at the expense of the urban populations. Richard Cobden,[18] a famous free-trade advocate, managed to galvanize public opinion against the Corn Laws and to build a political coalition that finally succeeded in at first lowering and later completely scrapping the import duty.[19] In 1860, Britain and France signed the Cobden-Chevalier trade treaty, liberalizing trade between the two countries. French import prohibitions were removed and replaced by duties not exceeding 30 percent. Britain dramatically reduced wine tariffs and started admitting many French products duty-free.[20] The treaty included an unconditional "most-favored-nation" clause, through which both countries pledged to apply the best terms they made available to any other country to their respective exports. The Cobden-Chevalier Treaty triggered a wave of similarly structured bilateral trade agreements on the continent.

These coincided with a gradual decline of tariffs in England and in Europe more generally, which lasted until the 1870s. Some tariff cuts were unilateral, without any international negotiations and oftentimes without much public discussion. However, bilateral agreements were increasingly becoming the policy instrument of choice for the proponents of free trade. "What happened in 1860 was that policy makers, faced with growing resistance to further trade liberalization, decided to change the instruments of liberalization. They decided to push the agenda out of parliament, towardss the diplomatic arena," writes economic historian Marc Flandreau.[21] But the proliferation of bilateral trade agreements, with their most-favored-nation clauses, seems to have backfired. Although intended to prevent discriminatory treatment of specific countries, the most-favored-nation clauses could have deterred politicians from pursuing deeper mutual concessions, since those would have to be extended across the board to all the countries with bilateral treaties. For that reason, assessing the impact of bilateral trade deals on economic integration on the continent is difficult, not least because it is impossible to dissociate the effects of bilateral treaties from the one-off intellectual and political victories of free-traders such as Richard Cobden. But even during Cobden's years, England was no free-trade paradise. Average tariffs in England were higher than in France throughout much of the 19th century, declining from around 60 percent in the early 1820s to below 10 percent in the late 1870s.[22]

Worse yet, the efforts to liberalize trade were disappointingly short-lived.[23] In 1871, following Germany's victory over France, Chancellor Bismarck imposed a sizeable war indemnity on France.[24] This represented a large investment boost to the German economy and prompted the introduction of the gold standard in Germany. But once the indemnity payments from France stopped, the German economy entered a period of crisis. Faced with an overvalued exchange rate and a fall in demand for their products, German producers started campaigning for tariff protection. The government, in turn, was looking for a source of revenue to make up for the shortfall created by the repayment of the war indemnity. In 1879, Bismarck introduced the "iron and rye" tariff, imposing import duties on various agricultural and industrial goods, including grains, meat, pigs, textiles, machinery, and various semi-manufactured products.[25]

The German tariff ended the brief period of relatively free trade in Europe. In 1882, France experienced a severe banking crisis that threw the country's economy into a recession that lasted for the remainder of the decade. In the second half of the 1880s, that generated political pressure to reintroduce trade barriers, some of it coming even from industries that had traditionally been export-oriented. In 1892, a reform of tariffs was introduced, named after its most important proponent,

Jules Méline, who later became prime minister. The Méline tariff covered both industrial and agricultural output, very much in the spirit of Germany's iron and rye tariff. Besides increasing import duties, the law provided a platform for future tariff revisions.[26] Those came often and typically went in the direction of increasing tariff protection, culminating in 1910. Suspended during the First World War, the Méline tariff was reintroduced in the interwar period and served as the foundation of France's trade policies until the outbreak of the Second World War.

In light of the return of protectionism at the end of the 19th century, it is difficult to understand why some free-market economists see the period as a model worth emulating. In an article in the libertarian *Cato Journal*, for example, the economist Deepak Lal juxtaposes what he sees as the "correct" policy of unilateral liberalization, which underpinned the 19th-century international economic order, and the "extremely acrimonious route of multilateral and more recently bilateral negotiations" that have led to the liberalization of trade after the Second World War.[27] The late economic historian Sudha Shenoy, in turn, claims: "[i]n the nineteenth century, you had for the first time a worldwide economic order. You had free trade, free movement of people, free movement of capital, a gold standard, falling prices in the latter part of the century, peaceful development, and no major wars between 1815 and 1914."[28] Even Hayek's mentor, Ludwig von Mises, writes that "[t]he British free trade philosophy triumphed in the nineteenth century in the countries of Western and Central Europe."[29] The fact that Europe saw genuine economic progress and market integration over that period can account for much of this nostalgia. But the growth of international trade was not a result of free-trade policies, which were in retreat at the end of the 19th century, perhaps with the exception of Britain. Economic historians concur that the late 19th century globalization was driven primarily by declines in the cost of transport.[30] Improved freight and the development of railway networks fostered trade, *in spite* of existing protectionism. But technology and politics interacted: low transport costs enabled the import of cheap grains from overseas, competing with local agriculture. This created political pressures from landowners, whose incomes were falling, to introduce measures such as the iron and rye and Méline tariffs. Those became vehicles for further tariff increases in response to changes in market conditions. By 1887, for example, German tariffs reached 33 percent on wheat and

47 percent on rye. In France, the import duty on wheat reached 32 percent.[31]

The drift towards protectionism was strong and continent-wide, including countries such as Sweden and Italy. In 1913, tariffs on manufactured goods averaged 18 percent in Austria-Hungary, 13 percent in Germany, 20 percent in France, 41 percent in Spain, and a staggering 84 percent in Russia.[32] Europe also saw frequent disputes and trade wars during this period. In 1904, Serbia attempted to build tighter economic links to France and Bulgaria, instead of its long-standing trade partner, Austria-Hungary. In response, in 1906, the Austrian government closed the borders of the empire to the imports of Serbian pork.

Of course, the "pig war," as the episode became known, was a relatively innocuous event considering what was ahead. World War I was the first in a series of major disruptions to trade flows. During the war, even the UK abandoned its traditional free-market stance in favor of import controls and tariffs, which it retained after the war. The biggest disruptions to trade were not the increases in import duties but the effects of the actual warfare. Physical infrastructure was destroyed, and European economies were turned into war machines. Warring sides engaged in blockades and U-boat campaigns to destroy each other's trade flows.

Efforts to revive the cause of free trade after the war produced disappointing results. One reason was the existence of a cobweb of bilateral agreements containing the most-favored-nation clauses. Whatever their role in the liberalization that occurred in the second half of the 19th century, in the interwar period they led to the problem of collective action—an instance of the tragedy of the commons.[33] Politicians were not incentivized to engage in bilateral liberalizations. Instead, they waited to reap the benefits of trade agreements reached by other countries. The Great Depression was another event that disrupted trade on the European continent. Trade volumes shrunk initially due to the fall in demand caused by the recession. But the contraction of international trade was exacerbated by deliberate protectionist policies. Instead of leading by example, the United States introduced the Smoot-Hawley Tariff Act, which increased import duties on a wide range of goods. The American tariff was emulated by European countries, specifically by those that were struggling to maintain the convertibility of their currencies to gold. Economic historians Douglas Irwin and Barry Eichengreen find:

> [T]he improvement in the price competitiveness of exports from countries with depreciated currencies prompted defensive counter-measures in countries remaining on the gold standard. A large number of countries ratcheted up their tariffs to block cheap imports. France imposed a 15 percent surcharge on British goods to offset the depreciation of the sterling and adopted more restrictive import quotas.[34]

As a result, the volume of international trade contracted by some 40 percent between the onset of the Great Depression and the early 1930s, returning international trade to its pre–World War I levels.[35] And when trade flows started to recover, the Second World War was just around the corner.

In short, Europe's historical experience does not lend much support to the idea that free trade flourished in the world of sovereign nation-states, unencumbered by mechanisms of international governance. By itself, that does not demonstrate that the EU, as it currently stands, is necessary for free trade between European countries, nor that it is the only possible arrangement for securing free movement of goods and services. After all, when the tariffs that had once divided Western European economies disappeared in 1968, the European Economic Community was a much smaller and less obtrusive organization than today's EU. In part thanks to GATT and the WTO—which are just another form of supranational governance, much like the EU—conventional protectionist tools, such as tariffs and quotas, are playing a much less significant role now than they did throughout much of Europe's history. However, as I argue in chapter 2, by actively dismantling regulatory barriers to trade, the EU single market has provided a much stronger basis for market integration than a simple absence of tariffs. As a result, going back to the relatively light-touch form of European integration of the 1950s and 1960s would mean forgoing much of the depth of market integration that the EU has achieved. To see that, it is enough to read the work of some of the free-market economists of the era, such as Wilhelm Röpke, who complained that without free capital flows (the postwar monetary order was characterized by capital and foreign exchange controls), the attempts to create a common market in Europe were doomed to fail. [36]

The simultaneous presence of enlightened free traders in positions of influence across European countries, like in the 1850s in the UK and in France, could replicate the degree of economic integration that Europe currently enjoys. Eurosceptics thus have a point when they say that enlightened leadership could easily repeat that success even in the EU's absence. But luck is a very poor substitute for European political institutions that keep markets together, even when politicians want to resort to protectionism.

NATION-STATE AND DEMOCRACY: IT'S COMPLICATED

One reason why conservative Eurosceptics see European integration as a threat to democracy has to do with their understanding of the link between the nation-state and democracy. The British philosopher Roger Scruton is perhaps the most significant voice representing this intellectual tradition, which underpins Eurosceptic thought, especially in the Anglo-Saxon world. [37] For him, the nation—with its sense of belonging and membership in the legal and political process that governs a certain territory—is a necessary precondition of democracy. Any attempt to delegate political decisions to supranational organizations erodes democracy:

> [N]ational loyalty does not merely issue in democratic government, but is profoundly assumed by it. People bound by a national "we" have no difficulty in accepting a government whose opinions and decisions they disagree with; they have no difficulty in accepting the legitimacy of opposition, or the free expression of outrageous-seeming views. In short, they are able to live with democracy, and to express their political aspirations through the ballot box. [38]

Scruton's characterization of territorially based loyalty to a given legal and political process as a necessary precondition for democracy is not unreasonable. Neither is it completely new. Already in the 1930s, the University of Chicago economist Frank Knight wrote about "moral like-mindedness" as a necessary feature of a free society. [39] In political science, the idea of an "imagined community," attributed to Cornell University's Benedict Anderson,[40] is used to denote socially constructed groups, such as nations, which are imagined by people who perceive themselves as part of the group. But it is far from obvious that such an abstract community can exist, as Scruton implies, *only within* the nation-state. The nation-state is an artifact of modern European history and only one of a spectrum of different political arrangements existing among the world's democracies.[41] It is far from clear that such a sense of loyalty is necessarily destroyed or even damaged when national sovereignty is pooled among democratic countries, as it is in the EU.[42]

A number of multiethnic societies around the world, such as the United States and India, have followed very different histories than the nation-states of Europe. Few would dispute that democratic institutions have taken deep root in these countries as well, in spite of their respective versions of ethnic and cultural pluralism and in spite of their foundational narratives, which are very different from those surrounding the emergence of European nation-states. Even in Europe it is possible to find examples of multilingual countries—most notably Switzerland—where democratic institutions and a common sense of political identity have emerged.[43] Conversely, it is incorrect to believe that Europe's nations predated and somehow catalyzed the emergence of states on the continent. Europe's territorial, "Westphalian" states precede the rise of the modern idea of the nation—a distinctly 19th-century phenomenon. The gradual emergence of ethnically homogenous states in Europe was not a result of some natural pre-ordained chain of events but of successive waves of expulsions, secessions, wars, and, in some cases, genocide. The sense of loyalty to a set of political institutions, as described by Scruton, is therefore much more fluid than a simple correspondence between historical nations of Europe and their states. It is far more helpful to think of it as of a plurality of overlapping collective identities, from very local ones, through the nation-state, and beyond.[44]

There is, of course, a space for a spirited discussion about whether a European political identity exists and whether EU institutions are making its emergence more, or less, likely.[45] The recurrent crises, in which some member states are pitted against others, are not helping the emergence of a common European political identity. On the other hand, the vast array of sometimes prosaic attributes of European public space and common references from everyday life—such as Schengen, the common currency, and European legislation—suggest that such a political

identity is not a priori impossible and is indeed emerging, albeit slowly.[46]

Ignoring the question of the fluidity of political identities, the critics
of the EU insist on a simple dichotomy between the nation, and what
Scruton calls "panglossian universalism"[47]—the idea that political
governance can and should transcend national boundaries. The European Union, he claims, "can gain authority only by colonizing the territorial jurisdictions of nation states"[48] and is therefore a threat to democracy. That, in a nutshell, is the core of the conservative argument about
the EU's democratic deficit—a deficit that allegedly cannot be addressed by making EU institutions more democratic. "Since there is no
European demos—and no European nation—this defect cannot be
solved by strengthening the role of the European Parliament," Václav
Klaus told the European Parliament in his speech of 2009.[49]

Some 70 years into Europe's experiment with "panglossian universalism," it is possible to assess, using evidence, just how pernicious the
EU has been to democracy in European nation-states. Upon cursory
examination, the notion that democracy and the EU are somehow incompatible is perplexing. If that were the case, one would expect visible
deterioration in the quality of democratic political institutions in EU
member states relative to comparable countries that have retained a
greater degree of sovereignty. Over time, as the EU has played an
increasingly important role in governing the affairs of Europeans, Europe's democracies should be expected to suffer. However, the EU
member states perform extremely well on conventional measures of
institutional quality and political freedom. In the 2014 Democracy Index, published by the Economist Intelligence Unit, out of the world's
24 "full democracies," half are EU member countries.[50] In Freedom
House's 2015 *Freedom in the World* ranking, the EU countries—with
the exception of some Central and Eastern European newcomers, such
as Hungary, Bulgaria, Romania, and Latvia—receive the highest possible marks for both their political rights and civil liberties.[51] On the
World Bank's measure of "Voice and Accountability," "old" EU member states receive scores that are consistently above the OECD average,
suggesting that EU member states outperform, in terms of their institutional quality, other advanced industrialized nations.[52]

A sceptical reader might object that the answer to the question of
whether the EU has made Europe more or less democratic cannot be

answered just by looking at raw statistics. The answer depends on the relevant counterfactuals. One could speculate that European governments would be *even more* democratic and accountable in the EU's absence. But therein lies the core of the problem with Euroscepticism: it starts from the premise that the counterfactual under consideration is an idealized Europe of sovereign and fully democratic nation-states. But such a counterfactual does not resemble anything that has existed at any point in Europe's past. Contrary to this nostalgic view of Europe's past, its nation-states have a troubled history when unconstrained by common political institutions. That history was marked by wars, slow and fragile democratizations, and outbursts of totalitarianisms of different stripes.

To be sure, European countries have also a track record of protecting individual rights and constraining governments. Some of its manifestations, such as the Magna Carta of 1215, long predate the modern nation-state. The emergence of others accompanied the development of European states in the more recent past. The Warsaw Confederation of 1573 guaranteed religious freedom within the Polish-Lithuanian Republic, which thus escaped the series of religious wars that ravaged the rest of the continent.[53] The Glorious Revolution in England, in 1688, asserted the sovereignty of parliament and restricted the power of the monarch.[54] This sequence of institutional innovations, which made the individual more than just a hapless subject of tyrannical governments, provided the basis for the rise of Western liberal democracy. However, political participation—one of its defining characteristics—is a much more recent phenomenon, going back only to the 1800s. Before then, to the extent to which the franchise had existed *at all* in some European countries, it was restricted to a fraction of adult men who owned property, earned a certain income, or paid a certain amount in taxes.

Over the course of the 19th century, European countries gradually introduced more extensive male franchise. Greece extended the right to vote to all adult males in 1844. By 1900, a number of European countries had enfranchised all adult males, but universal suffrage was still nonexistent. Women gained their voting rights in Finland and Norway in 1907, Iceland in 1915, and the United Kingdom in 1918.[55] Throughout much of the 19th century, patronage and corruption—particularly affecting the "rotten boroughs," constituencies with extremely small numbers of voters—were the norm in Britain, as was frequent intimidation of voters.[56] In Germany, even after suffrage was extended to all adult males over the age of 25, voting in rural areas was effectively controlled by landlords.[57] There may have been differences across countries, but from today's perspective, Europe was far from being a harbinger of democracy, even though, by historical standards, the continuing extension of suffrage was a major advance.

More importantly, the progress of liberal democracy in Europe at the turn of the century was quickly reversed in the decades that followed. The First World War led to the demise of a large portion of the political order existing on the continent. In 1917, revolution in Russia replaced the monarchy with a communist regime and triggered a protracted civil war. Monarchies in Germany and Austria-Hungary collapsed. Germany went through a period of instability before the Weimar Republic was established. The Weimar Republic faced the burden of war reparations and an ailing economy. In response, the government started printing bank notes to pay its various obligations, spurring hyperinflation that lasted until late 1923, with disastrous economic consequences. In the same year, Adolf Hitler and General Erich Ludendorff attempted an unsuccessful coup d'état, which established Hitler as a known political figure in Germany.[58]

True, some of the new states that emerged from the ruins of the former Habsburg Empire were democratic, such as Czechoslovakia, but others were less so. In Hungary a short-lived Republic of the Councils[59] was created by the Bolsheviks, only to be replaced by an authoritarian regime of Admiral Horthy, who declared himself the Regent of the Kingdom of Hungary. Poland, too, initially started as a democracy and took a turn, in the 1930s, towards authoritarianism. Its elections were rigged, freedom of the press was limited, and restrictions were placed on political competition. In 1930, the leaders of Poland's center-left opposition were accused of plotting an anti-government coup. In the subsequent Brest Trials, they were given a choice between prison sentences and emigration. In Italy, Benito Mussolini acceded to power in 1922 and created a dictatorship that would later serve as a model for Nazi Germany and the Francoist regime in Spain. Following the Great Depression, the accession of Adolf Hitler to power in Germany, and waves of political violence across the Soviet Union, the stage was set for what became the biggest bloodbath in human history.

Much like in the case of free trade, the democratic advances made in 19th- and 20th-century Europe, populated by sovereign nation-states, were not robust. Bad leaders, bad ideologies, and international conflicts repeatedly undid the painstakingly attained advances that had extended political representation and individual rights to broader groups of Europeans. Scruton does not think blaming the geopolitical catastrophes of the 20th century on the nation-state makes much sense:

> [I]t identifies the normality of the nation state through its pathological versions. As Chesterton has argued about patriotism generally, to condemn patriotism to go to war for patriotic reasons, is like condemning love because some loves lead to murder. The nation state should not be understood in terms of the French nation at the Revolution or the German nation in its twentieth-century frenzy. For those were nations gone mad, in which the springs of civil peace had been poisoned and the social organism colonized by anger, resentment and fear.[60]

But such blasé attitude is unwarranted. In evaluating the performance of alternative social arrangements, one does not get to cherry-pick the evidence to make it consistent with one's preconceptions. Wars, instability, and 20th-century totalitarianism are *as much* a part of the historical record of Europe's nation-states as the previous advances in extending suffrage, protecting individual rights, and fostering economic freedom. Of course, Scruton's idea of national loyalty is not irrelevant, and neither do nation-states belong in the dustbin of history. But Europe's history does show us that the performance of nation-states, when unconstrained by international political arrangements, has been mixed—and sometimes plain catastrophic. In any discussion of the EU's many flaws, the organization ought to be judged against that very conflicted baseline, not against an airbrushed vision of the nation-state, based on a selective reading of history.

In chapter 2, I suggest that the unimpressive record of fully sovereign nation-states compared with that of the EU—both in securing free trade and promoting democracy on the continent—is not accidental. The EU, much like other international political arrangements, serves as a "commitment device." In short, it enables policymakers to stick with policies that might be politically inconvenient but socially beneficial. Before the existence of the EU, trade openness on the conti-

nent hinged only on the benevolence and enlightenment of politicians—and on their resistance to pressure groups. In a Europe of bilateral trade agreements, there were no collective mechanisms to punish
protectionists, which would not simultaneously inflict the pain of economic protectionism on every country involved. Likewise, even as Europe's nation-states were becoming more democratic, there were no
sanctions, formal or informal, imposed on leaders who deviated from
the basic standards of democratic governance. Authoritarians were typically accorded the same treatment as democratically elected leaders.
Anything else, after all, would have been an instance of meddling in the
internal affairs of sovereign states. The stringency of the EU Copenhag-
en Criteria applied to prospective members, or the recoil Europeans
felt when Jörg Haider's far-right FPÖ in Austria joined the government
in 1999,[61] shows the magnitude of the change that Europe has seen
over the past 70 years.

I am not arguing that the EU's democratic deficit is nonexistent. In
the EU's present form, the decisions taken by European institutions
often seem disconnected from the popular will of Europeans. The long-
standing culture of closed-door summits of the European Council, an-
nouncing major policy decisions as *faits accomplis* to the befuddled
European public, is one factor that has contributed to this perception,
together with the perception that the EU is ultimately driven by decisions of the leaders of Germany and France, not through a pan-European political process. The European Commission, the EU's powerful
executive body, is largely insulated from the political accountability and
constant scrutiny that characterize elected governments. In spite of
attempts to make its functioning more transparent and open, its reputation has never fully recovered since Jacques Santer's presidency, which
was marked by scandals surrounding the Commission's financial mis-
management.[62] The European Parliament, in turn, has faced a continuous decline in public support, illustrated by falling rates of electoral
participation, perhaps because of the parliament's very limited role in
the actual legislative process.[63] Because the EU lacks a clearly delimit-
ed federalist structure and effective judicial review, Europeans have
little reason to believe that the layer of decision making at the European level is democratic—or fully independent of the realpolitik of the
EU's most powerful member states. The perception of this democratic
deficit, exaggerated though it might often be, is perhaps the most signif-

icant flaw of the European construction and might cause its ultimate downfall. To correct it, Europe needs to reform its formal institutions and strengthen a European culture of political legitimacy and consent: a European sense of self-governance. The road towards building such formal and informal institutions is long and complicated, but that is not a reason for ditching what the process of European integration has already accomplished.

The idea that a Europe of sovereign nation-states is self-evidently superior to a Europe in which countries are bound by common political institutions has little grounding in history and relies mainly on nostalgia for an imaginary past. Without its shared political institutions, the continent was largely protectionist. Its progress in building institutions of liberal democracy was limited and marked by frequent setbacks. Instead of the facile opposition between the nation-state and the "panglossian universalism," which purportedly characterizes supranational forms of governance, it is more fruitful to acknowledge the need for a plurality of overlapping forms of governance, local, nation-state-based, and international, with the appropriate versions of political identities and loyalties that these might carry. To be sure, these forms of governance sometimes interact in the ways described by Eurosceptics. The creation of international institutions might easily weaken or endanger governance at lower levels. One only needs to think of the likely effect that the introduction of the euro had on fiscal responsibility in Eurozone countries.[64] But such erosion is not the norm. Oftentimes, the various levels of governance are mutually reinforcing. During the existence of the EU, democracy and the rule of law in its member states have grown stronger than in any point in their prior history. That, as I argue in chapter 2, has not been an accident.

In his essay defending the nation-state, Scruton argues that "[t]he wise policy is to accept the arrangements, however imperfect, that have evolved through custom and inheritance, to improve them by small adjustments, but not to jeopardize them by large-scale alterations the consequences of which nobody can really envisage."[65] This quintessentially conservative maxim can be applied to the EU as well. Its institutions are not a product of a constructivist plan, as some might believe, but are themselves a result of 70 years of an iterative process conducted by democratically elected European leaders. It is difficult to think of any more ambitious, larger-scale alteration of the existing political order in Europe than that of discarding the project of European integration altogether. As this short excursion into Europe's modern history has shown—however flawed the currently existing EU institutions might appear—they have no perfect alternatives.

NOTES

1. Krugman, "The Twinkie Manifesto."
2. See Field, *A Great Leap Forward*.
3. Ferguson, "Sinking Globalization."
4. On transitions of these countries to democracy, see O'Donnell et al., *Transitions from Authoritarian Rule: Southern Europe*.
5. Hayek, "The Economic Conditions of Interstate Federalism," 269.
6. Ibid.
7. For additional context, see Coppolaro, "The European Economic Community in the GATT Negotiations."
8. It is perhaps possible to argue that Algeria and Saint Barthélemy withdrew from the EC when they gained independency. Furthermore, in 1985, Greenland left the EC after a dispute over fishing rights but much of the EU statutes still apply because of its nature as a territory of Denmark.
9. Smith, *An Inquiry into the Nature and Causes of the Wealth of Nations*, 471.
10. Allen, "Mercantilism."
11. Mun, *England's Treasure by Forraign Trade*.
12. For a discussion of the political economy of mercantilism, see Ekelund and Tollison, *Politicized Economies*.
13. Henderson, "The Anglo-French Commercial Treaty of 1786."
14. See Davis, "The Rise of Protection in England."
15. Nye, *War, Wine, and Taxes*.
16. See O'Rourke, "The Worldwide Economic Impact."
17. A classic discussion of liberalization of trade in the 19th century is provided by Kindleberger, "The Rise of Free Trade in Western Europe."
18. For a biography of Cobden written by a writer and politician sympathetic to his views, see Morley, *The Life of Richard Cobden*.
19. For an assessment of the repeal and the historical context, see Sharp, "1846 and All That."
20. Lampe et al., *How Much Trade Liberalization Was There*.
21. Flandreau, "The History of Spaghetti."

22. See Nye, "The Myth of Free-Trade Britain and Fortress France," 26.

23. See Röpke, *International Order and Economic Integration*, 18.

24. This amounted to 5 billion francs. See Wawro, *The Franco-Prussian War*, 305.

25. For an analysis of the agricultural dimension of the tariff and of the coalition supporting it, see Webb, "Agricultural Protection in Wilhelminian Germany." More on the politics can be found in Schonhardt-Bailey, "Parties and Interests in the 'Marriage of Iron and Rye.'"

26. A classic treatment is provided by Golob, *The Meline Tariff*. The tariff was highly discriminatory to particular commodities and countries. See Becuwe and Blancheton, "The Dispersion of Customs Tariffs in France."

27. Lal, "The Threat to Economic Liberty from International Organizations," 503–4.

28. Ludwig von Mises Institute, "The Global Perspective," 4.

29. Mises, *The Historical Setting of the Austrian School of Economics*, 13.

30. O'Rourke, "British Trade Policy in the 19th Century," 829.

31. Findlay and O'Rourke, "Commodity Market Integration," 35.

32. O'Rourke, "Europe and the Causes of Globalization," Table 4.

33. A tragedy of the commons refers to a situation in which individual pursuit of rational self-interest leads to outcomes that go against the best interests of the whole, such as by depleting some common resource. In this case, the commons that was being destroyed was the freedom of trade among European nations. For the original formulation of the problem, see Hardin, "The Tragedy of the Commons."

34. Eichengreen and Irwin, "The Slide to Protectionism in the Great Depression."

35. Hynes et al., "Commodity Market Disintegration in the Interwar Period." Röpke shows that in 1934 global trade flows were already smaller than in 1913. See Röpke, *International Economic Disintegration*, 24.

36. Röpke, *International Order and Economic Integration*, 225–30.

37. The idea is not unknown on the continent as well, even though there it tends to be associated more frequently with ethnocentric nationalism. For a blend of the two, see Baudet, *The Significance of Borders*.

38. Scruton, *England and the Need for Nations*, 22–23.

39. Knight, "Ethics and Economic Reform," 55.

40. See his influential book *Imagined Communities*.

41. Even Kenneth Minogue, a thinker with impeccable conservative credentials, admits that nation-state is an abstraction, not something that ever existed in a pure form. See Minogue, "Two Concepts of Citizenship."

42. Evidence for why the trade-off between national sovereignty and supranational governance is not a zero-sum game is provided also by Zürn, "Democratic Governance Beyond the Nation-State."

43. On the Swiss experience with multilingual democracy, see Lacey, "Must Europe Be Swiss?"

44. A similar argument is offered by Innerarity, "Does Europe Need a Demos to Be Truly Democratic?"

45. Some argue that the two levels of political identity are mutually reinforcing. See Hoffmann, "Reflections on the Nation-State in Western Europe Today."

46. Some scholars argue that a distinction needs to be made between explicit identification with the European project and the increasingly pervasive identification with the EU in everyday life. See Cram, "Does the EU Need a Navel?" See also McNamara, *The Politics of Everyday Europe*. Siedentop's prescient book provides a compelling discussion of the strong points of the European project, as well as an assessment of the real deficit that the EU has in terms of creating a common European culture of consent. Siedentop, *Democracy in Europe*.

47. Scruton, *England and the Need for Nations*, 29.

48. Ibid., 30.

49. Klaus, speech in the European Parliament.

50. Economist Intelligence Unit, Democracy Index.

51. Freedom House, "Freedom in the World."

52. World Bank, Worldwide Governance Indicators.

53. Rohac, "The Unanimity Rule and Religious Fractionalization in the Polish-Lithuanian Republic."

54. See North and Weingast, "Constitutions and Commitment."

55. See also Przeworski, "Conquered or Granted?"

56. See Acemoglu and Robinson, "Why Did the West Extend the Franchise?" 1183.

57. Ibid., 1184. For a book-long treatment, see Acemoglu and Robinson, *Economic Origins of Dictatorship and Democracy*.

58. Gordon, *Hitler and the Beer Hall Putsch*.

59. Janos and Slottman, *Revolution in Perspective*.

60. Scruton, *England and the Need for Nations*, 3.

61. Freeman, "Austria: The 1999 Parliament Elections."

62. Topan, "The Resignation of the Santer-Commission."

63. In the "ordinary legislative procedure" used for a dominant part of directives and regulations adopted by the EU, legislation is proposed by the European Commission, not by members of the European Parliament.

64. On this topic, see Sinn, *The Euro Trap*.

65. Scruton, *England and the Need for Nations*, 2–3.

REFERENCES

Acemoglu, Daron, and James A. Robinson. "Why Did the West Extend the Franchise? Democracy, Inequality, and Growth in a Historical Perspective." *Quarterly Journal of Economics* 115 (2000): 1167–99.

———. *Economic Origins of Dictatorship and Democracy*. Cambridge, UK: Cambridge University Press, 2009.

Allen, William R. "Mercantilism." In *The New Palgrave: A Dictionary of Economics*, vol. 3, edited by John Eatwell, Murray Milgate, and Peter Newman, 445–48. London: Palgrave Macmillan, 1987.

Anderson, Benedict R. *Imagined Communities: Reflections on the Origin and Spread of Nationalism*, revised and extended edition. London: Verso, 1991.

Baudet, Thierry. *The Significance of Borders: Why Representative Government and the Rule of Law Require the Nation State*. Leiden: Martinus Nijhoff Publishers/Brill Academic, 2012.

Becuwe, Stéphane, and Bertrand Blancheton. "The Dispersion of Customs Tariffs in France Between 1850 and 1913: Discrimination in Trade Policy." In *Research in Economic History*, vol. 30, edited by Christopher Hanes and Susan Wolcott, 163–83. Somerville: Emerald Group Publishing, 2014.

Coppolaro, Lucia. "The European Economic Community in the GATT Negotiations of the Kennedy Round (1964–1967): Global and Regional Trade." In *Inside the European Community: Actors and Policies in the European Integration 1957–1973*, edited by Antonio Varsori, 347–66. Baden-Baden: Nomos, 2006.

Cram, Laura. "Does the EU Need a Navel? Implicit and Explicit Identification with the European Union." *Journal of Common Market Studies* 50 (2012): 71–86.

Davis, Ralph. "The Rise of Protection in England, 1689–1786." *Economic History Review* 19 (1966): 306–17.

Economist Intelligence Unit. Democracy Index 2014. http://www.eiu.com/public/topical_report.aspx?campaignid=Democracy0115.

Eichengreen, Barry, and Douglas A. Irwin. "The Slide to Protectionism in the Great Depression: Who Succumbed and Why?" NBER Working Paper No. 15142, 2009.

Ekelund, Robert B, Jr., and Robert D. Tollison. *Politicized Economies: Monarchy, Monopoly and Mercantilism*. College Station: Texas A&M University Press, 1997.

Ferguson, Niall. "Sinking Globalization." *Foreign Affairs*, March/April 2005. https://www.foreignaffairs.org/articles/2005-03-01/sinking-globalization.

Field, Alexander. *A Great Leap Forward: 1930s Depression and U.S. Economic Growth*. New Haven CT: Yale University Press, 2011.

Findlay, Ronald, and Kevin H. O'Rourke. "Commodity Market Integration, 1500–2000." NBER Working Paper No. 8579, November 2001.

Flandreau, Marc. "The History of Spaghetti." *VoxEU*, August 23, 2008. http://www.voxeu.org/article/failure-history-s-most-celebrated-bilateral-trade-agreement.

Freedom House. *Freedom in the World*, 2015. https://freedomhouse.org/report-types/freedom-world.

Freeman, Heather B. "Austria: The 1999 Parliament Elections and the European Union Members' Sanctions." *Boston College International and Comparative Law Review* 25 (2002): 109–24.

Golob, Eugene O. *The Méline Tariff: French Agriculture and Nationalist Economic Policy*. New York: University of Columbia Press, 1944.

Gordon, Harold J., Jr. *Hitler and the Beer Hall Putsch*. Princeton: Princeton University Press, 1972.

Hardin, Garrett. "The Tragedy of the Commons." *Science* 162 (1968):1243–48.

Hayek, Friedrich A. von. "The Economic Conditions of Interstate Federalism." In *Individualism and Economic Order*, 255–72. Chicago: University of Chicago Press, 1948.

Henderson, William O. "The Anglo-French Commercial Treaty of 1786." *Economic History Review* 10 (1957): 104–12.

Hoffmann, Stanley. "Reflections on the Nation-State in Western Europe Today." *Journal of Common Market Studies* 21 (1982): 21–38.

Hynes, William, David S. Jacks, and Kevin H. O'Rourke. "Commodity Market Disintegration in the Interwar Period." NBER Working Paper No. 14767, March 2009.

Innerarity, Daniel. "Does Europe Need a Demos to Be Truly Democratic?" LSE "Europe in Question" Discussion Paper No. 77, July 2014.

Janos, Andrew C., and William Slottman (eds). *Revolution in Perspective: Essays on the Hungarian Soviet Republic of 1919*. Berkeley: University of California Press, 1971.

Kindleberger, Charles P. "The Rise of Free Trade in Western Europe, 1820–1875." *Journal of Economic History* 35 (1975): 20–55.

Klaus, Václav. Speech in the European Parliament, February 19, 2009. http://www.klaus.cz/clanky/310.

Knight, Frank. "Ethics and Economic Reform." In *Freedom and Reform*, 55–153. Indianapolis, IN: Liberty Fund, 1982 [1939].

Krugman, Paul. "The Twinkie Manifesto." *New York Times*, November 18, 2012. http://www.nytimes.com/2012/11/19/opinion/krugman-the-twinkie-manifesto.html.

Lacey, Joseph. "Must Europe Be Swiss? On the Idea of a Voting Space and the Possibility of a Multilingual Demos." *British Journal of Political Science* 44 (2014): 61–82.

Lal, Deepak. "The Threat to Economic Liberty from International Organizations." *Cato Journal* 25 (2005): 503–20.

Lampe, Markus, Felipe Tâmega Fernandes, and Antonio Tena-Junguito. "How Much Trade Liberalization Was There in the World Before and After Cobden-Chevalier?" Paper presented to the "New Perspectives on the Great Specialization in the Nineteenth Century: Growth, Welfare and Interdependence" conference, University of California, Davis, May 6–7, 2011. http://www.iga.ucdavis.edu/Research/CEGE/cege-conference-2011/How%20much%20trade%20liberalization%20_8_x.pdf/at_download/file.

Ludwig von Mises Institute. "The Global Perspective. Interview with Sudha Shenoy." *Austrian Economics Newsletter*, Winter 2003.

McNamara, Kathleen. *The Politics of Everyday Europe: Constructing Authority in the European Union*. Oxford: Oxford University Press, 2015.

Minogue, Kenneth. "Two Concepts of Citizenship." In *Citizenship East and West*, edited by André Liebich, Daniel Warner, and Jasna Dragovic, 9–22. London: Kegan Paul International, 1995.

Mises, Ludwig von. *The Historical Setting of the Austrian School of Economics*. Auburn: Ludwig von Mises Institute, 2003 [1969].

Morley, John. *The Life of Richard Cobden*. London: T. Fisher Unwin, 1905.

Mun, Thomas. *England's Treasure by Forraign Trade, or The Ballance of our Forraign Trade Is the Rule of Our Treasure*. London: Macmillan, 1895 [1664].

North, Douglass C., and Barry R. Weingast. "Constitutions and Commitment: The Evolution of Institutional Governing Public Choice in Seventeenth-Century England." *Journal of Economic History* 49 (1989): 803–32.

Nye, John V. C. *War, Wine, and Taxes: The Political Economy of Anglo-French Trade, 1689–1900*. Princeton NJ: Princeton University Press, 2007.

———. "The Myth of Free-Trade Britain and Fortress France: Tariffs and Trade in the Nineteenth Century." *Journal of Economic History* 51 (1991): 23–46.

O'Donnell, Guillermo, Philippe C. Schmitter, and Laurence Whitehead, eds. *Transitions from Authoritarian Rule: Southern Europe*. Baltimore: Johns Hopkins University Press, 1986.

O'Rourke, Kevin H. "Europe and the Causes of Globalization, 1790–2000." In *From Europeanization of the Globe to the Globalization of Europe*, edited by Henryk Kierzkowski, 64–86. London: Palgrave, 2002.

————. "The Worldwide Economic Impact of the French Revolutionary and Napoleonic Wars, 1793–1815." *Journal of Global History* 1 (2006): 123–49.

————. "British Trade Policy in the 19th Century: A Review Article." *European Journal of Political Economy* 16 (2000): 829–42.

Przeworski, Adam. "Conquered or Granted? A History of Suffrage Extensions." *British Journal of Political Science* 39 (2009): 291–321.

Rohac, Dalibor. "The Unanimity Rule and Religious Fractionalisation in the Polish-Lithuanian Republic." *Constitutional Political Economy* 19 (2008): 111–28.

Röpke, Wilhelm. *International Economic Disintegration*. London: William Hodge, 1942.

————. *International Order and Economic Integration*. Dordrecht: D. Reidel, 1959.

Schonhardt-Bailey, Cheryl. "Parties and Interests in the 'Marriage of Iron and Rye.'" *British Journal of Political Science* 2 (1998): 291–332.

Scruton, Roger. *England and the Need for Nations*, 2nd ed. London: Institute for the Study of Civil Society, 2006.

Sharp, Paul. "1846 and All That: The Rise and Fall of British Wheat Protection in the Nineteenth Century." *Agricultural History Review* 58 (2010): 76–94.

Siedentop, Larry. *Democracy in Europe*. New York: University of Columbia Press, 2002.

Sinn, Hans-Werner. *The Euro Trap: On Bursting Bubbles, Budgets, and Beliefs*. Oxford: Oxford University Press, 2014.

Smith, Adam. *An Inquiry into the Nature and Causes of the Wealth of Nations*, Vol. I, edited by Roy H. Campbell and Andrew S. Skinner. Indianapolis: Liberty Fund, 1981 [1776].

Topan, Angelina. "The Resignation of the Santer-Commission: The Impact of 'Trust' and 'Reputation.'" *European Integration Online Papers*, 6, 2002. http://eiop.or.at/eiop/pdf/2002-014.pdf.

Wawro, Geoffrey. *The Franco-Prussian War: The German Conquest of France in 1870–1871*. Cambridge: Cambridge University Press, 2005.

Webb, Steven B. "Agricultural Protection in Wilhelminian Germany: Forging an Empire with Pork and Rye." *Journal of Economic History* 42 (1982): 309–26.

World Bank. Worldwide Governance Indicators, 2015. http://info.worldbank.org/governance/wgi/index.aspx#home.

Zürn, Michael. "Democratic Governance Beyond the Nation-State: The EU and Other International Institutions." *European Journal of International Relations* 6 (2000): 183–221.

6

BETTER OFF OUT?

When communism was nearing its collapse, Yugoslavia seemed one of the more promising countries beyond the Iron Curtain. With its beautiful Dalmatian Coast, it enjoyed a steady stream of revenue from tourism, with visitors not just from the socialist bloc but also from Western Europe. Unlike others in the Soviet bloc, Yugoslavia pursued a policy of "market socialism," trying to combine elements of central planning with those of a market economy. Although the model led to high rates of inflation and unemployment (the latter virtually unheard of in other centrally planned economies), it exposed the country to private markets, investment, and entrepreneurship. Furthermore, because of domestic unemployment, in the 1980s more than 500,000 Yugoslav nationals were working in other European countries, including some 340,000 in West Germany.[1]

The experience of capitalism at home, together with a vibrant tourism industry and remittances from abroad, should have given Yugoslavia an edge over the more thoroughly Sovietized countries of the region. Instead, as the country plunged deeper into a crisis at the end of the 1980s, its constituent republics began to drift apart, both due to pressure from bottom-up movements within civil society and because of differences between the communist leadership in Serbia and those in in the smaller republics. In 1990, parliamentary elections were held across the country. With the exception of Serbia and Montenegro, where incumbents successfully clung to power, communist candidates were voted out and, one by one, the Yugoslav republics started declaring independence. Slovenia was first, triggering a short-lived armed conflict that resulted in the withdrawal of Yugoslav federal troops. But more were to come, not least because of Yugoslavia's multiethnic nature that left sizeable Serbian minorities stranded in the newly independent republics. A series of incidents led to an ethnic conflict in Croatia, and more significantly in Bosnia and Herzegovina, where more than 100,000 were killed before the war's end in 1995, including 38,000 mostly Bosniak civilians.[2]

The disintegration of Yugoslavia did not have to end in bloodshed. In my native country, some 300 miles north of Sarajevo, Czech and Slovak leaders agreed in the summer of 1992 to divide the common Czechoslovak state into two independent republics. Most Czechs and Slovaks opposed the split.[3] However, the future of the Czechoslovak federation seemed impossible because of the wide disagreements between Czech and Slovak leaders about its constitutional reforms and about the strategy for economic transition. Those, in turn, reflected deep-seated differences in public opinion in the two parts of the country.[4] Although border checkpoints emerged on the Czechoslovak border in 1993, many of the advantages of the common state remained in place. Slovaks and Czechs were able to continue to access each other's labor markets and, unlike foreign students, Slovaks could study free of charge at Czech universities. Today, the two countries find themselves in the EU, and their cultural, economic, and social ties are as strong as ever.

It is unlikely that the end of the EU would resemble the bloody breakup of Yugoslavia, but there is no guarantee that it would go as smoothly as Czechoslovakia's "velvet divorce." More importantly, there is little control over the dynamics of such a process of disintegration. Nobody *planned* the wars in Yugoslavia or other calamities that nonetheless happened around the world because of bad political choices. There is no guarantee that the politicians who would orchestrate the EU's demise would be also determined to preserve, in some other form, its function as a "commitment device" ensuring free trade or free movement of capital and people. Commitment devices, after all, are not physical objects but social artifacts. The political costs and benefits of reneging on an international agreement that ensures, for example, free movement of people or goods in the EU are not objectively measurable variables. Instead, their magnitude depends on what people *think*.[5] Therefore, commitment devices and other social institutions perform their roles only insofar as a critical mass of people recognize them as legitimate and desirable. Similarly, the US dollar would stop functioning as a currency if enough Americans and foreigners came to the conclusion that some other medium of exchange should be performing this role. The EU might find itself in a situation where the political cost of reneging on a particular commitment by, for example, reintroducing restrictions in immigration from within the EU become very low, if only because people's perceptions of that cost will have changed. Instead of seeing free movement of goods, services, capital, and people as beneficial, European voters might very well conclude that these are harmful or threatening. In such a case—hardly unimaginable—reneging on treaties that bind EU member states together would become a winning political proposition, even if it imposed sizeable social and economic costs. Given that even experts disagree about the effects of EU membership on economic and social outcomes, it is difficult to expect voters to objectively assess the costs and benefits of EU membership for their own lives. Voters will instead rely on mental shortcuts and heuristics. Those can easily lead, especially in times of social and political turmoil, to what social scientists describe as "availability cascades" (or the "bandwagon effect") through which the expressed perceptions concerning a given subject become more plausible merely by their rising availability in public discussions.[6]

As a result, one ought to worry not just about the demise of the EU but also about the ideological dynamics that would likely accompany such a demise. For all their good intentions, the free-market critics of the EU have little control over the appeal of ideas that the public associates with the EU and with its disintegration. The fearmongering and xenophobia to which the refugee crisis has given rise or the economic nationalism displayed by the likes of the Front National could easily become the dominant narrative through which European electorates view the prospects of a post-EU world. The breed of politics that this ideological shift has empowered dampens the hopes for a soft-landing scenario, in which the unequivocally beneficial parts of the EU's architecture, such as the single market, would be preserved.

If the entire matter boiled down to a decision over whether, for example, the UK should leave the EU to become a member of the EEA, like Norway, there would be little reason for panic. *Other things being equal*, Brexit is unlikely to lead to major economic dislocations.

However, unlike in economic theory, which relies on the idea of *ceteris paribus* as its key element, in politics other things are *never* equal. The biggest risks related to exit do not lie in the possible economic disruptions but in the potential destruction of the platform for cooperation and conflict settlement between European countries, which the EU represents. Such an outcome is not inevitable. However, an exit from the EU or its dissolution must be evaluated not just by the results that they would produce under a best-case scenario, but also by their outcomes under less-than-ideal circumstances.

THE COST OF EXIT

Economists do not make decisions about public policy on a whim. Instead, they rely on a comparison of benefits and costs. Unfortunately, while cost-benefit analysis is useful, especially for assessing individual pieces of legislation, it is only of limited avail for assessing tectonic political changes surrounded by many sources of uncertainty. The breakup of the EU is a prime example of such a large-scale dislocation. Unsurprisingly, few completely satisfactory analyses of such a scenario exist. However, multiple studies purport to estimate the economic effects of Brexit on the UK economy, perhaps because it is the only country where exit has been not just contemplated as a theoretical possibility, but also embraced by a substantial part of the political elite.[7] The contours of these studies tend to be similar. They see the EU as an institutional arrangement that generates both benefits and costs. Leaving the EU would relieve the UK of some of these costs, but deprive it of some of the benefits of membership. The studies then make a range of different assumptions about the magnitude of these costs and benefits and about the economic policy changes that would follow a potential Brexit. They typically shy away from an explicit discussion of the political dynamics that leaving the EU would trigger.

One area where the cost-benefit studies of membership and potential exit become murky is in assigning monetary values to the costs and benefits in question. It may be straightforward to compute the net contribution that the UK makes into the EU budget every year—£9.8 billion in 2014, up from around £3.3 billion in 2008.[8] But it is much more difficult to estimate the benefits derived from access to the EU's single market, which would likely be reduced if the UK leaves. Considerable uncertainty surrounds some critical questions of Brexit. How much of the existing trade with the EU would be preserved? Would the UK lower trade barriers with non-EU countries, which is currently impossible under the common external tariff? What would happen to EU migrant workers living in the UK and conversely to Britons living in Europe? And what economic impact would it have? Assuming we know how heavy the burden of the EU regulation is, how much of it would be relieved if the UK left? If the UK withdrew from the Union's Common Agricultural Policy, would it mean an end to all agricultural subsidies, or would a national system of agricultural protectionism emerge instead? Nobody knows the answers to these questions. As a result, any supposedly clear-cut estimate on the economic effects of Brexit, regardless of the direction in which it goes, should be treated with a heavy dose of caution.

Table 6.1 presents the findings of several studies that attempt to provide such estimates. Estimates of the effects of Brexit vary from negative to decidedly positive. A group of authors at the London School of Economics' Centre for Economic Performance, for example, argue that in the worst-case scenario Brexit could cost the UK almost 10 percent of GDP.[9] In contrast, Tim Congdon, an economist affiliated with UKIP, claims that Brexit could *boost* the country's GDP by almost 12 percent.[10] Other studies, such as the one by economist Brian Hindley and legal scholar Martin Howe, published by the Institute of Economic Affairs in 2001, argue that the net costs (or benefits) of EU membership are very small—less than 1 percent of GDP.[11]

One may wonder about the extent to which the results of what ought to be dispassionate, technical exercises are driven by the underlying preferences of the studies' authors. Suffice it to say that because of the complexity of the subject at hand, many judgment calls are required to arrive at any quantitative conclusions, both about the size of the costs and benefits of different features of EU membership but also about methodology, providing ample space for analytical decisions to be driven by hidden biases or ideological preconceptions. Some of the studies cited in Table 6.1 provide a simple static accounting of the likely effects of membership and/or withdrawal, whereas others try to capture the dynamic, second-order effects that leaving the EU would have on trade and investment flows. Depending on how one models them, those can either amplify or moderate the initial shock through structural adjustments that would occur in the economy. In short, because of their largely speculative character, the cost-benefit studies of Brexit are among the best illustration of what the economic historian Deirdre McCloskey once called the A-prime/C-prime theorem: "For each and every set of assumptions A implying a conclusion C, there exists a set of alternative assumptions A', arbitrarily close to A, such that A' implies an alternative conclusion, C', arbitrarily far from C."[12]

Other comprehensive studies, such as the one published by the Centre for European Reform (2014),[13] do not provide numerical estimates but suggest that Brexit would leave the UK worse off. In any event, the range of different estimates reflect a variety of assumptions about the EU, the UK, and the conditions of its possible withdrawal.

If anything can be said about Brexit with certainty, it is that it would create considerable uncertainty about the future path of public policy in the UK, difficult to capture in conventional cost-benefit exercises. If Britons vote to leave, lengthy negotiations will ensue about the conditions of the UK departure from the bloc. Those would raise questions about the future path of a whole range of policies affecting government spending, regulation, and trade. Uncertainty about future policy has important effects on investors' decisions and ultimately on economic

Table 6.1.   Estimates of Costs of EU Membership and/or Brexit

Minford et al. (2005).	EU membership costs the UK 3.2 to 3.7 percent of GDP.
Dhingra et al. (2015).	Brexit will reduce UK's GDP by 1.1 to 3.1 percent, and possibly more if it slows down productivity growth.
Ottaviano et al. (2014).	Brexit would decrease UK's GDP by 2.2 to 9.5 percent of GDP.
Congdon (2013).	EU membership costs the UK 11.5 percent of GDP.
Leach (2000).	EU membership costs the UK 1.75 percent of GDP.
Pain and Young (2004).	Brexit would decrease UK's GDP by 2.25 percent.
Booth et al. (2015)	Brexit could affect UK's GDP anywhere between decreasing by 2.2 percent and increasing it by 1.6 percent.
Milne (2004).	Brexit would increase UK's GDP by £17 billion to £40 billion (or 1.4 to 3.2 percent of GDP).
Hindley and Howe (2001).	The net benefit or cost of Brexit would be less than 1 percent of GDP.

activity.[14] Given the importance of financial services to the UK economy, for example, the lack of clarity about the future regulatory climate guiding the UK financial sector could lead banks and other financial institutions to leave London. The UK currently has significant influence within the European Banking Authority, a regulator based in London. "[I]t seems highly implausible that the rest of the EU would allow the City of London simply to play the same role as it does now with respect to the EU, if EU financial regulation no longer applies," writes economist Jonathan Portes,[15] director of the UK National Institute of Economic and Social Research. A substantial downside risk is related, he points out, to London's role as a gateway for financial companies that provide their services in the EU. If the UK decided to withdraw from the common regulatory structures, that appeal would be lost.

The decisions about what parts of the EU's regulatory structures would still apply would matter more than the risk posed by the resurgence of conventional trade protectionism. Even if no particular trade agreement was negotiated between the EU and the UK, the tariffs faced by British exporters would not be prohibitive. The weighted mean tariff rate is 1 percent, according to the World Bank,[16] unlikely to cause a significant disruption to UK-EU trade on its own.

Critics of the EU point to the large amount of legislation originating in Brussels that the UK must accept, including that guiding the functioning of the single market, as evidence of the loss of sovereignty that EU membership entails. The UK would be free to disregard any such legislation if it left. But the critics forget to add that the regulation is also a price that the UK is paying to access the single market. If the UK tries to preserve its access by joining the European Economic Area (EEA)—much like Norway, Iceland, or Liechtenstein—it will still be subject to the bulk of European legislation, and will have to contribute to the EU budget. In contrast to the status quo, however, it would no longer have any say in the creation of such legislation. The Norwegian political scientist Erik O. Eriksen reflected on the experience of his own country: "Approximately three quarters of the legislation that applies to the member states applies also to Norway. New agreements have been established over time, and existing agreements have been developed and expanded. Their cumulative effects are large and convoluted."[17] It is not the case, he claims, that having stayed outside has boosted Norway's independence. "On the contrary: Norway has relinquished sovereignty in a number of areas through regular majority voting, it pays (through the EEA financial contributions) and is subject to EU law on the same basis as the EU member states."[18]

True, the UK would not *have to* participate in the EEA to retain its access to the single market. Instead, like Switzerland, it could negotiate its access through separate bilateral agreements. But that would not solve the problem with EU regulation, either. As long as the UK wanted to export goods—and possibly services—to the EU, it would need to abide by the rules of the single market. Switzerland retains formal sovereignty over its legislation, but in reality a dominant (and growing) proportion of Switzerland's new laws and regulations results from simply transposing EU laws into its own legal system.[19] Even in an extreme case where no agreement between the two was made on regulatory matters and *all* European legislation was formally repudiated from the UK legal system, British businesses with a presence on the continent would continue to be affected by the EU regulation de facto.

One way—and possibly the only way—around this problem would be to deliberately reorient exports to other parts of the world. But that would only mean that British exporters would need to comply with economic regulation coming from *other* sources, without having any say in their content. At present, the UK is exporting relatively little to other EU countries, with EU exports accounting for only 47.9 percent of its total exports. In Germany, that figure is 57.7 percent, in France 60.3 percent, in Spain 63.8 percent, and in Portugal 70.9 percent. The new member states in the East are the most tightly integrated of all: 82.2 percent of all Czech exports and 84.4 percent of Slovak exports go to other EU countries.[20] Even if British Eurosceptics make a plausible argument about the reorientation of British exports to markets overseas, any attempts to extrapolate the UK's experience to other countries will be misleading. Economies that are tightly integrated into the single market would simply need to continue to largely abide by the *acquis communautaire* as long as they wanted to maintain their commercial ties with the EU.

The advocates of Brexit put a lot of faith in the success of the bilateral trade agreements that the UK would negotiate with third countries if it were no longer bound by the EU's common external tariff. "The EU," writes Daniel Hannan, "has to weigh the interests of Italian textile manufacturers, French filmmakers, Polish farmers. Even Germany likes to defend its analogue-era giants against American Internet challengers such as Google, Amazon, Facebook and Uber."[21] Unencumbered by such considerations, it is argued, the UK could pursue a much more aggressive liberalization policy. It is true that the UK government, or the government of any country leaving the EU, could unilaterally open its markets to imports from third countries, as long as influential interest groups would allow it. But unilateral liberalization will not help in gaining access to markets overseas. It is not obvious that the world's largest economies, such as the United States, China, or Japan, are inclined to engage in protracted trade negotiations with the UK in order to offer it a better deal than to the EU as a whole. When asked about the possible trade arrangement with the UK following Brexit, US Trade Representative Michael Froman stated that the US had "no [free-trade agreement] with the UK so they would be subject to the same tariffs— and other trade-related measures—as China, or Brazil or India," adding that there was not much appetite in Washington to engage in separate trade negotiations with the UK that would give it privileged access to the US market.[22] Even if special arrangements might be conceivable in the British case, they are almost certainly out of the question for the smaller countries on the European continent, which exercise only miniscule bargaining power vis-à-vis the world's leading economies, such as the United States, China, and Japan.

It is also worth noting that the analytical exercises that try to estimate the effects of Brexit on the UK economy do not measure the economic effects of what Eurosceptics really want: a complete end of the EU. Imagine that the current EU, together with all its burdensome legislation, were scrapped one day. European countries could conclude free-trade agreements with each other. However, unless a common set of rules for the single market were maintained in some form, regulatory barriers would mushroom across the continent. Total sovereignty for every EU country would lead to a multiplicity of regulatory regimes and therefore new obstacles to trade, investment, and entrepreneurship. Some countries might go down the road of aggressive deregulation. But the logic of public choice suggests that politicians would be tempted to use the reacquired sovereignty to other ends, especially if interest groups seized the EU's demise as an opportunity to regulate their foreign competitors out of existence.

WHITHER THE FOUR FREEDOMS?

Following an exit from the EU, one could expect more regulatory protectionism and more controls on capital flows and the cross-border provision of services. Without a tangible political commitment mechanism with penalties for noncompliance, nothing would keep politicians from succumbing to the temptations posed to them by interest groups demanding protection from foreign competition. However, freedom of movement of people provides the most obvious example of the direction in which the national policymaking would shift in absence of the checks provided by the EU.

There is evidence that the free movement of people within the EU has been overwhelmingly beneficial.[23] Yet there are strong pressures to close the borders of individual European countries not just to migration from the outside, but also to that from other EU states. These pressures have grown in the wake of the EU's refugee crisis and the Paris attacks, which have led to the reintroduction of border controls in some European countries. Unless European leaders arrive at a common solution, the refugee crisis risks destroying the Schengen system of free movement of people altogether.

Even without the refugee crisis, immigration, including immigration from within the EU, is one of the main drivers of support enjoyed by Eurosceptic political groups. Even those Eurosceptics who do not oppose the EU on xenophobic grounds often argue that European states should retain full control of their immigration systems. For some of them, the point is ostensibly not to close borders to immigrants, but rather to create a nondiscriminatory immigration system, which does not give automatic preference to migrants from the EU over those, for example, from India or Australia.[24] Whatever the details, it is exceedingly clear that free movement of people would be among the first victims of a withdrawal from the EU, either by the UK or by any other country.

Reasonable people may disagree about what immigration policy the EU should adopt with regard to third countries. Economists have provided evidence that substantial economic gains result from maintaining a relatively open-border policy.[25] At the same time, welfare systems and integration policies in European countries are not always geared towards a rapid integration of incomers and create cultural, economic, and sometimes literal ghettos. But whatever one thinks of immigration from *outside* the EU, it is hard to construct an intellectually credible case against free movement of people within the EU. A Europe that imposes restrictions on where Europeans can and cannot work will invariably be a much poorer Europe—not only economically. Yet it is exactly the kind of Europe that would emerge if the EU disintegrates.

If one is in any doubt about the prospects of the four freedoms in a post-EU Europe, one only needs to look at the policies advocated by some of the most prominent Eurosceptics across Europe. For Marine Le Pen, the protection of domestic production and industry is a cornerstone of her platform.[26] Even better, one can look at the actual policies implemented by Eurosceptic politicians when given the opportunity. In response to the financial crisis in Hungary, the government of Viktor Orbán pioneered a variety of "unorthodox" fiscal measures, including an Internet tax (later abandoned),[27] as well as levies that targeted foreign-owned media, telecoms, utilities, and banks. These triggered investigations by the European Commission, and in some cases legal action where they demonstrably discriminated between companies. Such was the case when he passed a special "health" tax targeted at tobacco companies and imposed a levy on corporate turnover. As a result, it hit companies with larger turnovers, most of them foreign-owned, harder than the low-turnover companies owned by domestic entrepreneurs.[28] Viktor Orbán's economic policies in Hungary, focused on state-led development and the promotion of strong domestic businesses shielded from international competition, is currently being emulated by the Law and Justice Party (PiS) in Poland. Andrzej Duda, the country's president and a member of PiS, argued that "Polish entrepreneurship should be protected and supported, for example by putting the tax burden on large networks of supermarkets, which in relation to their revenue pay peanuts in taxes. One needs a tax here."[29] Ahead of the 2015 parliamentary election in Poland, PiS promised such targeted levies, alongside a tax on the financial assets held by banks, also in large part under foreign ownership. The reliance on fiscal instruments, as opposed to other forms of protectionism, could perhaps be explained by the fact that governments in the EU have more leeway to organize their public finances how they see fit, rather than to introduce regulatory barriers, which could be incompatible with the rules of the single market. But it does not take much imagination to see that, absent the current EU supervision, the temptation of economic nationalism in many European countries would be much stronger than it is today.

IT'S POLITICS, STUPID

The UK is different from other European countries. For almost a thousand years, it has not been invaded by a foreign power. It has ancient, deeply rooted political institutions and a tradition of parliamentarianism, which evolved over centuries instead of being hastily put in place in order to satisfy the EU's Copenhagen Criteria. For all the headaches that Brexit could cause, including a reopening of the question of Scotland's independence, the UK is unlikely to see a fundamental deterioration of the rule of law or the quality of its democratic institutions following its exit from the EU. It is equally unlikely that the UK, with its tradition of classical liberalism, would fall prey to the delusions of economic nationalism and protectionism, or that it would become a threat to the security of Europe.

Regrettably, the same cannot be said of all EU countries. Until 1974, Greece was a military dictatorship. For 40 years, General Francisco Franco ruled Spain, while Portugal suffered under the regime of António de Salazar during roughly the same period. All of the new member states in Central and Eastern Europe had totalitarian, one-party political systems only 27 years ago. The success of their transitions to liberal democracy and the market was conditioned, among other factors, by the prospect of joining the EU. There was nothing inexorable about it, as shown by examples of failed transitions in Eastern Europe, such as Ukraine and Moldova.

Worryingly, some of the postcommunist countries that joined the EU have lately seen democratic backsliding. This is not due to the EU's democratic deficit or because of a nationalist backlash against the integration project, but rather thanks to the success of domestic strongmen. On the World Bank's measure of the rule of law, Hungary has seen a marked decline in recent years and performs worse than when the index was first created in 1996.[30] The quality of Hungary's democracy, as measured by Freedom House's Nations in Transit project, was downgraded in 2015 to the category of "Semi-Consolidated Democracies."[31] These developments cannot be separated from the policies put in place by Hungary's Prime Minister Viktor Orbán, who has embarked on a program of "national renewal." These policies include the controversial constitutional and electoral reforms that have empowered Orbán's party, Fidesz, in addition to a range of unconventional economic interventions. János Kornai, one of the most preeminent Hungarian economists and public intellectuals offers a dismal view of Hungary's developments, which is worth quoting at length:

> [T]he executive and legislative branches are no longer separate, as they are both controlled by the energetic and heavy hand of the political leader who has positioned himself at the very pinnacle of power: Viktor Orbán. No worthwhile preparatory work on bills is being done either within or outside the walls of Parliament. Parliament itself has turned into a law factory, and the production line is sometimes made to operate at unbelievable speed: between 2010 and 2014 no less than 88 bills made it from being introduced to being voted on within a week; in 13 cases it all happened on the same or the following day. Without exception, every single attempted investigation of the background of a scandal that has just broken, which would have been carried out objectively by a parliamentary committee with the effective involvement of the opposition, has been thwarted. "Reliable" people close to the center of power occupy decision-making positions even in organizations which are not legally under the control of the executive branch . . . : in the constitutional court, the state audit office, the fiscal council, the competition authority . . . , the ombudsman's office, and the central statistical office."[32]

Notwithstanding the flak that has been directed at him, Orbán is not, as the US Senator John McCain put it, a "neo-fascist dictator."[33] But as Hungary's recent history shows, one should not take liberal democracy in Europe for granted. More importantly, Hungary's story, just like the more recent developments in Poland, raises the question of whether its democratic backsliding would be more or less significant in the absence of the political commitment mechanisms represented by EU membership.

Of course, there is no rigorous, scientific way of answering that question. However, the experience of postcommunist countries that have not joined the EU provides some insight into the risks that liberal democracies of the region would face outside a pan-European system of political cooperation. At the beginning of the 1990s, after the fall of communism, Ukraine and Moldova were similar in their levels of economic development and the quality of their infant democracies to their neighbors in the West, such as Poland or Romania. Twenty-five years into the postcommunist transition, the difference between these countries and their neighbors, which have joined the EU, could not be starker. While Poland and Ukraine had the same per-capita income in 1990, an average Pole today is almost three times wealthier than the average Ukrainian. In 1990, the two countries had the same life expectancy; today, Poles live 77 years on average, while Ukrainians live only 71 years.[34] On Transparency International's Corruption Perception Index, Poland ranks 35th worldwide, while Ukraine occupies a dismal 142nd place.[35] The gap between Moldova and Romania might be smaller but it goes in the same direction, suggesting that EU membership— or the prospect of it—conferred on countries a significant advantage. Needless to say, other non-EU countries in the neighborhood appear to be in an even more dismal state. Belarus, for example, is a dynastic autocracy with a largely unreformed Soviet-style economy and little prospect for either political or economic liberalization.

This is not to argue that EU membership alone explains the difference between the quality of democratic institutions in the postcommunist countries that joined the EU and in those that did not. But it is difficult to make the argument that the sovereignty retained by Eastern European countries that did not join the Union was put to good use by its citizens and politicians. Many of the nonmembers that have made successful strides to strengthen their democratic governance—most notably Serbia—did so with their eyes set on EU membership. Serbia finds itself in the process of negotiating its accession and is expected to join by 2020. If the comparative experience of Eastern Europe has anything to teach us about life outside the EU, it is that the institutions of liberal democracy in transitional countries are at an increased risk without the commitment mechanisms provided by EU membership. These risks might appear esoteric to a Briton or a Swede. Yet if Hungarians and Poles worry today about the future of their democracy, they would be guaranteed to worry much more in the absence of their country's EU membership.

THE SHADOW OF PAST CONFLICTS—AND OF
THE KREMLIN

Violent conflict, fueled by nationalism, is another specter that has long haunted Europe. It is naïve to believe that wars in Europe have been confined, irreversibly, to the dustbin of history. To pick on Viktor Orbán again, when he delivered his controversial speech about "illiberal democracy" in July 2014,[36] he did so in the town of Băile Tuşnad, Romania. The spa town, also known as Tusnádfürdő in Hungarian, was once part of greater Hungary. Its population is composed overwhelmingly (over 90 percent) of ethnic Hungarians. By making a speech of such significance in Romania, Orbán was catering to those in his home country who consider Hungary's loss of territory in the aftermath of the First World War a grave historical injustice in need of correction. Large numbers of ethnic Hungarians live also in Slovakia and Serbia. In 2011, Orbán's government introduced a law encouraging ethnic Hungarians outside Hungary to acquire Hungarian citizenship. Worldwide, more than 500,000 people became Hungarian citizens following the enactment of the law, including more than 100,000 Serbian citizens.[37] Slovakia retaliated by introducing a legal requirement, scantily enforced, to strip Slovak citizenship from those who acquired foreign citizenship by choice. This was motivated by the fear that the large community of Hungarian citizens living on the Slovak territory contiguous to the Hungarian border could be used by Orbán to foster separatism.

If the idea of a separatist movement disturbing the peace in the heart of Europe in the 2010s sounds farfetched, it shouldn't. The conflicts in Northern Ireland, the Basque country, Kosovo, and Bosnia are neither too old nor too obscure to justify such complacency. Moreover, the narrative deployed by Orbán is not fundamentally different from the one used by the Russian regime in eastern Ukraine, Moldova, and Georgia, where Russian passports were distributed liberally, followed by ostentatious efforts by the Russian government to protect its new citizens—sometimes using military means. With its history of conflict, deportations, and ethnic cleansing, there is no shortage of real or imagined instances of past injustice in Europe. If Orbán's posturing seems a long way from the brazen behavior of the Kremlin, it is in part because of the constraints that are imposed on him by the EU. With the existing rules on the protection of minorities in the EU, any claims about the "oppression" of ethnic Hungarians in Slovakia or Romania strain credulity. It is equally unthinkable that one member state would make territorial claims against another without swift consequences in the form of sanctions, punitive fines, suspension of membership, or other measures adopted by the EU. It is therefore safe to say that, at the margin, the absence of the EU would increase the temptation to escalate similar disputes.

Of course, the EU is only one element of a broader international system that ensures peaceful relations between European countries. Another, arguably more important, element of that landscape is NATO, backed by the military might of the United States. The existence of that landscape hinges on the existence of trust between countries that share the formal platforms for cooperation and the settlement of disputes, including the EU. An exit from the EU would remove one such platform and replace it with weaker mechanisms, such as the Organization of Cooperation and Security in Europe or the Council of Europe. Worse yet, the ugly political dynamics that would likely accompany the demise of the EU would also undermine trust between European countries, making future conflicts more, not less, likely.

Russia's brazen annexation of Crimea and the invasion of Donbas in 2014 would not have happened if Ukraine had been a member of the alliance. However, the EU played a substantial role in containing Putin's aggression. After all, it was the EU, not NATO, that mustered up enough strength for targeted economic sanctions, which inflicted economic pain on Russia's economy and political elite. Those who want their countries to leave the EU need to explain how the absence of a common foreign and security policy would make Central and Eastern Europe less vulnerable to Russian threats.

The external threats to Europe are not limited to conventional forms of warfare. The Kremlin's influence in Central and Eastern Europe has flourished thanks to clever energy policy, covert bribes and attempts to coopt political elites, and skilled propaganda. NATO does not have the tools to respond to these threats. No military alliance can "defeat" the corruption of the political class by Russian money, nor can it change an intellectual climate that is hostile to liberal democracy. And neither have European countries, acting alone, been particularly effective in responding to these challenges.

A large part of Europe, especially its eastern flank, depends on Russian energy imports. Russia's regime has used its supply of energy as a lever of political influence in the region—not just in Ukraine or Moldova, but also inside the EU, including Hungary. But EU membership can make a huge difference. An Eastern European country that decided to leave the EU would not *have to* exclude itself from the EU's single energy market. Its government could, in principle, decide to free-ride on a competitive and diversified supply of energy from the EU. However, it is very plausible that the Russian regime would be able to make the government in question an offer that it could not refuse, locking the country into an irreversible position of dependence on Russian energy. Sometimes, even the pushback from the EU's institutions is not always enough to deter politicians from shady deals with the Russian government. It was certainly not enough in the case of Hungary's Paks nuclear plant or Germany's Nord Stream II. Its complete absence, though, would mean more of such deals.

The Kremlin has been unscrupulous in its attempts to buy political influence in other European countries. In Latvia, the 2009 mayoral campaign of Nils Ušakovs, the leader of the pro-Russian Harmony party, reportedly received funding from the SVR, Russia's foreign intelligence agency.[38] The hidden and not-so-well-hidden Russian influence on European politics has also come under the spotlight of the Central Intelligence Agency, which has been instructed to monitor the Kremlin's activities in Europe.[39] Short of bribery or loans to French nationalists, the Russian regime has made considerable advances on the public relations front, gaining the support of politicians across Europe. Conferences and events, such as the high-profile Valdai Forum or the somewhat lower-key Rhodes Forum, run by Vladimir Yakunin, former head of Russian Railways, serve as vehicles for the Kremlin to buy influence in the West. "Experts who go want to be close to power and are afraid of losing their access. Some might believe that they can use Valdai as a platform for criticism, but in reality their mere presence at the event means they are already helping legitimize the Kremlin," argues Lilia Shevtsova, a researcher at the Brookings Institution.[40] Russia also operates a sophisticated propaganda machine, which it uses to undermine the trust of Europeans in their political institutions. This includes official channels, such as the generously funded Russia Today and Sputnik, multilingual news services, and myriad "news" websites operated in multiple languages and engaged in spreading misinformation and conspiracy theories.[41] The EU does not immunize its member states against the challenges posed by dependence on Russian energy and soft power. However, the EU does wield some of the key tools that are needed to counter this threat—from its energy and competition policies to initiatives aimed at responding to the rise of Russian propaganda.

No European country would be better positioned to confront Russia's expansionism on its own. The fact that Russia's Western neighbors, which are not members of the EU, have been often reduced to the position of client regimes should serve as a warning to those in Central and Eastern Europe who are toying with the idea of an exit from the EU. An exit by an individual country, accompanied by protracted and likely bitter negotiations, is bound to make the EU more inward-looking and less willing to engage the outside world.

The effects of a country's withdrawal from the EU would depend on a range of factors, including the new institutional arrangement that the country would seek with the EU and the characteristics of the country itself. If an advanced, prosperous country, such as the United Kingdom after its referendum, decides to leave on friendly terms and seek membership in the European Economic Area, or some similar arrangement, it would not be a reason for an economic disaster. But neither would it be a reason for celebration. The withdrawal would not solve any of the grievances that the critics of the EU associate with membership. It would complicate the country's commercial ties with the EU's single market and put it in an awkward position relative to outside trading partners because any trade agreements negotiated by the EU would no longer apply. Instead of turning it into a free-trading, globalized superpower, the UK government would need to engage in painstaking trade negotiations with the major economies of the world, for which there might be very little appetite, while navigating the perilous waters of domestic interest groups and the question of Scotland's prospective independence.

But whatever the effects of Brexit on the UK economy, they pale in significance when compared with the risks that a departure from the EU poses to the smaller, more vulnerable countries of Central and Eastern Europe, whose EU membership has been a major factor contributing to the success of their transition to liberal democracy and the market. Besides direct economic costs, their exit from the EU—or the demise of the Union as a whole—would reopen old grievances and leave postcommunist countries exposed to predatory populism, as well as to the revisionist regime in Moscow. In short, the dream of Europe whole, free, and at peace, would be irretrievably lost.

NOTES

1. Mihajlovic, "Yugoslav Gasterbeiter," 188.
2. Calic, "Ethnic Cleansing and War Crimes." For an account of the war and its historical context, see, e.g., Woodward, *Balkan Tragedy*; and Lampe, *Yugoslavia as History*.
3. Bútora and Bútorová, "Neznesiteľná ľahkosť' rozchodu."
4. For a discussion of the differences in policy preferences between the Czechs and Slovaks in the early 1990s and their impact on the split of Czecho-slovakia and the economic transition, see Rohac, "Policy Preferences and the Czechoslovak Transition."
5. The Nobel Prize–winning economist Douglass North, one of the founding fathers of new institutional economics, arrived at the conclusion that the question of institutional change is ultimately a question of evolution of shared beliefs, ultimately a cognitive or epistemic question. On this see North, *Understanding the Process of Economic Change*.
6. See Kuran and Sunstein, "Availability Cascades and Risk Regulation." For evidence that results of public opinion polls shift voters' views of policies, see Rothschild and Malhotra, "Are Public Opinion Polls Self-Fulfilling Prophecies?"
7. There exist, however, studies that went through a reverse exercise with respect to countries of Central and Eastern Europe, which were joining the EU in the 2000s. See Baldwin et al., "The Costs and Benefits of Eastern Enlargment."
8. The net contribution is expected to remain stable or decrease for the rest of the decade. Webb et al., "In Brief," 12.
9. Ottaviano et al., *The Costs and Benefits of Leaving the EU*.
10. Congdon, *How Much Does the European Union Cost Britain?*
11. Hindley and Howe, *Better Off Out?*
12. McCloskey, "The A-Prime/C-Prime Theorem," 235.
13. Springford et al., *The Economic Consequences of Leaving the EU*.
14. For a foundational study of the economics of policy uncertainty, see Baker et al., "Measuring Economic Policy Uncertainty."

15. Portes, "The Economic Implications for the UK of Leaving the European Union."

16. Data on applied tariff rates (weighted mean, all products, %) from World Bank, World Development Indicators.

17. Eriksen, "Norway's Rejection of EU Membership."

18. Ibid.

19. Linder, "Swiss Legislation in the Era of Globalisation."

20. European Commission, *Trade Statistical Pocket Guide*, 61.

21. Hannan, "A Vision of Britain Outside the EU."

22. Hughes and Blenkinsop, "Exclusive."

23. See, e.g., Dustmann and Frattini, "Immigration."

24. Mason, "Nigel Farage."

25. Eliminating all immigration restrictions, globally, could easily double global GDP. See Clemens, "Economics and Emigration."

26. As discussed in chapter 3.

27. Byrne, "Hungary Abandons Controversial Internet Tax Plan."

28. Byrne and Shubber, "Hungary Threatens Foreign Companies in Tax Dispute."

29. Geottig, "Polish Challenger Duda Calls for New Taxes."

30. World Bank, Worldwide Governance Indicators.

31. Kovács et al., "Hungary."

32. Kornai, "Hungary's U-Turn," 5.

33. "McCain sparks US-Hungary diplomatic row over Orban."

34. World Bank, World Development Indicators.

35. Transparency International, Corruption Perception Index.

36. Orbán, Prime Minister Viktor Orbán's Speech at the 25th Bálványos Summer Free University and Student Camp.

37. Thorpe, "Hungary Creating New Mass of EU Citizens."

38. Harding, "Latvia."

39. Foster, "Russia Accused of Clandestine Funding of European Parties."

40. Quoted in Pomerantzev and Weiss, "The Menace of Unreality," 21.

41. Ibid.

REFERENCES

Baker, Scott R., Nicholas Bloom, and Steven J. Davis. "Measuring Economic Policy Uncertainty." *Chicago Booth Research Paper* No. 13-02, 2013. http://papers.ssrn.com/sol3/papers.cfm?abstract_id=2198490.

Baldwin, Richard E., Joseph F. Francois, and Richard Portes. "The Costs and Benefits of Eastern Enlargement: The Impact on the EU and Central Europe." *Economic Policy* 12 (1997): 125–76.

BBC. "McCain sparks US-Hungary diplomatic row over Orban."

Booth, Stephen, et al. *What if . . . ? The Consequences, Challenges, and Opportunities Facing Britain Outside EU*. London: Open Europe, 2015. http://openeurope.org.uk/intelligence/britain-and-the-eu/what-if-there-were-a-brexit/.

Bútora, Martin, and Zora Bútorová. "Neznesiteľná ľahkosť rozchodu." In *Rozloučení s Československem*, edited by Ruediger Kipke and Karel Vodička, 119–50. Prague: Český spisovatel, 1993.

Byrne, Andrew. "Hungary Abandons Controversial Internet Tax Plan." *Financial Times*, October 31, 2014. http://www.ft.com/cms/s/0/e847f75e-60e2-11e4-894b-00144feabdc0.html#axzz3ZBp2pawN.

Byrne, Andrew, and Kadhim Shubber. "Hungary Threatens Foreign Companies in Tax Dispute." *Financial Times*, July 19, 2015. http://www.ft.com/cms/s/0/b86018ca-2c7d-11e5-acfb-cbd2e1c81cca.html#axzz3q47JQxHi.

Calic, Marie-Janine. "Ethnic Cleansing and War Crimes, 1991–1995." In *Confronting the Yugoslav Controversies: A Scholars' Initiative*, edited by Charles W. Ingrao and Thomas A. Emmert, West Lafayette, 115–53. West Lafayette: Purdue University Press, 2012.

Clemens, Michael. "Economics and Emigration: Trillion-Dollar Bills on the Sidewalk?" *Journal of Economic Perspectives* 25 (2011): 83–106.

Congdon, Tim. *How Much Does the European Union Cost Britain?* Dagenham: Caxton Press, 2014. http://www.timcongdon4ukip.com/docs/EU2014.pdf.

Dhingra, Swati, Gianmarco Ottaviano, and Thomas Sampson. "Should We Stay or Should We Go? The Economic Consequences of Leaving the EU." *CEP Election Analysis* No. 22, 2000. http://cep.lse.ac.uk/pubs/download/EA022.pdf.

Dustmann, Christian, and Tommaso Frattini. "Immigration: The European Experience." *CReAM Discussion Paper* No 22/11, 2011. http://www.ucl.ac.uk/~uctpb21/doc/CDP_22_11.pdf.

Eriksen, Erik O. "Norway's Rejection of EU Membership Has Given the Country Less Self-Determination, Not More." LSE European Politics and Policy, April 22, 2014. http://blogs.lse.ac.uk/europpblog/2014/04/22/norways-rejection-of-eu-membership-has-given-the-country-less-self-determination-not-more/.

European Commission. *Trade Statistical Pocket Guide*. Luxembourg: Publications Office of the European Union, 2016, http://trade.ec.europa.eu/doclib/docs/2013/may/tradoc_151348.pdf.

Foster, Peter. "Russia Accused of Clandestine Funding of European Parties as US Conducts Major Review of Vladimir Putin's Strategy." *Telegraph*, January 16, 2016. http://www.telegraph.co.uk/news/worldnews/europe/russia/12103602/America-to-investigate-Russian-meddling-in-EU.html.

Geottig, Marcin. "Polish Challenger Duda Calls for New Taxes on Banks, Supermarkets." Reuters, May 17, 2015. http://www.reuters.com/article/2015/05/17/us-poland-election-duda-debate-idUSKBN0O20WV20150517.

Hannan, Daniel. "A Vision of Britain Outside the EU—Confident, Successful and Free." *Telegraph*, June 2, 2015. http://www.telegraph.co.uk/news/politics/11644904/A-vision-of-Britain-outside-the-EU-confident-successful-and-free.html.

Harding, Luke. "Latvia: Russia's Playground for Business, Politics—and Crime." *Guardian*, January 23, 2013. http://www.theguardian.com/world/2013/jan/23/latvia-russian-playground.

Hindley, Brian, and Martin Howe. *Better Off Out? The Benefits or Costs of EU Membership*. London: Institute of Economic Affairs, 2001. http://www.iea.org.uk/sites/default/files/publications/files/upldbook33pdf.pdf.

Hughes, Krista, and Philip Blenkinsop. "Exclusive: U.S. Trade Czar Says Britain Would Lose on Trade Outside the EU." Reuters, October 28, 2015. http://www.reuters.com/article/2015/10/28/us-britain-eu-usa-idUSKCN0SM2LS20151028.

Kornai, János. "Hungary's U-Turn." *Harvard University and Corvinus University of Budapest*, 2015. http://www.kornai-janos.hu/Kornai_Hungary's%20U-Turn%20-%20full.pdf.

Kovács, Balázs Áron et al. "Hungary." In Freedom House. *Nations in Transit* 2015, 267–97. https://freedomhouse.org/report/nations-transit/2015/hungary.

Kuran, Timur, and Cass R. Sunstein. "Availability Cascades and Risk Regulation." *Stanford Law Review* 51 (1999): 683–768.

Lampe, John R. *Yugoslavia as History: Twice There Was a Country*, 2nd ed. Cambridge: Cambridge University Press, 2000.

Leach, Graeme. *EU Membership—What's the Bottom Line?* London: Institute of Directors, 2000. https://www.iod.com/MainWebSite/Resources/Document/europe_publications_eumembership.pdf.

Linder, Wolf. "Swiss Legislation in the Era of Globalisation: A Quantitative Assessment of Federal Legislation (1983–2007)." *Swiss Political Science Review* 20 (2014): 223–31.

Mason, Rowena. "Nigel Farage: Indian and Australian Immigrants Better Than Eastern Europeans." *Guardian*, April 22, 2015. http://www.theguardian.com/politics/2015/apr/22/nigel-farage-immigrants-india-australia-better-than-eastern-europeans.

"McCain sparks US-Hungary diplomatic row over Orban." *BBC*, December 3, 2014. http://www.bbc.com/news/world-europe-30318898.

McCloskey, Donald. "The A-Prime/C-Prime Theorem." *Eastern Economic Journal* 19 (1993): 235–38.

Mihajlovic, Steven. "Yugoslav Gastarbeiter: The Guest Who Stayed for Dinner." *Northwestern Journal of International Law & Business* 8 (1987): 181–96.

Milne, Ian. *A Cost Too Far? An Analysis of the Net Economic Costs & Benefits for the UK of EU Membership*. London: Civitas, 2004. http://www.civitas.org.uk/pdf/cs37.pdf.

Minford, Patrick, Vidya Mahambare, and Eric Nowell. *Should Britain Leave the EU? An Economic Analysis of a Troubled Relationship*. London: Institute of Economic Affairs, 2005. http://www.patrickminford.net/europe/chap1.pdf.

North, Douglass C. *Understanding the Process of Economic Change*. Cambridge: Cambridge University Press, 2007.

Orbán, Viktor. "Prime Minister Viktor Orbán's Speech at the 25th Bálványos Summer Free University and Student Camp," Website of the Government of Hungary, July 26, 2014. http://www.kormany.hu/en/the-prime-minister/the-prime-minister-s-speeches/prime-minister-viktor-orban-s-speech-at-the-25th-balvanyos-summer-free-university-and-student-camp.

Ottaviano, Gianmarco, et al. "The Costs and Benefits of Leaving the EU." Mimeo, Centre for Economic Performance, London School of Economics, May 13, 2014. http://cep.lse.ac.uk/pubs/download/pa016_tech.pdf.

Pain, Nigel, and Garry Young. "The Macroeconomic Impact of UK Withdrawal from the EU." *Economic Modelling* 21 (2004): 387–408.

Pomerantzev, Peter, and Michael Weiss. "The Menace of Unreality: How the Kremlin Weaponizes Information, Culture, and Money." Institute of Modern Russia and *The Interpreter*, 2014. http://www.interpretermag.com/wp-content/uploads/2014/11/The_Menace_of_Unreality_Final.pdf.

Portes, Jonathan. "The Economic Implications for the UK of Leaving the European Union." *National Institute Economic Review* No. 226, 2013. http://www.niesr.ac.uk/sites/default/files/commentary.pdf.

Rohac, Dalibor. "Policy Preferences and the Czechoslovak Transition" In *Explorations in Political Economy of Reforms*, 102–28. PhD Thesis, Department of Political Economy, King's College London, 2014.

Rothschild, David, and Neil Malhotra. "Are Public Opinion Polls Self-Fulfilling Prophecies?" *Research and Politics* 1 (2014): 1–10.

Springford, John, Simon Tilford, and Philip Whyte. *The Economic Consequences of Leaving the EU. The Final Report of the CER Commission on the UK and the EU Single Market*. London: Centre for European Reform, 2014. http://www.cer.org.uk/sites/default/files/smc_final_report_june2014.pdf.

Thorpe, Nick. "Hungary Creating New Mass of EU Citizens." BBC News, November 7, 2013. http://www.bbc.com/news/world-europe-24848361.

Transparency International. Corruption Perception Index, 2014. http://www.transparency.org/cpi2014.

Webb, Dominic, Matthew Keep, and Marcus Wilton. "In Brief: UK-EU Economic Relations." *House of Commons Briefing Paper* No. 06091, January 19, 2016. http://www.parliament.uk/briefing-papers/SN06091.pdf.

Woodward, Susan L. *Balkan Tragedy: Chaos and Dissolution After the Cold War*. Washington DC: Brookings Institution, 1995.

World Bank. World Development Indicators, 2015.

———. Worldwide Governance Indicators, 2015.

7

HOW CONSERVATIVES CAN SAVE THE EU

Consider a radical vision of the EU's future: the Union as a fully fledged federal state. Its constitution reflects the American federal model with a two-chamber European Parliament. One chamber is elected directly by the population, while the other one is a senate made up of delegates of the constituent states, just like in the United States. The president of the Union is elected directly and forms a cabinet to be approved by the Parliament. The federation has acquired taxing powers and the ability to exercise legal coercion in the EU. The creation of the United States of Europe has also come with the federalization "of all state debt, after a suitable 'haircut' through the issue of Union bonds . . . backed by the entire tax revenue of the common currency zone; the supervised dissolution of insolvent private sector financial institutions; and the creation of a single European army."[1] Instead of a fuzzy notion of subsidiarity, which delimits the division of power between today's EU and member states, its hypothetical constitution creates clear mechanisms of judicial review in the EU. A supreme court interprets the constitution and settles disagreements between member states and the federal government over the division of legal and political authority.

Today's EU already has some attributes of such a federation, but its architecture is incomplete, convoluted, and alien to most Europeans. It has a common currency and a central bank but no central fiscal authority. It maintains free movement of people within the Schengen space but has no unified mechanism to protect its external border. Some of the EU bodies, most notably the European Parliament, are accountable directly to the public, but many Europeans see the Union's governance as extremely opaque. This is a result of a gradualist approach to integration, driven by the expectation that half-measures, such as the introduction of the euro, would sooner or later create incentives for fuller, deeper integration and the creation of democratic federal state.[2] According to some, a radical break with that approach is necessary if the EU is to see through its current woes. "[S]uccessful unions have resulted not from gradual processes of convergence in relatively benign circumstances, but through sharp ruptures in periods of extreme crisis. They come about not through evolution but with a 'big bang,'" writes Brendan Simms, a historian and fellow of Peterhouse, Cambridge,[3] who proposed the idea of a thorough federalization of Europe in a series of articles during the crisis in the Eurozone[4]—and who has adopted recently a more pessimistic view of Europe's prospects.[5]

Simms argues that a new constitutional convention has to be convened, emulating the one that took place in the nascent United States of America in 1789. It should assemble democratically elected representatives of each EU country—not the odd mixture of parliamentarians, retired grandees, and bureaucrats who met at the EU's original European Convention in the early 2000s—and draft a new constitution for the European federal state. This would supersede not just the previous treaties but also national constitutions with a text that would be simple, short, and understandable.

It is easy to see the appeal of a genuine federal structure for the EU. First and foremost, the big-bang constitutional reform would change the dynamics of the process of European integration. For decades, the vague promise of an "ever-closer union" propelled the efforts of European elites to centralize political decision making in Brussels, typically away from public scrutiny and oftentimes provoking a backlash in member states. As a result, instead of discussing the content of policies at the EU or national level, much time has been spent pondering future institutional arrangements in which such policy decisions are to be taken, while the end-state of a federal state or a political union lay only at an uncertain point in the future, with its final contours never articulated by the proponents of tighter integration.[6] Agreeing on a definitive and permanent framework for the union of European states provided through a constitutional convention would put an end to the self-referential, if not completely self-absorbed, nature of European integration and would likely shift the focus of discussions more onto actual policies.

Second, a larger economic role for the European federal government could smooth business cycles in the Eurozone. It would allow for transfers of resources into economically depressed areas at times of economic downturns, as well as coordination of structural policies across member states. A central government, with mechanisms of legal coercion, would be in a better position to limit the fiscal profligacy of politicians in member states and to complete the single market by removing the residual regulatory barriers to trade, investment, and labor mobility in the EU, following the example of the interstate commerce clause of the US Constitution, which enables the federal government to restrain the economic policies of states.[7] The EU, fully integrated into NATO, could finally speak with a unified voice on matters of security and foreign policy. For far too long, politicians in countries such as France, Italy, and Germany have avoided the responsibility for defending their countries and have relied instead on the military might of the United States. A federal state equal in size and wealth to the United States could not justify its shirking in the same way that individual European countries have. And, if one worries about the overreach of the federal government and about Europe's excessive centralization, a genuine federalist constitution would come with checks against the central government's encroachment on the powers of member states. Those are much weaker, if not completely absent, under the current rules.

Attractive as Simms's vision for the EU appears, it is not the vision advocated in this book. After all, conservatives—at whom its arguments are primarily directed—are wary of fantasizing about disruptive social and political changes. Michael Oakeshott, a prominent conservative thinker, argued that a person of a conservative disposition "prefers small and limited innovations to large and indefinite" and "favors a slow rather than a rapid pace, and pauses to observe current consequences and make appropriate adjustments."[8] This logic lends itself well to policymaking: "a modification of the rules should always reflect, and never impose, a change in the activities and beliefs of those who are subject to them, and should never on any occasion be so great as to destroy the ensemble."[9] Such a prudent attitude is not driven, as the common critiques of conservatism go, by a dogmatic resistance to change. Instead, it is motivated by the recognition that social affairs cannot be shaped arbitrarily by benevolent, omniscient policymakers. As Adam Smith famously argued, there are good reasons to be suspicious of the "man of system." A man of system is a policymaker or pundit who has become:

> enamored with the supposed beauty of his own ideal plan of govern-
> ment, that he cannot suffer the smallest deviation from any part of it.
> He goes on to establish it completely and in all its parts, without any
> regard either to the great interests, or to the strong prejudices which
> may oppose it. He seems to imagine that he can arrange the different
> members of a great society with as much ease as the hand arranges
> the different pieces upon a chess-board. He does not consider that
> the pieces upon the chess-board have no other principle of motion
> besides that which the hand impresses upon them; but that, in the
> great chess-board of human society, every single piece has a princi-
> ple of motion of its own, altogether different from that which the
> legislature might chuse [sic] to impress upon it. [10]

A modern formulation of the argument is offered by Hayek, who posits that the institutional order that structures human interactions is not a product of human design but rather an outcome of slow cultural and social evolution. [11] As a result, it is conceited to believe that this institutional order can be remodeled at will by policymakers—at least not without generating unintended consequences. [12]

A thread that goes through much of Hayek's intellectual work is his critique of "constructivist rationalism"—an approach to social affairs that "assumes that all social institutions are, and ought to be, the product of deliberate design." [13] Contrary to the ambitions of progressive reformers, Hayek argues that the existing institutions, however puzzling and inefficient they may appear, exist for reasons that might not be directly intelligible to our mind. [14] Treating them instead as arbitrary constraints that can be reshaped by policy is risky and often self-defeating. This is not to advocate complacency in the face of *any* social and institutional arrangements that might exist (e.g., slavery and communism) but to urge caution and humility in attempts to modify them through public policy. If we are willing to apply this reasoning to institutions in individual countries, we should also apply them to the institutions that have emerged at the international level. The logic leads to restraint no matter what side of the European debate one is on. Any intellectually sound and appealing reform of the EU could easily lead to unpleasant unintended consequences, and so could a dissolution of the EU. In contrast, once one gets into the business of simply applying constructivist reason to see what the EU *could* or *should* become, imagination becomes the limit. Simms, for example, suggests that in his federal system, each member state would send only four delegates to the upper chamber of the EU parliament, the senate, adding that "some of the larger existing nation-states, such as Germany and France, may wish to dissolve themselves into more manageable units for that purpose,"[15] as if the current states existing in Europe were just arbitrary formations that can be tweaked at will.

Another problem with the ambitious plans for the EU's overhaul is more prosaic. Whatever we think of their merits, they are unlikely to be translated into reality. The EU is stumbling from crisis to crisis and its leaders have little appetite to risk the small amount of political capital they still have on major institutional overhauls. Simms's suggestion is to start a Europeanist political platform, which he tentatively calls "Democratic Union" to deemphasize the reference to today's EU, in order to gather public support for the decisive move towards a federalization of the continent. But such political groups, contrary to Simms's recommendations, continue to be absent from European politics. Compared with pre-crisis days, even nominally pro-EU and federalist parties are relatively timid in their calls for closer political integration in Europe. That timidity reflects a lack of demand from the public for such reforms.

If we do not want the EU to implode and if its big institutional reforms are off the table, what should be done? This chapter offers some good news. Not only are there solutions to Europe's malaise, but conservatives and free-market advocates are uniquely positioned to help. To keep the European project alive, it has to be turned into a visible—in fact, an *ostentatious*—engine of economic prosperity. There is much in the EU's architecture that can be built on, including its success in creating the single market and dismantling barriers to trade and investment. But restoring full economic health in Europe will require a much larger dose of free-enterprise medicine. With their appreciation of government accountability, rule of law, and the evolutionary nature of social processes—as opposed to a technocratic faith in scien-

tific fixes to human problems, which permeates modern progressivism[16]
—conservatives are also an obvious source of ideas about how to address, through evolutionary reforms, the democratic deficit that is affecting how the EU is being perceived in the eyes of the general public.
In addition to discussing how the EU's democratic deficit can be reduced through incremental governance reforms, I address two other
issues. First, I offer practical advice about what the EU needs to do to
present a coherent, unified front to the outside world and tackle the
crises looming in its neighborhood—including the influx of refugees
from the Middle East. Second, in a condensed form, I outline an agenda for restoring Europe's economic prosperity through a combination
of looser monetary policy and economic reforms.

CLOSING THE EU'S DEMOCRATIC DEFICIT

Left-wing[17] and conservative[18] critics of the EU agree on one point.
The biggest flaw of the EU is its lack of democratic legitimacy. However, contrary to what Eurosceptics sometimes claim,[19] this deficit *can* be
reduced, if not completely eliminated. As chapter 5 argues, democratic
politics is not inextricably linked to the nation-state. It can flourish in
other contexts as well, including large multiethnic democracies or at the
local level. What has made the emergence of democracy so difficult in
the EU is the inadequacy of its institutions. But those institutions can
be modified, either by a big-bang constitutional reform or through
more humble, incremental changes. Here are some examples of the
latter.

European Council and Council of the EU

One possible remedy consists of strengthening the transparency of EU
summits and meetings of the Council, including those of the EU finance ministers (Ecofin) and of the finance ministers of the Eurozone
(Eurogroup). These two platforms have played a key role in the Eurozone crisis, and their opaqueness has contributed to the popular backlash against fiscal consolidation programs on the periphery.

   All of the Council's legislative documents could be publicly available. The meetings and discussions ought to take place in public as well.

Moreover, even without any change to existing treaties, a commission could be created, composed of members of the budget committees of national parliaments of Eurozone countries and of the European Parliament, to scrutinize decisions about fiscal policy, lending, and structural reforms taken by European institutions, including Ecofin and Eurogroup. Even without power to overrule the Commission or the Council, this would create a space where these institutions would have to explain and justify their actions in public.[20]

European Commission

The European Commission is a body that merges the functions of the EU civil service, a strong executive and supervisory role, and a virtual monopoly on new legislation.[21] Its technocratic aura and independence of direct political scrutiny are warranted only as long as the Commission acts as an executive and regulatory body, overseeing the single market for example. One avenue for reform, which is bound to be controversial, would be to strip the European Commission of its non-executive roles, particularly of its prerogatives in the legislative process, and subject it to political control by the Council.[22]

In addition to encountering resistance from the Commission itself, such a reform would require a revision of treaties. A more realistic alternative would be to recognize, begrudgingly perhaps, that the Commission has already become an autonomous political actor, and to treat it as such. The Commission's president is now chosen by the European Council, typically through haggling behind closed doors. The nomination is followed by a largely formal election by the European Parliament. The entire process of the selection of the president could be public, with online or televised debates between the candidates. The bids in support of candidates by EU governments could be announced publicly as well. The groups represented in the European Parliament could publicly advertise which candidate they support. Some elements of a more open selection process have already been adopted through the system of *Spitzenkandidaten* (lead candidates), through which parliamentary groups announced their candidates for president of the Commission ahead of the 2014 European election, thus providing input for the decision taken by the European Council after the election.[23] There appears little downside in extending this degree of transparency to the entire selection process, making European citizens more directly involved, through European elections, in the choice of the Commission's president.

European Parliament

As the EU's only directly elected body, the European Parliament is critical to reducing the existing democratic deficit. Alas, turnouts at European elections are weak,[24] and the chamber is hardly seen as a venue for an actual Europe-wide debate over public policy.[25] This is a result of the fact that the Parliament is not a full-fledged legislative body but only a vehicle through which legislation is passed and amended. It is the European Commission that has a virtual monopoly on proposing new legislation, whereas MEPs only suggest amendments. There is often a greater political payoff in passing nonbinding resolutions on topics ranging from gay rights[26] to critical commentaries on the political situations in specific countries,[27] not to mention the rhetorical exercises that sometimes rise to public prominence through YouTube and social media.[28] A treaty change that would allow MEPs to propose new laws, as opposed to simply assenting to and amending the proposals submitted by the Commission, would raise the stakes of parliamentary work, increase the importance of the chamber in the eyes of the public, and bring the European political process closer to the traditional form of parliamentarianism seen in individual European countries.[29]

Subsidiarity, or How to Keep the EU in Check

Democracy in the EU is not helped by the lack of a properly functioning system of judicial review that could stop new legislation from coming from Brussels—or Strasbourg. Under the US system of government, the Constitution enumerates the powers that are given to the federal government, explicitly constraining its activities to only the ones that are explicitly listed.[30] The European Union relies instead on the application of the somewhat elusive idea of subsidiarity, defined in the Maastricht Treaty: "the Union shall act only if and in so far as the objectives of the proposed action cannot be sufficiently achieved by the Member States, either at central level or at regional and local level, but can rather, by reason of the scale or effects of the proposed action, be better achieved at Union level."[31] However, whether a certain policy objective is better achieved at the national or at the European level is primarily a political, not a legal decision.[32] Unless the EU is turned into a US-style federation, formal judicial review is unlikely to play a large role in countering overreach by European institutions.

The lack of an effective *judicial* review process strengthens the case for *political review* of the EU's activities by its member states.[33] The Lisbon Treaty granted national parliaments the power to raise objections to proposed legislation on the grounds of subsidiarity, known as the "yellow" and "orange" cards.[34] In simple terms, a group of national parliaments can raise reasoned objections to a legislative proposal in the early stages of the legislative procedure, within its first eight weeks, if they believe that the law infringes on the idea of subsidiarity and unduly encroaches on the sovereignty of member states. This yellow card, a reference to the penalty card used by referees in association football, triggers a review of the proposal by the European Commission. If a majority of parliaments object, which constitutes an orange card, the Council or the European Parliament are entitled to strike the proposal down immediately.[35] The idea is laudable because it creates a connection between national politics and the EU. It was hoped the reform would spur tighter cooperation between national parliaments over time. However, the mechanism has had only a limited impact. When national parliaments used it for the first time in May 2012 to block an EU regulation that would limit the workers' right to strike, the Commission ultimately withdrew the proposal.[36] On other occasions when national parliaments have issued yellow cards, they have not been translated into a change of course by European institutions. That should not be a surprise. If a group of member state parliaments reach the conclusion that the proposal violates the principle of subsidiarity, the European Commission, which is typically also the author of new legislative proposals, becomes the arbiter of such disputes. At the time of writing of this book, the orange card, which requires a majority of member states or MEPs, has not been used once.

To strengthen the supervisory role of national parliaments, the Prime Minister of the United Kingdom, David Cameron, proposed a modification of the system in the form of "red cards," which would enable "groups of national parliaments, acting together, [to] stop unwanted legislative proposals."[37] At the time of writing, it is still unclear whether the proposal will make it into the final settlement between the UK and the EU. If implemented, it would turn national parliaments into a virtual European senate, providing a check on the EU's legislative activity. Finally, there would be little downside to a system of "green cards," which would allow coordinated groups of national parliaments to propose EU-wide legislation, which could then be discussed and voted on in the European Parliament.[38] That would help bridge the disconnect that exists between the legislative process in the EU, dominated by the Commission, and national politics.

In addition to changes to formal rules at the European level, member states can do a lot themselves to strengthen the oversight of European affairs by their own parliaments. The Swedish *Riksdag*, which is often cited as an example to follow, stays systematically on top of current European legislation and frequently issues opinions under the "yellow card" procedure. In contrast, the outreach of the UK Parliament to European institutions is only weak and unsystematic, which only deepens the perception that the EU is a distant and alien entity, imposing its will on members.[39] To make the system of cards of *any color* work as an effective check on the overreach of EU institutions, national parliaments will have to learn to cooperate and work together in practical ways, going above and beyond the mostly formal ties currently existing among the parliaments.

TOWARDS A EUROPEAN VOICE ON THE WORLD STAGE

The EU has to become a more effective supplier of European public goods. The issues that come the closest to the textbook definition of public goods have to do with the way the EU behaves with respect to the outside world: how it deals with security challenges, including the protection of its borders, immigration, and asylum.[40] The free movement of people within the Schengen space is perhaps the most obvious and tangible achievement of the European project. Yet, as chapter 4 shows, the refugee crisis has exposed a deep flaw in the EU's architecture, which combines an unrestricted freedom of movement with a set of different immigration, border protection, and asylum policies in each member state. That creates ample space for free riding and moral hazard. The good news, however, is that with the right policies, the EU can get the refugee crisis under control and help the Schengen system survive the 21st century.

First, the EU needs a common system of border protection, funded from European sources. It is not fair to Hungary, Italy, or Greece that the bloc expects them to bear the bulk of the cost of rescuing, accommodating, and processing refugees, just because these countries happen to be in their way. More importantly, the situation creates a space for free riding. As a result, all of these activities are underprovided, and asylum-seekers are passed from one country to the next like hot potatoes. National border protection forces should be replaced by—or merged into—Frontex, which needs a mandate, coming from a revision of the existing treaties, and the funding to do the job done in the United States by its federal US Customs and Border Protection agency. The point of funding Frontex generously is not to build a "Fortress Europe" or to give new powers to an unaccountable, EU-run security force. The point is to restore the feeling of safety and security on the continent, eroded by the EU's inept response to the refugee crisis of 2015 and by the attacks in Paris, which have demonstrated how easy it is for populists to instill fear and leverage it for political gains. If the EU is seen as anathema to the personal safety and security of Europeans, its future is doomed. That outcome can be avoided if European institutions, such as Frontex and Europol, are recognized as reliable providers of security.

Another, perhaps more controversial, element of a common European response to the refugee crisis is a coherent and proactive asylum policy. The main reason for the large illegal influx of asylum-seekers into the EU has to do with the living conditions of refugees in countries such as Turkey and Lebanon, and also by their inability to obtain asylum in European countries through the legal route. The first problem could be alleviated by additional funding to refugee programs in countries surrounding Syria. Still, it is unlikely that any amount of financial assistance would reduce the attraction of the EU's relative prosperity to those fleeing the Middle East. As a result, to curb the chaotic flows of people across the Schengen border, the EU has no choice but to provide the refugees with a legal way in.

Alas, the seemingly irreconcilable difference of opinions between countries that are willing to accommodate large numbers of refugees, such as Germany and Sweden, and member states in Central Europe that reject the idea of accepting any asylum-seekers from Muslim-majority countries is preventing a common response from emerging. Temporarily, this divergence of opinions has also stalled the efforts to share the burden among different countries in the Schengen area. Furthermore, because of the unequal conditions surrounding the asylum process and different levels of assistance provided to asylum-seekers by individual countries, asylum-seekers are incentivized once in the EU to migrate to countries such as Germany, even if doing so violates the existing rules governing the Schengen space.[41] Intractable as this problem appears, mainly because of the erosion of trust and goodwill among EU countries that the gridlock has led to, there are ways out.

There are, for example, more flexible ways of spreading the burden across member states than the quota system proposed by the European Commission. Countries could agree on the total number of refugees that the EU would be willing to accept, determine an initial assignment of quotas between countries, and then allow governments to trade the quotas on a market.[42] Tradable quotas would enable countries that do not want to accommodate refugees—such as Slovakia, Poland, or Hungary—to pay others to step in. Of course, even that system of burden sharing would require a prior agreement about the total level of asylum-seekers or refugees that the EU is willing to accept and, more controversially, the initial assignment of quotas. That could easily generate as much disagreement as the European Commission's initial proposal of fixed refugee quotas. Member states that are opposed to the idea of accepting refugees would hardly say yes to a scheme in which they would have to buy their way out of their obligations.

Before contemplating any system of burden sharing, the EU could implement the much more modest mechanism of a two-sided matching market, described in a recent working paper by Oxford researchers Will Jones and Alexander Teytelboym.[43] The matching market would enable refugees to apply for protection in several EU countries, ranked by order of preference. It would also enable states to compete for particular groups of refugees. In addition to reflecting countries' preferences over the characteristics of refugees, the system would enable member states to set the minimum and maximum quotas of refugees they would be willing to accept. Of course, for the matching market to make a meaningful difference in the ongoing crisis, the minimum quotas, set by individual countries, would have to add up to a number commensurate with the numbers of asylum-seekers coming into the EU. However, in principle, a matching market would allow for a degree of free-riding, which would be politically one of the scheme's selling points. As long as others were willing to pick up the slack, the matching market would not be jeopardized if a number of EU countries decided to take no refugees whatsoever. Another appealing characteristic of this proposal is that it puts national governments in control of the refugees' characteristics, potentially including their qualifications, language skills, or country of origin. Once in place, the framework would allow the introduction of explicit elements of burden-sharing, such as quotas that may or may not be tradable. As a start, however, the matching mechanism would reduce the size and the chaotic nature of the uncontrolled influx of refugees seen in 2015, because arriving at any particular destination country would become much less important for refugees.

A functioning matching market for EU countries and refugees would create an alternative to the dangerous and illegal journeys that Syrian and other refugees are currently undertaking. That might not seem like a lot, but it might just be enough to relieve the populist pressures that currently risk tearing the EU apart.[44] The civil war in Syria is also a painful reminder that Europe's long holiday from history is over. Ignoring the brewing security threats in Europe's neighborhood, whether in Syria or Ukraine, means paying a steep price later. However, just as there is disagreement over the refugee crisis, the EU rarely speaks with a unified voice on foreign policy and security matters. Once again, that is caused by the absence of a European political process that would give the EU a mandate to speak on behalf of member states on such important matters. The sooner Europe creates such a process by reducing the bloc's democratic deficit, the sooner the EU can become a force for good in its neighborhood.

RENEWING EUROPE'S PROSPERITY

Europeans need to address their economic woes: inflexible markets, aging populations, and unsustainable public finances. Some of the needed reforms can be done by European institutions acting alone, but Europe's future prosperity also requires deep changes in the economic policies of member states. The EU's democratic deficit plays a complicated role in pushing for such reforms. To the extent to which European institutions are overseeing compliance with norms that have already been agreed on by member states, their insulation from political pressures can be helpful.[45] However, if the EU is to push for pro-market reforms that are politically controversial, it stands little chance of success unless it gains a stronger mandate from the public. Either way, conservatives should be at the forefront of pushing European institutions and national governments in a market-friendly direction.

First, there is the low-hanging fruit. The European Central Bank (ECB) has to draw the right lessons from the Great Recession. In light of the collapse in nominal spending, as illustrated in figure 4.1 in chapter 4, there is nothing unconventional about the ECB's so-called unconventional monetary policies, also known as quantitative easing (QE). It should not have taken four painful years, until Mario Draghi's famous "whatever it takes" speech,[46] to instill an understanding that even when interest rates are close to zero lower bound, the central bank can control inflation and growth through other means.[47] Worse yet, it then took another two and a half years, until January 2015, for the ECB to expand the existing quantitative easing programs to a meaningful scale.[48] Even better than quantitative easing would be an explicit target level for nominal spending, such as that advocated by a number of modern followers of Milton Friedman's monetarism.[49] Under nominal GDP targeting, the central bank would respond aggressively to nominal shocks, thus preventing the debilitating cycles of deleveraging and prolonged unemployment.

Accommodative monetary policy in times of crisis reduces the impact of economic shocks and facilitates economic reforms.[50] But European institutions also have two trump cards up their sleeve to push for deeper structural changes to European economies. First, there is no question that the survival of the Eurozone will require a much greater degree of economic flexibility. Second, European institutions have the mandate to complete the single market. That means dismantling national barriers to competition in numerous areas, including services, energy, and digital transactions. Europe's online markets, for example, are still segmented and guided by different rules in different countries. The spirit of the European Commission's *Digital Single Market Strategy*[51] deserves applause for aiming to dismantle the barriers to cross-border digital transactions, including different VAT rules, and arbitrary geo-blocking. But the document does not go far enough. It does not, for instance, include a commitment to creating a truly coordinated spectrum policy, which impedes the deployment of the advanced LTE networks.[52] Common EU rules on data protection must be implemented uniformly by member states—so far, they have not—to remove the legal uncertainty facing companies that rely on cross-border data transfers.[53]

Worse yet, EU competition policies can be counterproductive, especially when they treat digital markets in the same way as old-fashioned utilities, like energy companies. This may be appropriate for a small number of Internet service providers that resemble natural monopolies, but even there caution is necessary in order to avoid discouraging investment in digital infrastructure. In any case, looking at large digital companies as natural monopolies or oligopolies, as the Commission long has, is misguided and has hindered the growth of Europe's digital markets.[54] Today's digital markets are very different from textbook examples of imperfect competition. Compared with the era when the EU regulatory landscape was being formed, digital markets present a much greater degree of convergence between different aspects of digital products and services. Companies such as Google and Apple are active in developing digital devices and applications, providing connectivity, and aggregating digital content. Services including voice communication and text messaging, once charged for by mobile operators, are increasingly provided by Internet-based business models, such as Skype and WhatsApp, which do not charge customers directly. If the past offers any insight to our understanding of future trends, we can expect even more fluidity between the different facets of digital markets, including Internet service provision. The behavior of EU regulators needs to reflect this new reality, instead of relying on static measures of market power or harassing companies such as Google just because they appear to dominate an arbitrarily defined market[55] —not to speak of launching investigations into miscellaneous sharing economy platforms, like Uber.[56] Treating the digital economy in the same way as utilities has backfired even in the area of Internet service provision (ISP), which superficially resembles the textbook example of a natural monopoly, mainly because of the high costs of entry. In the United States, the prevailing attitude of regulators relies on fostering competition *across* different networks. ISPs in the United States, including Comcast and Verizon, own the infrastructure that they are using and are incentivized to invest in it in order to serve their customers. In the EU, by contrast, the transmission infrastructure remains in the hands of incumbent telecom firms, which lease their lines at regulated rates to ISPs. The transmission networks have thus become a form of commons, contributing to Europe's low degree of penetration of high-speed fiber-optic networks and continued reliance on largely obsolete DSL technology.[57]

The focus of European institutions has to be on the creation of common, technology-neutral rules, which will allow providers of digital services to compete across the EU. If they succeed in creating an environment in which the digital economy can prosper, the potential upside is enormous. A fully fledged, single, digital market could give the EU economy a boost of €415 billion, increasing economic growth by 1 percentage point.[58] That is not a utopian objective. No far-flung changes to European treaties are needed to turn it into a reality, merely a sensible application of the tools that the EU already has.

The Commission should use its mandate of overseeing the single market to become a voice for reforms that can deliver shared prosperity across the EU. For a long time, European institutions seemed exceedingly preoccupied with the differences between member states' tax regimes.[59] Corporate tax reforms in various Central and Eastern European countries in the 2000s made it attractive for companies to relocate from "old" member states. Moreover, a number of large corporations have been running their EU operations from jurisdictions such as Luxembourg and Ireland, where they benefit from excessively generous tax treatment—which in some cases qualifies, in the Commission's opinion, as illegal state aid.[60] In the eyes of policymakers and of the general public, "tax competition" has been eroding the tax base and distorting investment decisions.

Advocates of free markets are critical of efforts to harmonize tax regimes in Europe,[61] but the issue also provides a hint of how the EU could be helpful. True, tax regimes across European countries matter for the functioning of the single market. However, the EU also offers a picture of dramatic diversity in the quality of the business and regulatory environments, which inevitably affect investors' and entrepreneurs' decisions at least as much, if not more, than taxation. According to the eponymous survey conducted by the World Bank, Denmark is the third best country in the world in which to do business. Finland ranks 10th. Greece, a Eurozone member just like Finland, occupies *60th* place globally, trailing behind Moldova and Russia.[62] Using the judiciary system in Greece to enforce a contract takes 1,580 days on average, almost three times as long as in a typical OECD country.[63] These vast differences in regulatory quality and the costs of compliance clearly interfere with the single market, making it difficult for businesses to compete across borders.

What is more, the lack of economic flexibility associated with onerous regulation in countries such as Greece is in part responsible for the Eurozone's woes. If the common currency is to survive its next crisis, it must dramatically improve the flexibility of its constituent economies by introducing common standards that facilitate the hiring and firing of employees, the starting and winding down of businesses, and tax compliance, and that curb the power of local populists to distort their business environments and pamper their "national champions."

Conservatives may be sceptical of the EU's ability to push for good economic policy in member states. That is why European institutions need to start with themselves. Proponents of new economic regulation adopted at the EU level, for example, ought to be able to demonstrate that its burden outweighs its benefits.[64] At the present time, the EU lags far behind the United States. In 1981, US President Ronald Reagan issued an executive order that required federal agencies to provide impact analysis, including a comparison of costs and benefits, for any new significant piece of regulation they produced.[65] In comparison, not until 2009 did the EU introduce the European Commission Impact Assessment Guidelines,[66] which require the quantification of significant costs and benefits of new regulations. The guidelines, which have since undergone some revisions, task the different branches of the European Commission with answering the following questions:

- What is the problem, and why is it a problem?
- Why should the EU act?
- What should be achieved?
- What are the various options to achieve the objectives?
- What are their economic, social, and environmental impacts, and who will be affected?
- How do the different options compare in terms of effectiveness and efficiency (benefits and costs)?

- How will monitoring and subsequent retrospective evaluation be organized?[67]

These impact assessment exercises would be effective in constraining the growth of harmful regulation only if the EU also had an independent oversight unit[68] that could assess and strike down regulatory proposals. In July 2015, the Commission created an independent Regulatory Scrutiny Board, to replace its previous incarnation, the Impact Assessment Board. Its performance is lackluster. It went from conducting 135 assessments in 2008 to only 25 in 2014, covering only a tiny fraction of the new legislation adopted by the EU.[69] The Regulatory Scrutiny Board should be thus given the resources and the mandate to review *every* regulatory proposal from the European Commission. The Commission, in turn, should initiate a review of existing legal acts that are obsolete or do not pass the cost-benefit test and prepare an omnibus repeal bill, to be presented to the Parliament and Council. Furthermore, by default, new pieces of regulation ought to include mandatory sunset clauses, making it necessary for European institutions to defend them in the eyes of the public after a certain time period or to let them expire.[70]

European institutions can do much more to promote competition and growth, but the bulk of the responsibility for reviving Europe's economy rests with national governments. One reason for the severity of the Great Recession in Europe had to do with the fiscal situation of countries, such as Greece, with bloated public sectors and overly generous welfare states, financed through debt. When the crisis hit, governments struggled to meet the financial commitments that they had made to their populations, and in some cases they had to renege on them, imposing substantial hardship on the most vulnerable. However, defenders of free enterprise should not be waging a war against social safety nets.[71] Instead, they should propose making these nets sustainable in light of long-term demographic trends and resilient to economic shocks *precisely to avoid* the painful episodes of austerity seen in some Eurozone countries during the crisis.

Regrettably, as a general rule, Western economies *do not* have the long-term outlooks of their public finances under control, and they rely excessively on deficit financing. Unless reforms are undertaken, debt burdens will explode in the coming decades, making the entire continent insolvent.[72] Whether or not the Eurozone moves closer to creating a fiscal union with enforceable rules—which will require bridging the EU's democratic deficit—policymakers will have to find ways of ensuring their governments live within their means. With their appreciation of fiscal prudence, conservatives are better positioned than anyone to help Europe solve this conundrum.

Instead of indulging in fantasies about a world without the EU, conservatives and advocates of free enterprise should strive to be at the forefront of discussions about how European countries can leverage individual initiative, creativity, and the power of incentives to their advantage. Because of a flawed incentive structure, Europe's universities are increasingly lagging behind the top research institutions in the world. Instead of embracing "creative destruction," Europeans are often inclined to preserve the economic status quo even at the price of stagnation and backwardness.[73] For Europe to become an economic powerhouse again, that needs to change. It will not change without an active, vocal, and credible movement in favor of free markets that offers practical solutions to Europe's problems instead of simply pontificating about the supposed evils of European integration.

The EU needs reforms. In the Eurozone, mechanisms of joint economic governance need to be created that will be perceived as legitimate by voters in countries as diverse as Greece, Portugal, and Germany. It is also time to recognize that the EU is a multispeed or "variable-geometry" organization. Not all EU countries are or are planning to become members of the Eurozone, and some of its members have come close to leaving it. The existing rules do not offer the possibility of a legal exit without also leaving the EU. That needs to change. Eurozone membership has to be uncoupled from EU membership, enabling countries to take advantage of EU membership without necessarily rushing into the Eurozone. Such unbundling might be inconvenient for the proponents of "ever-closer union," but in reality it is little more than a simple acknowledgment of reality. It is the only way to prevent the financial crises in the Eurozone from becoming existential matters for the entire EU and to allow countries inside the Eurozone to proceed towards tighter coordination of fiscal and structural policies without dragging other EU members down that path against their will.[74]

Europe's outdated social contract needs to be updated to the realities of the 21st century. The increasingly fluid labor market, rising economic complexity, and globalization are not compatible with the arrangements that governed Europe's workplaces and industries in the 1960s.[75] Neither is there any justification to spend a generous portion of the EU budget on an anachronistic system of agricultural subsidies within the Common Agricultural Policy—a program that has withstood many an attempt at reform. To preserve freedom of movement of people within the Schengen area—one of the EU's most significant achievements—the EU needs to take over from its member states the protection of its common border and put in place a joint system of asylum application processing. It needs to step up its engagement with countries such as Ukraine and Moldova and do more to end the conflicts in the Middle East and North Africa.

According to a quote commonly attributed to Mark Twain, history does not repeat itself, but it rhymes. It bears repeating that when Hayek was writing his defense of political federation in Europe, the continent was headed for an unprecedented geopolitical catastrophe. If the idea of an international war in Europe appears impossible today, it is in part because liberal democracies heeded Hayek's advice in the decades after the Second World War and formed a federal platform that has since kept them economically integrated and at peace. In today's discussions about the technicalities of what needs to change in the EU, it is easy to lose sight of the fact that the continent finds itself at a crossroads. Europe can go back to the model of nation-states unconstrained by a central authority, hoping that its absence will not recreate the wars, protectionism, and hatreds that had so long been the norm on the continent. Or it can attempt to make meaningful strides to address the problems of the EU's democratic deficit, the economic turbulence created by the common currency, and refugee crisis. Conservatives face a choice between coming to the rescue of a reasonably well-run, although necessarily flawed, union of liberal democracies that work together to keep the continent safe, democratic, and prosperous, or becoming cheerleaders for the EU's demise. This book has tried to show, hopefully not entirely in vain, that choosing to cheer for European disintegration is perilous, ill-advised, and ultimately self-defeating.

NOTES

1. Simms, "Towards a Mighty Union," 61.
2. Spolaore, "What Is European Integration Really About?"
3. Simms, "Towards a Mighty Union," 50.
4. In addition to Simms "Towards a Mighty Union," see Simms, "Reinventing Europe"; Simms, "The Ghosts of Europe Past"; Simms, "We Eurozoners"; and Simms, " Why We Need a British Europe."
5. Simms and Less, "A Crisis Without End."
6. For a critique of the open-endedness of Europe's integration process and of the lack of clear goals, see Majone, *Rethinking the Union of Europe Post-Crisis*, 8.
7. Article 1, Section 8, Clause 3, of the US Constitution gives Congress the power "to regulate commerce with foreign nations, and among the several states, and with the Indian tribes." See also Epstein, "The Proper Scope of the Commerce Power."
8. Oakeshott, "On Being Conservative," 412.
9. Ibid., 431.
10. Smith, *The Theory of Moral Sentiments*, 234.
11. See in particular his last book, Hayek, *The Fatal Conceit*.
12. For a detailed discussion of the deep-seated differences between the federal design of the United States and Switzerland on the one hand, and of the European Union on the other, see Fabbrini, *Which European Union?*, 228–47.
13. Hayek, *Law, Legislation, and Liberty*, 5. See also the application to modern economic thought by Smith, *Rationality in Economics*.
14. One reason for that is that the rules might reflect tacit and dispersed knowledge, which cannot be explicitly formulated or made available to a single human mind. Many human institutions, such as markets and prices, Hayek argues, are ways of translating such knowledge into useful guides for action. See Hayek, "The Use of Knowledge in Society."
15. Simms, "Towards a Mighty Union," 61.
16. An exploration of intellectual heritage of progressivism is offered, among others, by Leonard, "American Economic Reform in the Progressive Era."
17. See Iglesias, *Politics in a Time of Crisis*.
18. See, among many examples, O'Sullivan, "Cyprus Suffers EU Folly."
19. E.g., O'Sullivan, "Europe," 4–8.
20. Legrain, *European Spring*, 427. These reform ideas appear originally in Hix, *What's Wrong with the European Union and How to Fix It*, although its publication predates the financial crisis.

21. See Vaubel, *The European Institutions as an Interest Group*, 26–40.

22. Ibid.

23. Tortola, "Why A Partisan Commission President Could Be Good for the EU."

24. A sizeable literature studies the drivers of the low turnout, e.g., Bhatti and Hansen, "The Effect of Generation and Age on Turnout to the European Parliament"; Clark, "Explaining Low Turnout in European Elections"; Lefevere and Van Aelst,"First-Order, Second-Order or Third-Rate?"; and Brug, *(Un)Intended Consequences of EU Parliamentary Elections*.

25. An overview of the factors driving this problem can be found in Hix and Høyland, "Empowerment of the European Parliament."

26. European Parliament, Resolution of 4 February 2014 on the EU Roadmap.

27. European Parliament, Resolution of 10 June 2015 on the Situation in Hungary.

28. As of January 2016, a 2010 YouTube video of Nigel Farage, in which he compares the then-president of the European Council, Herman Van Rompuy, to a "damp rag" had over 1.6 million hits on YouTube.

29. Fabbrini also proposes that EP be granted power to initiate new legislation, and that it be grown into the equivalent of US senate. Fabbrini, *Which European Union?* 253.

30. Pilon, "Madison's Constitutional Vision."

31. Consolidated Versions of the Treaty on European Union and the Treaty on the Functioning of the European Union, October 26, 2012.

32. As an ECJ judge put it, "a certain leeway must be left to the EU institutions in the decision making process. In such cases, the Union Courts cannot simply replace the assessment of the EU Legislator with their own, if they want to remain within the limits of the competences assigned to the judiciary. Hence, the very nature of the subsidiarity test imposes certain limitations as to the level of scrutiny to be undertaken by the Court." See Larsen, "The Judicial Review of the Principle of Subsidiarity," 8.

33. So far, such review is complicated by the layers of overlapping jurisdictions resulting from the many treaties adopted through the existence of the EU and its predecessors. See Alesina and Perotti, "The European Union."

34. See Consolidated Versions of the Treaty on European Union, arts. 6 and 7.

35. Ibid.

36. Cooper, "The Story of the First 'Yellow Card.'"

37. Cameron, "A New Settlement for the United Kingdom in a Reformed European Union."

38. UK House of Lords, "The Role of National Parliaments in the European Union."

39. Gostyńska, *A Ten-Point Plan to Strengthen Westminster's Oversight of EU Policy*.

40. Alesina, et al., "What Does the European Union do?" 2.

41. As mentioned in chapter 4, the most important ones are the Dublin Convention and the Dublin Regulation (Dublin II). See Convention Determining the State Responsible for Examining Applications for Asylum Lodged in One of the Member States of the European Communities—Dublin Convention, August 19, 1997, and European Council, Council Regulation (EC) No 343/2003 of 18 February 2003 Establishing the Criteria and Mechanisms for Determining the Member State Responsible for Examining an Asylum Application Lodged in One of the Member States by a Third-Country National.

42. See Moraga and Rapoport, "Tradable Refugees," and Shuck, "Refugee Burden-Sharing."

43. See Jones and Teytelboym, *The Refugee Match*.

44. Integration strategy is another necessary component of any successful asylum policy. Some thoughts are presented in Rohac, "Tap the Refugee Source."

45. An argument along these lines is made also by Lilico, "Cameron's Renegotiation 'Red Card' Demand Is Impossible."

46. Draghi, Speech at the Global Investment Conference in London.

47. The existing evidence from the Great Recession suggests strongly that, when conducted, QE has indeed had beneficial economic impacts. See Joyce et al., "Quantitative Easing and Unconventional Monetary Policy."

48. Claeys et al., "European Central Bank Quantitative Easing."

49. See Sumner, *The Case for Nominal GDP Targeting*; and Sheedy, "Debt and Incomplete Financial Markets."

50. For a nontechnical version of the argument, see Pesenti, "Structural Reforms and Monetary Policy Revisited," as well as the discussion in chapter 4 of this book.

51. European Commission, "A Digital Single Market Strategy for Europe."

52. Macaes, See also Massaro and Bohlin, *Is Europe Moving Towards a Strategic Developmetn of Spectrum Policy?*

53. Macaes, "A Digital Strategy for Europe," 6.

54. For a critical discussion of EC's Digital Single Market strategy, see, e.g., Blackman, "Last Chance for Europe in the Digital Saloon?"

55. Erixon, "The 'Google Case' and the Promotion of Europe's Digital Economy."

56. Azevedo and Maciejewski, "Social, Economic, and Legal Consequences of Uber."

57. According to the OECD's Broadband Portal, particularly large EU countries such as Germany and France are lagging substantially behind the world leaders in the use of fiber-optic connections. Around 70 percent of all broadband subscriptions in Korea and Japan are fiber connections (highest numbers worldwide) and 43.7 percent in Sweden (highest penetration rate in Europe). In the US, the market share is more modest (8.9 percent of all subscriptions) but substantially higher than in France (3.6 percent), Germany (1.2 percent), or Italy (3.8 percent). See Organisation for Economic Co-operation and Development, "Broadband Statistics."

58. European Commission, "A Digital Single Market Strategy for Europe," 5.

59. Already in 1997, Ecofin discussed measured aiming to tackle the problem of "harmful tax competition," which gave rise to further efforts, particularly to tax breaks. See European Council, Conclusions of the Ecofin Council Meeting on 1 December 1997 Concerning Taxation Policy.

60. European Commission, "Commission Decides Selective Tax Advantages for Fiat in Luxembourg and Starbucks in the Netherlands Are Illegal Under EU State Aid Rules."

61. E.g., Salin, "The Case Against 'Tax Harmonization,'" and Mitchell, "A Tax Competition Primer."

62. World Bank Group, Economy Rankings.

63. Ibid.

64. For a discussion of the effects of the use of cost-benefit analysis on the practice of economic regulation, see Hahn and Litan, "Counting Regulatory Benefits and Costs," or Hahn and Tetlock, "Has Economic Analysis Improved Regulatory Decision?"

65. Reagan, "Federal Regulation."

66. European Commission, Impact Assessment Guidelines.

67. European Comission, "Better Regulation Guidelines," 18–19.

68. Hahn and Litan "Counting Regulatory Benefits and Costs," 473.

69. European Commission, Impact Assessment Board—2014 activity statistics.

70. McKinley, "Sunrises Without Sunsets."

71. If one believes the economic theory of democratization, that dismantling is not even possible, modern democracies have been set up with the particular purpose of ensuring that social safety nets can be preserved over time. Acemoglu and Robinson, "Why Did the West Extend the Franchise?"

72. Under a baseline scenario, by 2050 public debt will hit 400 percent of GDP in France and the Netherlands, 300 in Ireland, and over 500 in the United Kingdom. See Cecchetti et al., "The Future of Public Debt."

73. These and many other structural problems are discussed by Alesina and Giavazzi, *The Future of Europe*.

74. See Majone, "Rethinking European Integration After the Debt Crisis," 22. For a book-long treatment, see also Majone, *Rethinking the Union of Europe Post-Crisis*.

75. For a general discussion of structural changes in Western economies and the challenges they pose for policymakers, see Lindsey, *Human Capitalism*.

REFERENCES

Acemoglu, Daron, and James A. Robinson. "Why Did the West Extend the Franchise? Democracy, Inequality, and Growth in Historical Perspective." *Quarterly Journal of Economics* 115 (2000): 1167–99.

Alesina, Alberto, and Francesco Giavazzi. *The Future of Europe: Reform or Decline.* Cambridge: MIT Press, 2008.

Alesina, Alberto, and Roberto Perotti. "The European Union: A Politically Incorrect View." *Journal of Economic Perspectives* 18 (2004): 27–48.

Alesina, Alberto, Ignazio Angeloni, and Ludger Shuknecht. "What Does the European Union Do?" *NBER Working Paper* No. 8647, 2001. http://www.nber.org/papers/w8647.

Azevedo, Filipa, and Mariusz Maciejewski. "Social, Economic and Legal Consequences of Uber and Similar Transportation Network Companies (TNCs)." Briefing, European Parliament, 2015. http://www.europarl.europa.eu/RegData/etudes/BRIE/2015/563398/IPOL_BRI(2015)563398_EN.pdf.

Bhatti, Yosef, and Kasper M. Hansen. "The Effect of Generation and Age on Turnout to the European Parliament—How Turnout Will Continue to Decline in the Future." *Electoral Studies* 31 (2012): 262–72.

Blackman, Colin. "Last Chance for Europe in the Digital Saloon?" *CEPS Commentary*, May 28, 2015.

Brug, Wouter van der, Claes H. de Vreese (eds.). *(Un)Intended Consequences of EU Parliamentary Elections.* Oxford: Oxford University Press, 2015.

Cameron, David. "A New Settlement for the United Kingdom in a Reformed European Union." Letter to President Donald Tusk. November 10, 2015. https://www.gov.uk/government/uploads/system/uploads/attachment_data/file/475679/Donald_Tusk_letter.pdf.

Cecchetti, Stephen, G. M. S. Mohanty, and Fabrizio Zampolli. "The Future of Public Debt: Prospects and Implications." *BIS Working Paper* No. 300, 2010. http://www.bis.org/publ/work300.pdf.

Claeys, Gregory, Alvaro Leandro, and Allison Mandra. "European Central Bank Quantitative Easing: The Detailed Manual." *Bruegel Policy Contribution*, 2015/02, 2015. http://bruegel.org/wp-content/uploads/imported/publications/pc_2015_02_110315.pdf.

Clark, Nicholas. "Explaining Low Turnout in European Elections: The Role of Issue Salience and Institutional Perceptions in Elections to the European Parliament." *Journal of European Integration* 36 (2014): 339–56.

Consolidated Versions of the Treaty on European Union and the Treaty on the Functioning of the European Union. Official Journal of European Communities, 2012/C 326/01, October 26, 2012. http://eur-lex.europa.eu/legal-content/EN/TXT/HTML/?uri=CELEX:12012M/TXT&from=en.

The Constitution of the United States, 1789. http://www.archives.gov/exhibits/charters/constitution_transcript.html.

Convention Determining the State Responsible for Examining Applications for Asylum Lodged in One of the Member States of the European Communities—Dublin Convention. Official Journal C 254, August 19, 1997. http://eur-lex.europa.eu/legal-content/EN/ALL/?uri=CELEX%3A41997A0819(01).

Cooper, Ian. "The Story of the First 'Yellow Card' Shows That National Parliaments Can Act Together to Influence EU Policy." European Politics and Policy, LSE, April 23, 2015. http://blogs.lse.ac.uk/europpblog/2015/04/23/the-story-of-the-first-yellow-card-shows-that-national-parliaments-can-act-together-to-influence-eu-policy/.

Draghi, Mario. Speech at the Global Investment Conference, London, July 26, 2012. https://www.ecb.europa.eu/press/key/date/2012/html/sp120726.en.html.

Epstein, Richard A. "The Proper Scope of the Commerce Power." Virginia Law Review 73 (1987): 1387–455.

Erixon, Fredrik. "The 'Google Case' and the Promotion of Europe's Digital Economy." ECIPE Bulletin No. 1/2015, 2015. http://ecipe.org/app/uploads/2015/04/Bulletin-01151.pdf.

European Commission. "A Digital Single Market Strategy for Europe—Analysis and Evidence." Commission Staff Document, May 6, 2015. http://eur-lex.europa.eu/legal-content/EN/TXT/?qid=1447773803386&uri=CELEX:52015SC0100.

———. "Better Regulation Guidelines." Commission Staff Working Document, 2009. http://ec.europa.eu/smart-regulation/guidelines/docs/swd_br_guidelines_en.pdf.

———. "Commission Decides Selective Tax Advantages for Fiat in Luxembourg and Starbucks in the Netherlands Are Illegal Under EU State Aid Rules." EC Press Release, October 21, 2015. http://europa.eu/rapid/press-release_IP-15-5880_en.htm.

———. Impact Assessment Board—2014 Activity Statistics, 2015. http://ec.europa.eu/smart-regulation/impact/key_docs/docs/iab_stats_2014_en.pdf.

———. Impact Assessment Guidelines. SEC 2009(92), 2009. http://ec.europa.eu/smart-regulation/impact/commission_guidelines/docs/iag_2009_en.pdf.

European Council. "Conclusions of the Ecofin Council Meeting on 1 December 1997 Concerning Taxation Policy." Official Journal of the European Communities, 98/C/ 2/01, 1998. http://ec.europa.eu/taxation_customs/resources/documents/coc_en.pdf.

———. Council Regulation (EC) No 343/2003 of 18 February 2003 Establishing the Criteria and Mechanisms for Determining the Member State Responsible for Examining an Asylum Application Lodged in One of the Member States by a Third-Country National. OJ L 50, February 25, 2003. http://eur-lex.europa.eu/legal-content/EN/TXT/?uri=celex:32003R0343.

European Parliament. Resolution of 4 February 2014 on the EU Roadmap Against Homophobia and Discrimination on Grounds of Sexual Orientation and Gender Identity. 2013/2183(INI), 2014. http://www.europarl.europa.eu/sides/getDoc.do?pubRef=-//EP//TEXT+TA+P7-TA-2014-0062+0+DOC+XML+V0//EN.

———. Resolution of 10 June 2015 on the Situation in Hungary. 2015/2700 (RSP), http://www.europarl.europa.eu/sides/getDoc.do?pubRef=-//EP//NONSGML+TA+P8-TA-2015-0227+0+DOC+PDF+V0//EN.

Fabbrini, Sergio. Which European Union? Europe After the Euro Crisis. Cambridge, UK: Cambridge University Press, 2015.

Gostyńska, Agata. A Ten-Point Plan to Strengthen Westminster's Oversight of EU Policy. London: Centre for European Reform, 2015.

Hahn, Robert W., and Paul C. Tetlock. "Has Economic Analysis Improved Regulatory Decision?" Working Paper 07-08, AEI-Brookings Joint Center for Regulatory Studies, 2007.

Hahn, Robert W., and Robert E. Litan. "Counting Regulatory Benefits and Costs: Lessons for the US and Europe." Journal of International Economic Law 8 (2005): 473–508.

Hayek, Friedrich A. von. "The Use of Knowledge in Society." American Economic Review 35 (1945): 519–30.

———. Law, Legislation, and Liberty. Vol. 1, Rules and Order. London: Routledge, 1973.

———. The Fatal Conceit: The Errors of Socialism, edited by W. W. Bartley, III. Chicago: University of Chicago Press, 1988.

Hix, Simon. *What's Wrong with the European Union and How to Fix It*. Cambridge, UK: Polity Press, 2008.

Hix, Simon, and Bjørn Høyland. "Empowerment of the European Parliament." *Annual Review of Political Science* 16 (2013): 171–89.

Iglesias, Pablo. *Politics in a Time of Crisis: Podemos and the Future of Democracy in Europe*. London: Verso, 2015.

Jones, Will, and Alexander Teytelboym. *The Refugee Match: A System That Respects Refugees' Preferences and the Priorities of States*. University of Oxford, 2015.

Joyce, Michael, et al. "Quantitative Easing and Unconventional Monetary Policy—an Introduction." *Economic Journal* 122 (2012): F271–88.

Larsen, Lars B. The Judicial Review of the Principle of Subsidiarity at the Court of Justice of the European Union. Speech at 6th Subsidiarity Conference, Berlin, 2013. https://portal.cor.europa.eu/subsidiarity/news/Documents/Subsi_Conf_2013/Berlin%20-%20Judicial%20Review%20of%20the%20Principle%20of%20Subsidiarity%20(Dec%202013)%20Draft%20before%20delivery%20REV%20doc.pdf.

Lefevere, Jonas, and Peter Van Aelst. "First-Order, Second-Order or Third-Rate? A Comparison of Turnout in European, Local and National Elections in the Netherlands." *Electoral Studies* 35 (2014): 159–70.

Legrain, Philippe. *European Spring: Why Our Economies and Politics Are in a Mess—and How to Put Them Right*. Clinton, CT: CB Creative Books, 2014.

Leonard, Thomas C. "American Economic Reform in the Progressive Era: Its Foundational Beliefs and Their Relation to Eugenics." *History of Political Economy* 41 (2009): 109–41.

Lilico, Andrew. "Cameron's Renegotiation 'Red Card' Demand Is Impossible." *CapX*, December 10, 2015. http://www.capx.co/camerons-eu-renegotiation-demand-for-a-red-card-system/.

Lindsey, Brink. *Human Capitalism: How Economic Growth Has Made Us Smarter—and More Unequal*. Princeton: Princeton University Press, 2013.

Macaes, Bruno. "A Digital Strategy for Europe." *ECIPE Policy Brief* No. 8/2015, 2015. http://www.ecipe.org/app/uploads/2015/09/PR-PB0815-copy.pdf.

Majone, Giandomenico. "Rethinking European Integration After the Debt Crisis." *UCL European Institute Working Paper* 3/2012, 2012. https://www.ucl.ac.uk/european-institute/analysis-publications/publications/WP3.pdf.

———. *Rethinking the Union of Europe Post-Crisis: Has Integration Gone Too Far?* Cambridge: Cambridge University Press, 2014.

Massaro, Maria, and Erik Bohlin. "Is Europe Moving Towards a Strategic Development of Spectrum Policy? A Review of the Connected Continent Legislative Proposal." Paper presented at the annual TPRC Conference, Arlington, VA, September 12–14, 2014.

McKinley, Vern. "Sunrises Without Sunsets—Can Sunset Laws Reduce Regulation?" *Regulation—The Cato Review of Business & Government* 18 (1995): 57–64.

Mitchell Daniel J. "A Tax Competition Primer: Why Tax Harmonization and Information Exchange Undermine America's Competitive Advantage in the Global Economy." *Backgrounder* No. 1460, Heritage Foundation, 2001. http://www.heritage.org/research/reports/2001/07/a-tax-competition-primer.

Moraga, Jesús Fernández-Huertas, and Hillel Rapoport. "Tradable Refugee-Admission Quotas and EU Asylum Policy." *CESifo Working Paper Series* No. 5072, 2014.

O'Sullivan, John. "Europe: Market or Cartel?" Speech given in Prague, November 7, 2007. http://forbritain.org/economists/wp-content/uploads/sites/11/2015/06/Speech-by-Global-Vision-Fellow-John-OSullivan.pdf.

———. "Cyprus Suffers EU Folly." *National Review*, March 29, 2013. http://www.nationalreview.com/article/344248/cyprus-suffers-eu-folly-john-osullivan.

Oakeshott, Michael. "On Being Conservative." In *Rationalism in Politics and Other Essays*. Indianapolis, IN: Liberty Fund, 1991.

Organisation for Economic Co-operation and Development. "OECD Broadband Statistics." 2014. http://www.oecd.org/sti/broadband/1.10-PctFibreToTotalBroadband-2014-12.xls.

Pesenti, Paolo. "Structural Reforms and Monetary Policy Revisited." *VoxEU*, September 7, 2015. http://www.voxeu.org/article/structural-reforms-and-monetary-policy-revisited.

Pilon, Roger. "Madison's Constitutional Vision: The Legacy of Enumerated Powers." In *James Madison and the Future of Limited Government*, edited by John Samples, 25–41. Washington DC: Cato Institute, 2002.

Reagan, Ronald. "Federal Regulation." Executive Order 12291, February 17, 1981. http://www.archives.gov/federal-register/codification/executive-order/12291.html.

Rohac, Dalibor. "Tap the Refugee Source." *Politico.eu*, December 17, 2015. http://www.politico.eu/article/tap-the-refugee-source-crisis-european-commission/.

Salin, Pascal. "The Case Against 'Tax Harmonization.'" In *Competition, Coordination and Diversity: From the Firm to Economic Integration*, 127–42. Cheltenham: Edward Elgar, 2015.

Sheedy, Kevin D. "Debt and Incomplete Financial Markets: A Case for Nominal GDP Targeting." *Brookings Papers on Economic Activity* 48 (2014): 301–72.

Shuck, Peter. "Refugee Burden-Sharing: A Modest Proposal." *Yale Journal of International Law* 22 (1997): 243–97.

Simms, Brendan. "Reinventing Europe." European Council on Foreign Relations Blog, March 19, 2012. http://www.ecfr.eu/blog/entry/reinventing_europe_brendan_simms.

———. "Towards a Mighty Union: How to Create a Democratic European Superpower." *International Affairs* 88 (2012): 49–62.

———. "The Ghosts of Europe Past." *International New York Times*, June 9, 2013. http://www.nytimes.com/2013/06/10/opinion/the-ghosts-of-europe-past.html?_r=0.

———. "We Eurozoners Must Create a United State of Europe." *Guardian*, April 23, 2013. http://www.theguardian.com/commentisfree/2013/apr/23/united-state-of-europe-anglo-american-union.

———. "Why We Need a British Europe, Not a European Britain." *New Statesman*, July 9, 2015. http://www.newstatesman.com/politics/2015/07/why-we-need-british-europe-not-european-britain.

Simms, Brendan, and Timothy Less. "A Crisis Without End: The Disintegration of the European Project." *New Statesman*, November 9, 2015. http://www.newstatesman.com/politics/uk/2015/11/crisis-without-end.

Smith, Adam. *The Theory of Moral Sentiments*, edited by David D. Raphael and Alec L. Macfie. Indianapolis: Liberty Fund, 1982 [1759].

Smith, Vernon L. *Rationality in Economics: Constructivist and Ecological Forms*. Cambridge, UK: Cambridge University Press, 2008.

Spolaore, Enrico "What Is European Integration Really About? A Political Guide for Economists." *Journal of Economic Perspectives* 27 (2013): 125–44.

Sumner, Scott. *The Case for Nominal GDP Targeting*. Arlington, VA: Mercatus Center, 2012. http://mercatus.org/publication/case-nominal-gdp-targeting.

Tortola, Pier Domenico. "Why a Partisan Commission President Could Be Good for the EU: A Response to Grabbe and Lehne." *Centre for Studies on Federalism Policy Paper* No. 2, 2013.

UK House of Lords. "The Role of National Parliaments in the European Union." House of Lords' European Union Committee. 9th Report of Session 2013–14, 2014. http://www.publications.parliament.uk/pa/ld201314/ldselect/ldeucom/151/151.pdf.

Vaubel, Ronald. *The European Institutions as an Interest Group: The Dynamics of Ever-Closer Union*. London: Institute of Economic Affairs, 2009.

World Bank Group. Economy Rankings. *Doing Business* website. http://www.doingbusiness.org/.

INDEX

ABOUT THE AUTHOR

Dalibor Rohac is a research fellow at the American Enterprise Institute and a visiting fellow at the University of Buckingham, UK. In addition to scholarly publications, his commentary on the political economy of Europe has been published in the *New York Times*, *Financial Times*, *Wall Street Journal*, and many other outlets. His PhD is from King's College London.